Ten Moons to Darwin

By Myself, But Not Alone on the
Overland Route to Australia

A Travel Memoir
by Will Furth

FURTHER
EDITIONS

Sebastopol, California 2023

Paperback ISBN: 979-8-9881510-0-5
E-book ISBN: 979-8-9881510-1-2

First printing edition 2024

Further Editions
Sebastopol, California
furthereditions@gmail.com

I dedicate this book to Jenny Jones.
My traveling partner, life companion,
and wife for the past twenty years.

In memory of my brother,
Richard D. Furth.
He loved his road trips!

Table of Contents

Preface

The rumbling of the train was the first thing I heard when I awoke from a deep sleep. I was in the middle of Turkey on my way to Erzurum in the east. I lay there on my couchette for a moment enjoying the rocking motion. Looking out, I saw the four others: a man about my age, an old man with no teeth, and a young boy with his father. The five of us were sharing the sleeping cabin, and one by one, we got up, pushing our couchettes against the wall so we could sit down for another day on the train. We nodded at each other, exchanging the same greeting, "Günaydin," which means "good morning" in Turkish.

Beyond that, I couldn't communicate with my Turkish cabinmates. They talked amongst themselves but were still friendly to me. The father of the young boy took out a suitcase and laid it flat in the aisle between the benches. He and the young man around my age pulled several rolled-up cotton cloths out of wrinkled sacks, placing them on top of the makeshift table. Once opened, the cotton wrappers revealed a variety of food spread out on the suitcase – fresh bread, feta cheese, grilled meat, and hard-boiled eggs. Someone had lovingly put together meals for each of the young men and the boy. They beckoned the old man and me to join them. The old man pointed to his gums and declined the invitation. But I was happy to join in, if only for a taste, because I didn't want to be eating food meant to last for their entire two-day journey. Remembering that I had a paper bag full of dried apricots, which I had bought especially for the train ride, I handed the bag to the old man. He happily took them and began gumming the soft fruit. It was a surprisingly nice feast to start the day. I felt a real camaraderie with these strangers, who were now my companions, for the next day-and-a-half.

The train sped along passing through a stark landscape. The terrain of the high central plateau of eastern Turkey became more rugged the further east we went. For hours, we passed mountains, rivers, rolling hills, and long stretches of barren land, sparsely covered by a variety of grasses. Trees and people were few and far between.

For the rest of the day, I had very little to do but read, look out the window, or take a nap. I thought about where I had been, what I had seen, and whom I had met over the past five months since leaving Colorado bound for Australia via the overland route.

* * *

Before the British sent their convicted criminals to a large arid landmass in the southern Pacific, that unknown continent had been populated by an Indigenous people for over 50,000 years. As part of the Indigenous people's tradition, young boys between the ages of 10 and 16 were sent on a six-month journey into the wilderness alone to make the spiritual transition into manhood. These rites of passage were known as walkabouts. On a walkabout, a boy had to survive in whatever environment he found himself, create a relationship with the land, and then return to the community as an adult. These could be challenging and even dangerous. The old continent had always been populated by unusual animals, such as the kangaroo, wallaby, platypus, and koala. It was also home to more than 100 varieties of venomous snakes. Australia was unlike any other place on the planet, and I wanted to go there.

I started thinking about how great it would be to go to Australia when I was in high school in the early 1960s. Study Hall was a 40-minute period dedicated to reviewing the day's lessons, but instead of studying algebra and European history, I used the time to study a map of Australia. I memorized the outline of the island continent, which sits under a chain of Indonesian islands and the rest of Asia. I repeatedly drew a free-hand outline of Australia, including the island of Tasmania, situated off the southeast corner. I learned the names of the states, territories, and towns and could draw the appropriate lines dividing the country and place dots on the map to indicate the major cities. Drawing those maps ate up a lot of my study time, but I was sure they would one day be useful. Although I didn't know when or how I would get to Australia, I knew I would be ready once I got there.

When I first considered what it would take to reach Australia, I found that the most direct route began with a flight from Los Angeles or San Francisco to Sydney. For a high school student, the cost of the long flight over the Pacific seemed pricey. In the 1960s, for young European or Australian travelers trying to reach each other's continent, there were a couple of options. One was to fly 10,500 miles (17,000 kilometers) for over 30 hours, making several stopovers along the way. The second was to travel overland and take as long as one wanted, moving cheaply through a variety of cultures, using trains, buses, and boats to cover the same distance.

Young people with backpacks were choosing the overland route taking them across Turkey, Iran, Afghanistan, Pakistan, India, Burma, Thailand, Malaysia, and Indonesia. Once they had traversed the length of Indonesia and reached the small island of Bali, flights to Darwin in Australia's Northern Territory were available several days a week.

All along the overland route, backpacking travelers could explore the countries they were passing through and expand their journey with side trips. For example, other countries in the region, such as Nepal or Ceylon, were not far once a traveler reached India.

In 1972, Ceylon became a republic and took the name Sri Lanka. In 1973, the U.S. had pulled out of Viet Nam, but the North and South Vietnamese were still fighting, so going to Viet Nam was not a good option for a side trip. There was also fighting in Cambodia between the Khmer Republic and the Khmer Rouge, and Laos had fighting of its own between the monarchy and the communists. In the 1970s, these were the countries in Southeast Asia that travelers were advised to avoid, for good reason.

Trains and buses were the main modes of ground transportation for crossing Asia with the occasional boat, ship, or sometimes a plane used to cross bodies of water. For less than the cost of a lengthy flight from London to Sydney, backpackers could travel at their own pace through an amazing variety of countries and cultures to reach their destination.

In 1973, I was 26 years old and living in the foothills of the Rocky Mountains just outside the town of Evergreen, Colorado, about 30 miles west of Denver. I had been working outdoors for a construction company during a particularly cold autumn, and I was starting to think about doing something besides construction work for the coming winter. I had no plans for 1974, but I was getting tired of getting up early, making breakfast, pouring hot soup into a thermos for lunch, and then digging my truck out of fresh snow so that I could drive to the jobsite in the dark.

During the ten years after high school, I hadn't thought much about Australia, but, once I got the itch to travel, I realized that Australia was where I wanted to go. I had heard about traveling overland carrying nothing but a backpack, sleeping in hostels or cheap hotels, moving around via local transportation, having no schedule, and spending very little money. That was something I thought I could do, and reaching Australia seemed possible.

Map Key

 RIDE WITH FRIEND/FAMILY

 PLANE

 TRAIN

 HITCHHIKING

 BOAT

 BUS

 TRUCK

 TAXI

 BEMO (VAN)

All maps and location names are from 1974.
All photos originated from Will's trip, unless otherwise noted.
All measurements of distance, weight and temperature are listed in miles, feet, inches, pounds, and Fahrenheit for Americans; and in kilometers, meters, centimeters, kilograms, and Celsius for international readers.
The first instance of each measurement is spelled out in full, and then, later abbreviated, i.e., kilometers becomes kms.

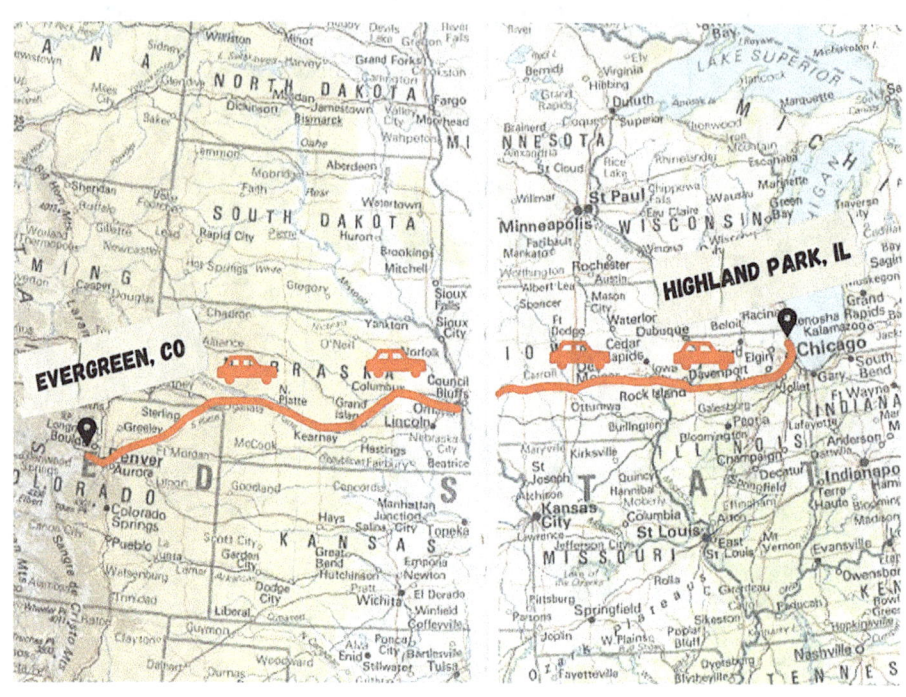

Evergreen, Colorado to Highland Park, Illinois (ride with friend)

First Full Moon

The first full moon of the year, which came on my 27th birthday, fell on the frigid 8th of January 1974. I had made up my mind to leave family, friends, and a comfortable home heated by a warm potbelly stove for an adventure to see new sights in warmer climes. I could be on my way by the end of the month.

I had been working steadily for a couple of years and had saved up enough money to quit my carpenter's job and take the time to see some of the world. I was strong and healthy, and I figured the best time to travel was while I was young. If I needed to work when I was older, rather than retire, that would be the tradeoff for traveling while I had the energy. In December, I had given my boss two weeks' notice, figuring that would give me enough time to prepare for my journey.

My last day on the construction job was just before Christmas 1973. As soon as I put down my tool belt, I started preparing for my trip by going to the Army-Navy surplus store in Denver. I bought a lightweight dark green nylon backpack. It had an aluminum handle at the top which allowed me to carry the pack like a suitcase when it wasn't on my back. Just below the bottom of the pack was the perfect place to securely attach my sleeping bag using nylon straps. I would have to stuff everything I would need for all kinds of weather and situations into this small space, zip it up, and throw it on my back.

I would be living out of that backpack for months, but I had to pack light: A change of shoes, two pair of pants, a couple of shirts, sweatshirt, raincoat, undies, socks, t-shirts, and a small bag holding soap, toothpaste, toothbrush, comb, shampoo, a nail clipper, aspirin, and Imodium, in case I ate some bad food. I also tucked a plain brown knit tie into the pocket of a sage-green corduroy sport coat, then tightly rolled up the coat and placed it at the base of the pack, in case I needed to dress up for some occasion.

Besides the backpack, I would need a small shoulder bag that would carry things I might need throughout the day. Looking around the Army-Navy surplus store, I found a gray canvas ammunition bag with an adjustable strap that I thought would hold everything I might need.

The first item I put in the bag was the blank journal I would fill with entries describing my journey as I went from city to town to village. The bag had room for a small snack, a paperback, a map, a 35mm camera, a little toilet paper, a space blanket, and a Bible. Even though I wasn't religious I felt that carrying a Bible might provide some spiritual protection. The space blanket was a lightweight sheet of Mylar that I could wrap around myself in to keep warm when I couldn't use my sleeping bag. In addition to the shoulder bag and backpack, I stuffed a small satchel with five pairs of used Levi's 501 shrink-to-fit blue jeans. I had read that used Levi's could be sold in Istanbul for $100 a pair. I figured it would be worth carrying the extra load for the extra money it would provide before I started traveling across Asia.

At some point, someone tagged the overland route I planned to follow as the "hippie trail". For those of us who traveled overland through Asia in the early 70s, we were definitely an alternative to the conventional tourists. At the time, we considered ourselves "travelers" more than tourists. We carried our belongings in rucksacks, while traditional tourists traveled with suitcases. Our hair was a little longer; some of us wore beards and beaded necklaces. We stayed in economical lodgings and found cheap restaurants or ate street food. The less money we spent each day prolonged our travels until we needed to work again. We didn't see ourselves as hippies, but if the people who hand out labels felt that anyone who traveled on the cheap, dressed in a mix of western and local attire, and smoked cannabis met the definition of a hippie, we fit the bill. However, most of us were out to experience different cultures and travel as thrifty as possible, using local transportation to reach our final destinations.

Not long before I left, my friend Marsha told me that I needed to wear a necklace, so she took some sturdy nylon thread, a variety of beads, and strung one together. I found a small, cylindrical, sandalwood container about the size of a hazelnut which had a top that could be unscrewed revealing just enough space to hide something inside.

Another friend found a hollow bean holding 10 tiny carved wooden animals that fit nicely inside the sandalwood cylinder. He told me that each animal would share their individual strength with the person holding them. After dropping the animal-filled bean inside the sandalwood container, I screwed on the top and attached it to the necklace. I put Marsha's necklace around my neck and didn't take it off for two years.

The month of January went by quickly preparing to leave. After a few farewell parties, hugs, and handshakes, I woke up early on January 28th, put my pack, shoulder bag, and satchel full of old Levi's in the trunk of my friend Bob's car, and left the Rocky Mountains for the plains of the Midwest. Bob was moving back to Illinois, and my timing was good for hitching a ride.

As we descended the foothills of the Rocky Mountains, the sun was just starting to brighten the sky and light up the plains to the east. Because I had been living in Colorado for several years, I had already made the same day-long drive many times across Colorado, Nebraska, and Iowa into Illinois to see my family in Highland Park. I always enjoyed passing the endless fields full of corn and soybeans, which were barren during the winter months, while watching huge storms create anvil clouds on the horizon. Luckily, that winter drive was cold, clear, and free of stormy weather.

I was now eastbound, and my travels had begun. I had the feeling of complete freedom. I was carrying everything I might need for the next several months, and perhaps years. I had no keys and no obligations. I was on my own. I felt the excitement of starting a journey along with the anxiety of an unknown future.

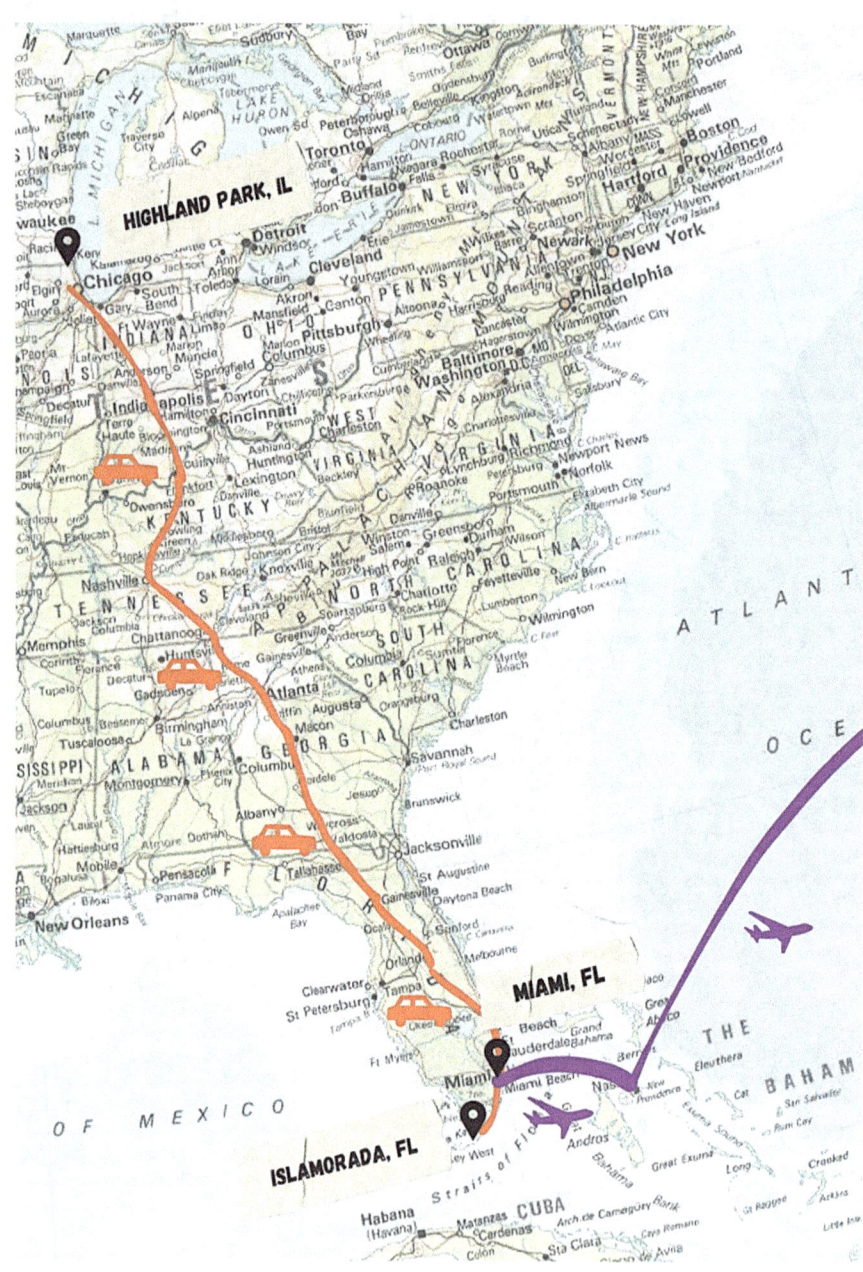

*Highland Park, Illinois to Miami, Florida to Islamorada, Florida
and back to Miami (ride with family)
Miami to Nassau, Bahamas, to Luxembourg (by plane)*

Second Full Moon

Married on February 6, 1942, my parents were celebrating their 32nd anniversary in 1974. My Dad made reservations for five at his favorite French restaurant, L'Escargot. Joining us for the festive night were my brother, Richard, and his girlfriend, Carol. My Dad ordered a bottle of Bordeaux, and the evening began. After a delicious meal and another bottle of wine, we walked outside to see the second full moon of the year rising over the Chicago skyline.

The next day I went to a travel agent and purchased an airline ticket for the flight to Europe. There were two cheap ways to get to Europe in the early 1970s. The northern route on Icelandic Air started in New York, making a stop in Reykjavik, Iceland, before flying to Luxembourg. Icelandic Air was known as the "Hippie Airline" because so many young people flew to Europe on it. Air Bahamas, which Icelandic also owned, flew the southern route starting in Miami. The flight made a stop in Nassau and then continued on to Luxembourg for the same inexpensive price as the northern route. My one-way ticket was leaving February 25th – an Air Bahamas flight from Miami to Luxembourg with a three-hour layover in the Bahamas. Holding my airline ticket meant my dream was becoming a reality. I knew I might be gone for a long time and would be totally on my own. I had never taken an extended trip by myself.

I felt a mixture of feelings – excitement tinged with a sense of loneliness lurking in the back of my mind.

The two-and-a-half weeks before the flight gave me time to join my parents on their annual drive from Illinois to Florida. After the drive, I would have 10 days to spend in the Florida Keys before my flight left from Miami. Every year my parents spent six weeks in the Keys to get away from the Midwest winter. They had taken the same route south for many winters, and all I had to do was share in the driving.

We left Highland Park on February 9th, following the main roads south. Eventually, the air got a little warmer each time we stopped for gas. The five-day drive was not my first with my parents. My dad liked road trips, and when I was younger, he would pile three of us, or four when my sister came along, into the back of a Chevy station wagon at four in the morning to beat the rush hour traffic that clogged the Chicago expressways. We had gone on several trips to explore America, but in 1965, my dad planned a two-month car trip around Europe.

The family picked up a new 1965 VW bus in Paris and had a great summer touring Europe. I was 18 then and learned to negotiate the tricky three-lane roads of France. The middle lane was meant for passing which worked very well unless cars coming in the opposite direction decided to pass at the same point in the road and met you head-on in the middle. I'm sure I got the travel bug from my dad, so it felt appropriate to be taking a car trip together at the beginning of my upcoming solo trip.

The further south we went on Route I-75, the more Stuckey's gas stations, a chain of pecan shops and convenience stores, we passed. We would stop at the station to fill the car with gas, use the clean restrooms, and buy pecan log rolls, which were my dad's favorite. The pecan logs were made with a nougat center mixed with maraschino cherries rolled into a log shape, dipped in buttery caramel, and then hand-rolled in fresh chopped pecans. The super-sweet logs were nutty, delicious, and the perfect car food. Once the car got rolling again, my mom would get out a knife, cut three-quarter inch rounds from the log, and hand them out to us until the log was finished. Yum!

To break up the drive through the length of Florida, my dad scheduled a stop at Disney World, near Orlando. Having opened in 1971, it was less than three years old, and had that Disney feel but was much bigger than Disneyland. We next drove into Miami to find one of the great Jewish delicatessens in South Florida. My dad liked deli food and thought Pumpernik's had one of the best corned beef sandwiches in the world. Two fresh slices of rye bread smeared with mustard encased hot, juicy corned beef piled so high you could hardly get your mouth open wide enough to take a bite. It came with a fat dill pickle on the side. My saliva glands get triggered just thinking about that sandwich.

Once we left mainland Florida, we crossed bridges and small keys until we arrived on Islamorada in the late afternoon on the 13th. We checked into the Islander

Motel, and I took my pack to a room not far from my parents'. All the rooms were on the ground level and near the pool, which was ideal for swimming and sunning. They had small kitchenettes, a small dining set, beds, and a patio out front for lounging in the breezy sea air. Most of the rooms were filled with "snowbirds" from the north who stayed for several weeks to get away from the cold winters in New York, Boston, Detroit, and Chicago. My parents usually stayed for six weeks, but I was only going to spend less than two weeks living the laidback life, swimming in the pool, fishing with my dad, and eating at the local spots, such as Manny and Isa's Cuban restaurant. It was a small place where you could order a plate of rice and black beans with a hunk of pork or chicken on top. It was delicious! Key lime pie and stone crabs were also a big part of the menus in the Keys.

Dad and I would walk to one of the bridges connecting the islands and cast our lines into the water, or we would rent a small boat and fish on the leeward, or west side, of the Keys, which was a lot calmer than deep sea fishing in the ocean to the east. We usually had good luck catching a few Red Snapper, which we would take back to the room to clean and fry up for a tasty lunch or dinner.

During those few days of sun, fun, and fishing, I took the time to reflect on traveling on my own. I had grown up traveling around the States and Europe with my parents, and I had learned about hotels, restaurants, and maps. Once I had a driver's license and a car, I traveled on my own around America, and in

1967, I had gone to Europe for the summer to work and drive through new countries I'd never visited before.

In the spring of 1967, I had paid for a new MGB in Chicago and picked it up from the factory just outside of London. I drove up to Edinburgh and then down to Newcastle, England, where I took a ferry over to Bergen, Norway. I planned to drive around Scandinavia so I could send my MGB back to the States as a used car and pay lower import tax. I didn't have a radio in the car but used a small transistor radio to keep me company as I drove through Norway, Sweden, and Denmark.

I was cruising down a Swedish road heading toward Stockholm when I spotted a hitchhiker up ahead by the side of the road. I had an empty seat and room for a pack, so I pulled over to see where he was going.

Walter from New Zealand was hitchhiking his way to Stockholm, which worked out well for the both of us. He put his backpack in the trunk and climbed in next to me. As we drove through the Swedish countryside in that small car, he told me he was hitchhiking around the world.

For the rest of the day, he told me stories about the places he had been and how difficult or easy hitchhiking had been in each country. He said that Malaysia was the best country for hitchhiking and had the nicest people. He was a printer by trade, and because he was from New Zealand and part of the

Commonwealth, he could get a printing job in any Commonwealth nation.

The Commonwealth of Nations is a group of independent countries who joined together under the leadership of Queen Elizabeth II.[1] Most of the member countries had once been territories of the United Kingdom and remain connected through the English language and history. Besides the United Kingdom, over fifty other countries belong to the Commonwealth, including Australia, Canada, India, Malaysia, Singapore, Nigeria, Ghana, Fiji, and Jamaica, just to name a few.

Walter had been working in Canada before landing in Oslo, where he started hitchhiking across Scandinavia. He told me he mainly stayed in youth hostels as he traveled. I didn't know about youth hostels, but I was eager to learn. He told me that each hostel was different, but usually there were separate dorm rooms for men and women. After checking in at a hostel, travelers were assigned a bed and could put down their own bedding, or the hostel would charge a little more to provide clean sheets. Hostels were an inexpensive way for young travelers to have a safe place to stay as they traveled around Europe and the world. At about 40 years old, Walter was older than most people who stayed in hostels, but he said that youth hostels welcomed all travelers. He had an International Youth Hostel membership card, which allowed him to stay in hostels around the world. He

---

[1] *The Commonwealth is now led by King Charles III.*

pulled out a small pamphlet that listed hostels in Europe and turned to the page listing the hostels in Sweden and found one not much further down the road. At that small hostel in the middle of Sweden I got my first membership card and learned that there were other ways to travel besides hotels and motels.

Walter said that he always kept enough cash on him to travel back to New Zealand from wherever he was in case his mother got sick and needed him. I thought at the time stashing a little extra cash for emergencies was a good idea. Walter changed my perspective on travel, and, when I finally decided to travel seven years later to places far away, I knew it could be done. As much as I liked driving around northern Europe, there was no one to share the experience. I saw some beautiful sites, but being by myself did get a little lonely. I ate in restaurants alone, stayed in hotel rooms by myself, and had conversations with very few people. That wasn't much fun. The best part of riding through Scandinavia was meeting a world traveler like Walter and hearing about how to live inexpensively while traveling through far-off places.

Seven years later, I was now about to take off on a trip that was more ambitious than any I had taken before. The apprehension I felt centered around the memory of the lonely times I'd had traveling by myself through Scandinavia. I would be crossing far stranger lands than Sweden, trying to communicate with people whose language and alphabet were foreign to me. I had never been very outgoing and was uneasy about how I would handle being on my own. How would I communicate with the people I met? Would I be spending a lot of time by myself? One night I had a vivid dream that dealt with the anxiety.

I dreamt that I was walking downhill on a cobblestone street in a small town somewhere in Europe. There were no cars, just a few bicycles and several pedestrians walking up and down. I was lost, so I approached a man and tapped him on the shoulder to ask for directions. It wasn't clear what my destination was, but I was probably trying to find a hotel or restaurant. The man stopped walking and turned to me. He was very gruff, obviously irritated that I had stopped him from getting where he was going. He said something I didn't understand, turned, and carried on his way. I kept walking down the cobblestone street, still lost, so I tapped another stranger on the shoulder to ask him for directions. The man turned toward me, looked me in the eye, and responded to my question. He couldn't have been nicer. The stranger was very friendly and even went out of his way to take me to my destination.

I don't usually remember my dreams, but I woke up remembering this one distinctly. That dream helped dampen the anxiety I was feeling about traveling alone. I now realized that I might meet people who didn't like me or wouldn't help me, but I would also meet people who were kind and more than willing to help me get where I was going. Of course, this also translated into a life lesson that there are all kinds of people in the world, and I would soon be heading off to meet a few of them. After that, I felt a little more at ease with the idea of traveling by myself; I also understood loneliness was still something I would have to deal with.

One of the friends I visited while staying with my parents in Highland Park had been a Peace Corps volunteer in India in the early 1970s. After Chuck had finished his two years in the Peace Corps, he left India and traveled overland to Europe using public transportation. When I told him about my upcoming trip across Asia, he gave me some advice: "Although you are always on your own, you will never be alone." Chuck's advice and the clarity of the recent dream prepared me to take the next step.

Monday, February 25th came up faster than expected. I had spent nearly a month with my parents. We hadn't spent that much time together since I graduated from high school in 1965, but the past few weeks had resulted in a more adult relationship than we'd had before.

On the morning of my departure, I was up early and checked to make sure my backpack and shoulder bag were packed and ready to go. I double-checked my passport and ticket. Mom cooked up a hearty breakfast of bacon, eggs, and toast to prepare me for my long day of flying. After breakfast, I threw my stuff into the trunk of my parents' car, and my dad drove us to the Miami airport. After many hugs and kisses, we said goodbye.

I put on my backpack, hung my shoulder bag, grabbed the bag of old Levi's, and headed inside to check in for my flight. I was carrying everything on my back that I would need, ready to travel for as long as I wanted. I had some cash, a book of American Express Traveler's Checks, and my father gave me an American Express credit card for emergencies. I hoped I would never have to use it. The traveler's checks had my signature on them, so with a passport, I would be able to cash them at any big bank. If they were stolen, I would be refunded for the amount I had lost. It was a safe way to carry money when traveling abroad. It was a good feeling to be self-contained and finally getting on a plane.

I had left my parents before when I had gone to university in Denver, but this was different. This time I was leaving my parents plus all that was familiar to me to follow my dream and travel the world. I was too excited to realize that I wouldn't be the same when I returned. I felt no anxiety stepping into the airport or onto the plane. With only the destination as a plan, the feeling of starting the next part of my life was exhilarating.

The plane took off, and during the short flight to Nassau, I hardly had time to digest that I had started an adventure that might take me away from my family and friends for months or even years.

I had a three-hour layover before the flight to Luxembourg, so I found a seat in the visitors' area and started reading the John D. MacDonald mystery, *Dress Her in Indigo*. Travis McGee, the hero, was trying to solve a murder in Mexico, and I wanted to find out "who dun it."

The Nassau airport wasn't very big or crowded, and I noticed a young woman sitting nearby who seemed to be also waiting for a plane. We made eye contact and smiled. I asked her where she was going, and she said she was flying home to New York. I told her I was waiting to catch a flight to Luxembourg, and from there the conversation just flowed. Nan was easy to talk to, and we ended up having lunch together in the airport restaurant and kept talking until her flight was called to board. Meeting Nan was easy and gave me a little more confidence that I could and would meet people as I traveled.

When my flight to Luxembourg was called, I boarded the plane, found my row with three empty seats, and sat down next to the window. I thought I would have to sit up for the 13-hour flight, but, when the last passenger had boarded and the plane door closed, I had the whole row to myself. The plane took off and reached cruising altitude before the seatbelt sign went off. I unbuckled my seatbelt, raised the armrests between the three seats, and stretched out in the empty row. The flight would take all night, and I hoped to get some rest before landing. The stewardess saw that I was trying to sleep and brought me a blanket. As I lay on those seats with the engines droning, I knew that I was really on my way. Sleep came easy.

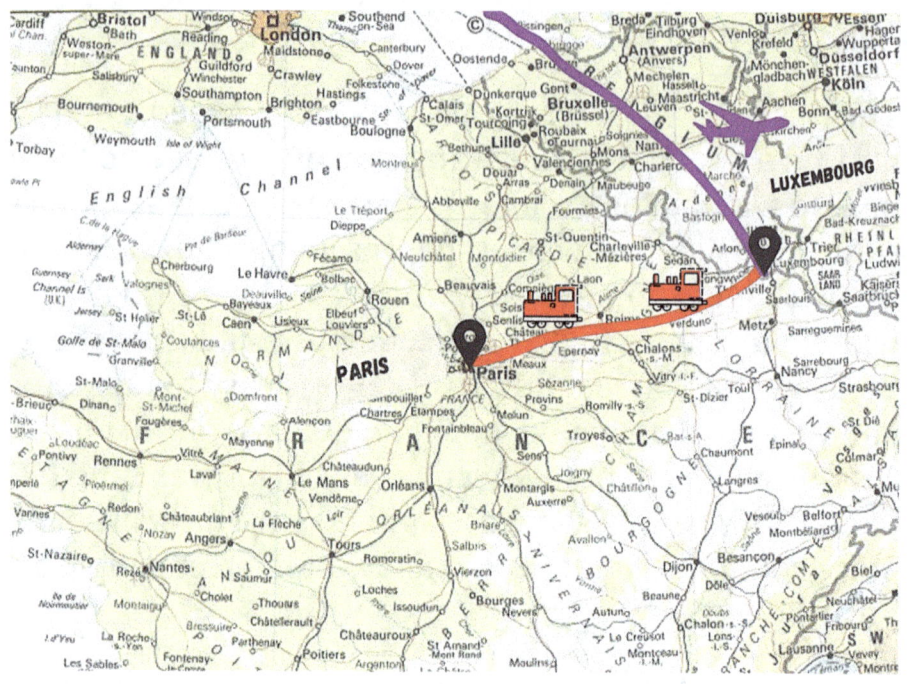

Luxembourg to Paris, France (by train)

The plane landed in Luxembourg around noon, and I went through customs getting the first of many entry stamps in my passport. I walked out of the airport and followed the signs to the train station, a short walk from the airport terminal. I was looking for the board listing train destinations and their departing times, hoping to find a train leaving for Paris that evening. I decided to go from Luxembourg straight to Paris where I could get my bearings in a familiar city. I located the large board listing departing trains and saw three other travelers with backpacks. I heard them speaking to each other in North American English. They were Americans who were also checking for the next train to Paris. Jane, Jo, and Dan weren't traveling together, but had just flown into Luxembourg separately and ended up at the train station in front of the departure board, just like me. There was a train bound for Paris at 17:37, which meant 5:37 p.m.[2] We went up to the ticket window and bought tickets.

Jo and Jane had places to stay in Paris, but Dan and I would have to find a hotel. Jane told us she was staying with a friend from home who was living in Paris and assured Dan and me that we could crash on the floor of her friend Jim's apartment. On the first day in Europe, I had found people to travel with and a place to stay. It felt like my trip was off to a good start.

Once the train arrived in Paris, we said goodbye to Jo, then Jane, Dan, and I shared a taxi to Jim's apartment building. Jim buzzed us in, and we walked up a couple flights of stairs to reach the small, dark, one-bedroom apartment. It was late, but Jim made us some tea, which was very welcoming. The four of us chatted until we decided to turn in. Jim slept in his room; Jane took the couch, and Dan and I happily unrolled our sleeping bags on the floor.

The apartment was a little crowded with the four of us, so in the morning Jim walked us to a nearby hotel, where Dan and I took a room that had two beds with the bathroom and toilet down the hall. We left our packs in the hotel room and went out to find croissants and coffee with Jane.

Dan was leaving for Tel Aviv the next day and left after

---

[2] *For clarity I will use the 12-hour system using a.m. and p.m. and not the 24-hour system that train and bus stations use.*

coffee to run some errands. Jane and I decided to do some sightseeing. Our first stop was the Musée du Jeu de Paume. The Jeu de Paume was an amazing museum in the northeast corner of The Tuileries Garden. At the other end of the Tuileries sat the Louvre. The Jeu de Paume housed some of the great impressionist paintings by Monet, Cezanne, Degas, Lautrec, Gauguin, van Gogh, and others. It was not large, but each wall was filled from floor to ceiling with paintings in the French salon style. I had studied art history using books and slides, but to see the actual oil and canvas used by these artists made the images I'd seen in class pale by comparison. That these classic paintings hung one above the other was overwhelming. It was hard to take it all in.

The highlight of the day came after dinner. Jane and I were walking down Blvd. St. Michel when we heard music coming from one of the side streets. We followed the music, and, when we got closer, we saw there were different groups of musicians performing on several corners around the area. We stopped to listen to a duo called "Renaud et Gaël," who sang French ballads under a three-quarter waxing moon next to a darkened church. Those few moments listening to musicians on a street corner in the dim light added to the richness of Paris more than walking down the Champs-Elysées ever could. To me, impromptu moments like this are what make Paris so magical.

One night I met friends of my parents, Pierre and his wife Claude, for dinner. I had first met them in 1965 at the start of my family's eight-week driving tour around Europe. On this February evening, Pierre, Claude, and I met for dinner at the Gaudroile, a restaurant where the menu was handwritten and there were no prices listed for any of the dishes. Madame Durant, who ran the restaurant, was very welcoming and charming. She and Pierre carried on like old friends. I didn't understand much of the conversation, but there was plenty of laughter. Pierre really knew how to have fun. As the night wore on, Mme. Durant's nose got redder and redder, and, at the end of the evening, when most of her patrons had finished their desserts and were having coffee or a brandy, she sat down at the piano and sang a lovely old French song with a beautiful voice full of emotion. The restaurant broke into applause when she finished.

Memorable dinner in Paris

After dinner, Pierre took us to a small cabaret not far from my hotel for an after-dinner drink. Le Port Du Salut had a few tables and chairs with a small stage at one end. Inside, the walls were covered with plaster casts of faces of famous comedians, poets, and musicians who had performed at the cabaret or were frequent patrons. Musicians like Georges Moustaki and Serge Gainsbourg got their starts at this cabaret and had casts of their faces on the wall.

Pierre insisted there was a plaster cast of himself on the wall somewhere. We had just received our drinks when a man walked up to the table. Pierre introduced him as Jean-Pierre, the artist who made the casts. I stood up and shook his hand, and he promptly invited Pierre and me to follow him to his studio. We followed him through a door in the back of the cabaret and up a steep, narrow flight of stairs to the next floor where he had set up shop. The rough old attic contained a few wooden benches, unfinished walls, and a floor made of well-worn planks. Everywhere I looked there were plaster casts covering the walls and benches, but these casts weren't of famous faces. The casts in the artist's private studio were of penises and breasts. Pierre explained to me that Jean-Pierre's studio was only for the viewing of his friends. While the casts were of famous people, I certainly didn't recognize anyone.

Pierre knew Paris very well and knew how to enjoy life. When people talk of *joie de vivre*, they are describing Pierre. He showed me a side of Paris not often seen by tourists. The plaster casts reminded me of the Plaster Casters, who in the 1960s made plaster casts of the penises of famous rock musicians. Jean-Pierre's private studio stuffed with body parts was the kind of place that makes Paris so full of life.

Pont des Arts over the Seine

Montmartre

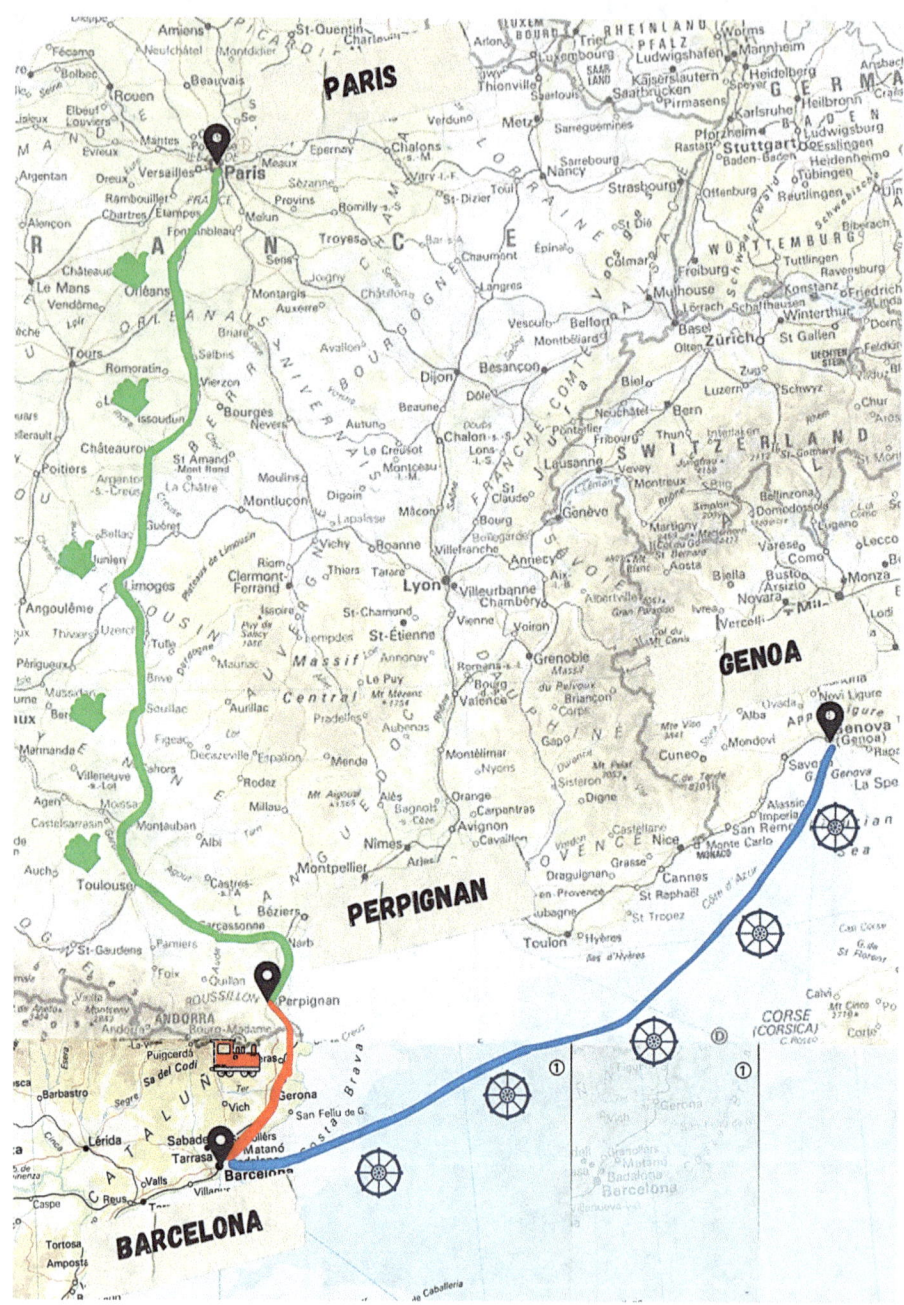

Paris, France to Perpignan, France (by hitchhiking)
to Barcelona, Spain (by train) to Genoa, Italy (by boat)

Third Full Moon

The river Seine is the heart of Paris, but people mainly talk about what is happening in the arrondissements along the Right and Left Banks. I spent the 8th of March slowly walking up and down the edge of the river taking in the sights, sounds, and smells of river life. Barges floated by carrying mounds of ore, a variety of houseboats lined the banks, and sightseeing boats full of tourists made for a good day near the water. March 8th was the third full moon of the year, and I was filled with eager anticipation for what was to come. I walked back to the hotel after dinner noticing the Parisian rooftops aglow with moonlight.

I would eventually leave Paris and hitchhike south to Spain, but before heading south, I was so close to England that I decided to take a side trip to visit a few friends. I also needed the vaccination shots required by some of the countries I would be passing through, and London was the best place to get them.

The next day, I hitchhiked northwest from Paris to Dunkerque on the Normandy coast and caught a ferry to Dover, England. While on the ferry, I met Fritz, a young South African. He had a car and offered to drive me into London. I was happy to accept because the ride would save me from getting a hotel room in Dover and hitching into London the next day. Once we were off the boat and through English customs, Fritz and I popped into one of the first pubs we passed. We both had a pint of lager, and when the patrons at the pub heard our accents, they bought us each another pint. By the time we got back into the car we were both a little tipsy. I was in no shape to even be the passenger, much less the driver, but Fritz said he was okay to drive so I got into the passenger seat on the right-hand side of Fritz's Renault.

Fritz had been working in Paris for the past few months and had gotten used to driving in the right-hand lane in a French car equipped with the steering wheel on the left, like we have in America. However, when he pulled out onto the roadway, he forgot we were in England where people drive in the left-hand lane, and, as a result, started driving toward London on the wrong side of the road. That night the cloudy sky hid the moon and created a darkness that was suddenly illuminated by the bright headlights of a car coming directly at us. I was sure we were going to crash, but at the last second, the oncoming car swerved to our right, and Fritz swerved to our left.

If the drivers had reacted differently, we would have struck head-on. From where I was sitting it seemed that the two cars missed each other by less than a foot. In my mind the near miss had been in slow motion, and being in a drunken state, I only saw the incident as a carnival ride where I had the best seat in the house. The other car kept on driving, but Fritz pulled over to the side of the road and took a minute or two to process what had happened.

Those few seconds didn't seem real to me. We had barely avoided a nasty accident and were still in one piece. Once Fritz had collected himself, we continued our ride into London on the correct side of the road, in the left lane. I thought at the time the whole incident occurred just the way it was meant to, and that surviving the close call was an indication that I would probably be OK in the months to come.

Once I reached London, I met people who told me about a travel pamphlet called *Overland to India and Australia*, published by BIT, an information and help organization based in London. The guide was just a bunch of mimeographed pages folded and stapled together costing about one British pound, but the pamphlet had fairly recent information about transportation, lodging, food, and the visas needed to enter the various countries along the route. It had good tips about the ins and outs of traveling overland.

People who were taking the overland route sent letters back to BIT with the most recent information, which was added to updated editions of the guide. I found the BIT Guide office and bought their latest edition which proved to be very useful once I reached Istanbul and continued east. While the BIT Guide provided important information, I ultimately collected the most current information from the other backpackers I met coming back from India and Australia. In dorm rooms, restaurants, and train and bus stations, information was exchanged with fellow passengers. The exchange always seemed to me like two lines of ants going in opposite directions and touching each other as they passed, transferring vital travel tips. After spending a few weeks in England visiting friends and getting the necessary vaccinations and international vaccination card, I hitchhiked back to Paris to continue my trip.

When I arrived in Paris, I was invited to a party at a friend of Jim and Jane's where I met Mary Ellen, an American. While we were talking, I told her I was leaving Paris and hitching to Barcelona in a few days. Mary Ellen said that she had friends there and asked if she could join me. Though I had just met her, I thought it would be good to hitchhike with someone, so by the end of the party, we decided to travel together.

On Saturday, March 30th, Mary Ellen and I took the Metro to the south end of Paris and found our way to the road heading toward Spain. We had made good time picking up rides out of Paris. Mary Ellen usually sat in the front with the driver because she spoke some high school French. I had been traveling only a few weeks, but I was finding that meeting people and making conversation was easier than I thought it would be. However, that wasn't the case with Mary Ellen. Mary Ellen and I didn't connect. The conversation didn't flow, which made waiting for a ride seem even longer than it was. She didn't seem to enjoy being in the middle of France standing by the side of the road with me. There were long periods of silence where we didn't have much to talk about, and, when I tried to start a conversation, I got a one-word response or maybe a short complete sentence. Neither of us were to blame; there just wasn't any chemistry between us, platonically or romantically. We made the

La Cité at Carcassonne

best of an awkward situation.

On the second day we made it all the way south to Carcassonne and found a youth hostel in the large double-walled fortress known as La Cité de Carcassonne. The massive medieval fortress overlooks the plains that stretch from the Atlantic Ocean to the Mediterranean Sea and had been a strategic point since the Romans first arrived 2,000 years earlier. The size of La Cité with its double walls and 53 towers made it the largest walled city in Europe.

We entered through the main gate, crossed a bridge spanning the dry moat, and walked up the narrow cobblestone road to the youth hostel. After we put our packs in separate dorm rooms, we went out to explore the fortress. The only vehicles allowed into La Cité were taxis, small delivery vans, and the cars of hotel guests. Otherwise, the well-worn streets were meant for pedestrians only. We strolled through the web of tiny streets that led to all corners of the old fortress. Many of the people working in the shops inside La Cité also lived there, which is part of what made the walled city so vibrant.

Weaving through the winding streets, we passed restaurants, museums, and small shops selling a variety of goods for tourists: fake swords for the kids, tablecloths for the home, or beautiful handmade jewelry for someone special. La Cité had the feel of a small village, making the ancient fortress a unique place to stop for the night.

In the north of France, we had made good time with a few rides, but trying to get rides became much harder the further south we went. Traveling to Barcelona from Carcassonne by car would ordinarily take three hours, but hitchhiking out of Carcassonne down to Barcelona took a lot longer. We stood by the side of the road with our thumbs out, but people in the south of France seemed reluctant to pick up hitchhikers. Even so, we were able to reach Perpignan, which was the last large city in France, before crossing into Spain. But unfortunately, Perpignan was as far as our thumbs would take us. We weren't having any luck getting out of France on the road, so we gave up and made our way to the train station where we boarded the train to Barcelona.

It was late afternoon when the train finally pulled into

Sants railway station. Mary Ellen was excited about seeing her friends, so we said our goodbyes, and off she went. I was glad to be on my own again. I had been having good luck meeting people since arriving in Luxembourg and wasn't too concerned that Mary Ellen and I didn't click. It just reminded me that I would meet all kinds of people as I traveled and that I had been doing fine traveling solo. I realized that, in the short time I had been in Europe, I preferred traveling by myself rather than with someone I wasn't in tune with. I was gaining confidence in myself as a solo traveler.

Just a few months earlier, I'd had lunch in Chicago with my buddy, Frank. After graduating from college, he lived for a while in Barcelona, where he had a girlfriend, Marta. He had given me her telephone number and suggested that I call her when I passed through. He promised to write to her, introduce me, and tell her I might call.

It wasn't hard to find a pay phone in the train station, so I pulled out Marta's number and dialed. When a women answered the phone, I used my best high school Spanish but was saved when Marta quickly realized we would have to communicate in English. Marta, her parents, and her sister lived in the Horta District of Barcelona and invited me to stay with them. I learned over dinner that night, served at 10 p.m. as is traditional there, that the northeast corner of Spain is Catalonia, and that Barcelona is its capital. The Catalans come from a long line of independent people who have always had their own government, courts, and language. Many of the Catalans weren't pleased to be part of Spain. Marta and her family, who considered themselves more Catalan than Spanish, spoke Catalan at home and among their friends. They were very welcoming and let me sleep in an extra bedroom.

Marta introduced me to her best friend, Laura, who had a car and was kind enough to drive us around the city, giving me a taste of the locals' point of view. The first stop we made was at the Sagrada Família, a modern and striking church in the middle of Barcelona designed by the architect Antoni Gaudí. The architecture was unlike any I had ever seen. It looked more like a giant sandcastle. Even though construction had begun in 1882, it was still not finished and would need many years, if not decades, to complete.[3]

As young women living in Barcelona, Marta and Laura dressed in bellbottoms. When it was cool outside, Marta threw a black cape over her shoulders. They were like any modern young women in the 1970s who lived in the big cities of the world, and they were exposed to the same music and movies we had in the U.S., which opened them to a bigger world view.

One day Laura picked Marta and me up and started driving north along the winding coastal road by the Mediterranean. It was slow going up the coastline of the Costa Brava, but after a couple of hours we reached the small village of Cadaqués, where Salvador Dali was living with his wife and muse, Gala. Dali's home sits on

---

[3] *As I write this in 2023, the church is still under construction.*

a rocky shore at the edge of the Mediterranean. Laura found a road that wound above and behind Dali's property, so, when we reached the end of the narrow road, we stopped, got out, and looked down into the yard. What we saw was a mannequin of a full-sized horse, brightly painted, lying on its side in the middle of Dali's fenced-in garden. Although we were hoping to see one of them, neither Gala nor Dali came out while we stood there staring down at their backyard.

On the way back to Barcelona, we stopped for coffee at a small seaside café. The three of us were speaking English, and we weren't dressed like local Catalan villagers. We finished our coffee, paid for the drinks, and were almost to the door when we heard a couple of men at the bar make some comments and start to laugh.

Marta and Laura turned around to face the men and responded to their comments in Catalan. The men's comments must have been very insulting because the two women really tore into those guys. Everyone at the bar sat there with their mouths open and shock on their faces. When we got outside, Laura told me that the men had said some nasty things in Catalan thinking we were all foreigners. She and Marta told the men exactly what they thought of them. I didn't understand the language, but I certainly understood the intent.

Laura and Marta

*Genoa, Italy to Trieste, Italy (by train) to Dubrovnik,
Yugoslavia (by hitchhiking) to the Greek Border (by bus)
to Athens (by hitchhiking)*

Fourth Full Moon

On Saturday the 6th of April, Laura's boyfriend, Juan, invited Marta and me for a weekend at his family's cabin outside La Floresta, a village in the hills above Barcelona. The cabin sat on a wooded hillside in the beautiful mountain park, Parc Natural de la Serra de Collserola. The pine trees, hills, and fresh air reminded me of the hills in Colorado where I had started out a few months earlier. I was happy to get out of the city and into the green of the park. The cabin was like other mountain cabins I had been in: A simple framed non-insulated structure containing a small kitchen, a main room with a bunch of comfortable chairs, and a large table for eating or playing games. Off to one side there were several small bedrooms, each containing one or two beds.

Most of the day had been overcast, and we knew as the sky darkened that rain was coming. Before it got dark, Juan and I gathered some wood to make a fire in the grate outside so we could grill sausages for dinner. Marta cracked a few eggs and separated the whites from the yolks to which she added a little olive oil, lemon juice, and salt before whipping it up until it thickened and became mayonnaise.

In the small kitchen there was a small two-burner propane stove boiling water for a few eggs that we would eat with Marta's mayonnaise. When the fire burned down to coals, we grilled the sausages and put cheese, bread, eggs, and mayonnaise on the table near the kitchen, and ate our simple meal.

As we were having our sausage dinner, the rain started beating down on the cabin roof, so we never knew when the sun went down or when the April full moon came up.

The cabin was a good place to shelter while it rained. But, as soon as the sky cleared, the four of us climbed into Laura's car looking for some adventure, whether on the hiking trails through the park or exploring some of the small villages near La Floresta.

After the few days I spent with Marta and Laura, I ended up spending another 10 days in Barcelona before leaving on Tuesday the 16th aboard an overnight ferry to Genoa, Italy. I had considered hitchhiking from Barcelona across the south of France to Italy but remembered standing by the side of the road for hours with Mary Ellen in our futile attempt to hitchhike from Perpignan to Barcelona. I decided that the ferry across the Mediterranean would be the better choice. I booked a berth in one of the cabins that held two sets of bunk beds. The ferry was not very crowded, so I threw my pack on one of the lower bunks and went out to the open area on the main deck. There were seats throughout the deck giving passengers clear views of the rolling Mediterranean as we sailed along.

I walked around the main deck to get my bearings. I

wanted to see what the ship had to offer and where the bathrooms were located. Among the dozens of chairs and soft benches filling the main deck, I found a small cafeteria that served chicken or fish with rice, plus a salad and a small cup of ice cream. I wasn't ready to eat, so I started looking for a place to sit. As I looked around, I noticed a young, red-headed woman with a backpack also looking around the main cabin for a place to settle. We made eye contact and smiled. I went over to where she was standing and introduced myself. That's how I met Ginny, the only other American on board. We found some comfortable chairs and, like the ants, started telling each other where we had come from and where we were going. We ended up having dinner together at the little cafeteria and decided that, when we arrived in Genoa, we would find the local hostel which was supposed to be close to where the ships docked.

Even though I was traveling alone, I always found someone to talk to or travel with. My fear of initiating conversations with new people seemed to melt away the more I traveled. On the surface, what people on the road have in common is always being in a transitory state and living out of a suitcase or backpack. But I was starting to realize that most people, like me, just wanted to connect and sharing travel information was the best way to start a conversation.

The ship docked in Genoa, the home of Christopher Columbus. Ginny and I put our packs on, walked off the ship, and went through Italian customs. We found the local hostel not far from the dock and went in to see if it had any available beds. Luckily, it did. We left our packs in our dorm rooms and walked around the port until we found a little restaurant serving a satisfying meal of spaghetti with a simple red sauce, salad, fruit, a roll, and wine. It was the perfect meal for our first night in Italy.

The next day I said goodbye to Ginny and went to the main Genoa train station and I bought a ticket to Florence. I boarded the train and found a seat near a group of backpackers that included a Dutch girl, a Canadian guy, and another American. We chatted a little, but, once we exchanged some travel information, I sat back and read.

I had picked up a couple of paperbacks in England and was reading Kurt Vonnegut's *Slaughterhouse-Five*, enjoying Billy Pilgrim's exploits in the anti-war sci-fi novel. The train ticket hadn't cost very much, which explained why we stopped at, so it seemed, every single station until we finally pulled into *Firenze* (Florence).

I was going to be in Florence for only a couple of days, so, after getting settled into a cheap hotel, I went out to walk around the city. I had been there once before with my family in 1965 and seen the amazing art and architecture that make the city so popular. The best part of being in Florence was Florence itself. It was a thrill to be walking the streets, alleys, and plazas where so much history had taken place. I went to Ponte Vecchio, the historic bridge over the Arno River known for commerce. The bridge is lined with numerous small shops, crammed side by side, selling jewelry, art, and souvenirs. I stood in line to get into the Uffizi Gallery and saw masterpieces by Rubens, Botticelli, and Michelangelo.

The Uffizi holds the artwork that once belonged to the influential Medici family, during the early 15th through the 17th centuries. The Medici family started a large bank in Florence, and for many years supported the arts and artists of Italy, gathering an amazing collection of art. In the 16th century, visitors to the Uffizi had to make a request to visit the gallery. It opened to the public in 1765 and was designated an official museum one hundred years later. Florence is fascinating and always filled with tourists. I was just passing through but hoped to return one day to spend more time there.

Once I left Italy, all the cities and countries I planned to pass through would be totally new to me. I was ready. On the morning of April 21st, the train for Venice left the Florence station about 45 minutes late. It was not a problem finding a seat since there weren't many other passengers on this train. I hadn't seen any passengers with backpacks, so I put my pack in the overhead rack and sat down to view the northern Italian countryside and read. I had traded *Slaughterhouse-Five* with someone I had met in Florence and ended up with *Stranger in a Strange Land* by Robert Heinlein. By chance, I was reading more science fiction, and the current title was very appropriate as I rumbled through Italy headed to stranger lands.

The train slowed as we pulled into Venice. I decided

not to spend any time there because the city was said to be crowded and expensive. I wanted to save my money for places I had never been and decided to keep traveling onward. I was getting used to putting on my pack, hanging the shoulder bag off one side, and grabbing the bag of Levi's, but by now, I was looking forward to selling the jeans in Istanbul and lightening my load.

In the main part of the station, I bought a train ticket for Trieste, Italy, near the border with Yugoslavia. With my ticket in hand, I followed the signs to the correct platform, and as I was approaching the train looking for my assigned car, I heard a whistle. The flagman was waving his flag to signal that the train to Trieste was about to leave. I ran to the nearest door, hopped on, and found my seat just as the train was rolling out of the station. Good timing! The train wound its way around the north side of the Adriatic Sea then turned south tracing the coast of the Gulf of Trieste. Beautiful scenery and interesting reading made the train ride particularly enjoyable.

Arriving in Trieste in the late afternoon, I put on my pack, grabbed the Levi's bag, and started walking around to see if I could get a feel for the city. I walked past the bus depot and knew I would catch a bus out of Trieste the next morning, so I didn't want to find a hotel too far away. I hadn't met any other travelers who had passed through Trieste, so I was on my own to find somewhere to sleep for the night and a restaurant for dinner.

After spending a couple of days in the vibrancy of Florence where the streets, restaurants, and museums were full of life, I found Trieste low-key. The people on the streets were the local citizens going home after their workday. I could tell from the lack of restaurants and hotels that Trieste didn't have many tourists or people who stayed in the center of town after work. It got very quiet, and for the first time, I felt that I was all by myself. I wasn't looking forward to staying in a hotel room or eating alone, so I walked back to the bus depot to buy a ticket for the overnight bus to Dubrovnik, Yugoslavia. I would sleep on the bus and keep moving. I found my way back to the bus depot, and, as I was walking up to the door, someone tapped me on the back of my backpack and said, "*mi scusi*," Italian for "excuse me." I turned around and saw a guy about my age asking me in English if I wanted a ride to Dubrovnik. I told him I sure would, and we introduced ourselves.

John was an Englishman working in Italy taking some time to explore Yugoslavia. He had a car and had been waiting at the bus depot looking for someone to share the ride down the Dalmatian Coast. Apparently, when I walked up to the bus station with my backpack, shoulder bag, and the satchel of jeans, I looked like someone who could use a ride. Meeting John reminded me of when I was driving through Scandinavia and was glad to have picked up Walter to have some company and swap some stories. My timing had been good. I had been at the right place at the right time to meet someone to travel with. When I felt lonely in the middle of Trieste, I had a choice to make: either stay in Trieste or keep moving. I'd made a good choice. Again, great timing!

John said that, because it was already late afternoon, he wanted to cross the Yugoslavian border and drive a short way before looking for a hotel. I was happy to have a ride, so, if he was ready to cross into Yugoslavia, so was I. I loaded my gear into his car, and we drove to the Italian/Yugoslavian border where we easily went through customs for both countries. Once we were on the road, we hit it off right away, sharing information about who we were and about our travels. The conversation flowed easily, and I felt lucky to have caught a ride with John for a few days. We drove for an hour into Yugoslavia, and just as it was getting dark, we found a hotel by the road.

Dubrovnik was over 400 miles (640 kms) farther south, and it would take two days to drive down the Dalmatian coast. After a restful night's sleep, we left Monday morning hoping to make it to the old coastal port of Split, halfway to Dubrovnik.

Split was first established by the Greeks around the third or second century BCE. The winding road was beautiful, desolate, and slow, but we were in no rush. We saw very few vehicles on the road as we drove with the sea on our right and tall sheer cliffs on our left. If I had taken the overnight bus from Trieste to Dubrovnik, I would have missed the beauty of the Dalmatian Coast. And yes, we did see a couple of black and white spotted Dalmatian dogs as we traveled through Dalmatia, where the breed of dogs associated with U.S. fire stations originated.

We arrived in time to spend that night in Split, and the next morning, walked around the old village. Over the centuries, Split had come under the rule of many of the major powers in that part of the world. In 1974 Split was Yugoslavian. We toured the huge Diocletian's Palace, which was built by the Roman emperor around 305 CE. It is called a palace, but it looked more like a fortress with plenty of room for an army. After a lunch of meat and vegetable stew, thick hearty bread, and a glass of golden beer, we got back on the road.

Dubrovnik is a walled port city, first established in the seventh century. It was a fortress built to withstand attempted invasions from Turkish forces approaching from the east or from the Venetians just across the Adriatic Sea to the west. When John pulled up in front of the large wall that made up the east side of the city, we didn't know what to expect. The car had barely come to a stop when a man ran up to us asking, "Vuoi una stanza per la notte?" He spoke to us in Italian because we were in a car with Italian license plates. John spoke Italian and translated for me. The man was offering a room inside the walls with two beds and a bathroom down the hall. Outside the walled city, a newer city had grown over the years, but we were happy to have a room inside the twelve-hundred-year-old walls. No cars were allowed inside, so after John parked, we grabbed our packs and followed the man to the main gate.

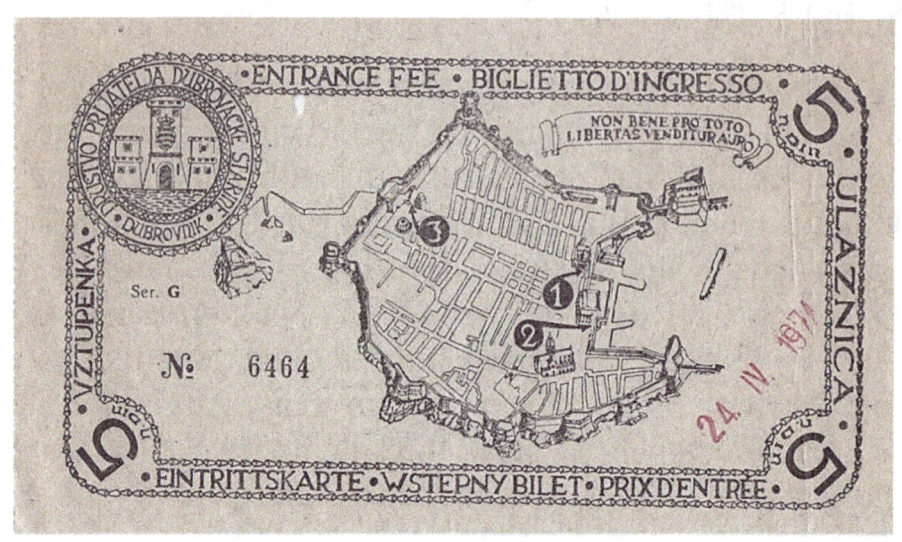

Ticket to Enter Dubrovnik

On the Wall of Dubrovnik

View From the Wall of Dubrovnik

First, we had to cross a wooden bridge spanning the dry moat before reaching the ticket window next to the main gate. We bought entry tickets and followed the man through the gates. Once inside, we followed him down narrow cobblestone streets to a village home that had a guest room with two beds. As promised, the sink and toilet were down the hall. In addition to being in a medieval setting, the hushed silence that greeted us was a pleasant and noticeable change from the everyday noises that hummed outside the walls. There was no sound of cars or traffic. I was thrilled to be spending the night in this beautiful old city.

The next morning, John and I climbed to the top of the walls and found a path we could follow around the perimeter of the city. Walking on the walls gave us great views of the glistening Adriatic and the ancient city below. Back on the ground, we went through the Maritime Museum, which had detailed exhibits displaying the history of sea travel through the centuries.

After our short visit around Dubrovnik, we went back to our room, picked up our packs, and said goodbye to our hosts. It was time for John and me to part ways as well. We walked back out the large entry doors, over the wooden bridge, and piled our packs into John's car. He took me to the Dubrovnik bus depot and dropped me off at noon. I thanked him and wished him well.

The late April weather was warming up, turning the local countryside green; the water of the Adriatic was deep blue and clear, and the Slavic language remained impossible. People were friendly everywhere I went, and travel was just what I hoped it would be. I was in Yugoslavia, a completely new territory, and excited to continue my journey.

I went up to the ticket window and bought a ticket for the overnight bus to Skopje, in the south. Directed to the bus parked closest to the ticket booth, I carried my pack and sack of jeans onto the bus looking for a place to sit. The bus was filling up with local people, but I noticed a young woman sitting by herself next to a window. She was wearing jeans and appeared to be from Western Europe or North America.

I asked if I could sit next to her, and, when she said yes, I put my backpack and bag of jeans in the overhead rack and sat down. Ellen was in her 20s and from Massachusetts. I introduced myself, and, before we could start talking, she turned around and introduced me to a couple seated two rows behind us. Ellen had met Mary and Larry, from Denver, while waiting for the bus. We were all on our way to Athens, but first, we had to travel through the southern part of Yugoslavia to get to the Greek border.

I immediately fell into comfortable conversation with Ellen and found out that she was taking some vacation time to travel before going back to work in Boston. She had a boyfriend but wanted to do some traveling by herself. Her plan was to take public transportation down the coast of the Adriatic going through Yugoslavia and Greece before ending up in Athens. Mary and Larry were both taking a break from college and wanted to travel some before going back to school. Mary had a red mop of hair and Larry had long blond hair tied in a ponytail. When the bus made its first stop for a tea and bathroom break, I realized that both Mary and Larry were over six feet tall. They had their packs in the racks above, but also a guitar. Mary, Larry, and I talked a lot about skiing, hiking, and living in Colorado, which gave us something in common.

There were two legs of the 15-hour overnight bus trip to Skopje. The first left Dubrovnik and went south following the west coast of Yugoslavia to Titograd. Previously called Podgorica, the Yugoslavs had re-named the city to honor the Communist leader, President Josip Broz Tito. Titograd was about 15 miles north of the border with Albania. The People's Socialist Republic of Albania was on the coast just below Yugoslavia and above Greece. We couldn't go through Albania because their borders were closed to most travelers by the Communist government. The bus would have to go up and around Albania to reach Skopje, a few miles from the Greek border.

The first leg of the trip ended when the bus pulled into Titograd for 30 minutes, which gave us time for a bathroom break, a cup of hot soup, a piece of thick, heavy bread, and a glass of dark tea. We found a table with four empty chairs in the main terminal and took turns visiting the bathroom. We had just enough time to eat before climbing back on the bus for the second leg to Skopje, which would take us east up into the mountains skirting around the Albanian Alps, before turning south and dropping into Skopje.

It was dark outside as the bus left Titograd, and, although we couldn't see much out the windows, we could feel the bus climb into the mountains. Ellen and I slept as best we could by leaning on each other and were barely awake when the bus arrived at the Skopje bus depot early Friday morning. Once the bus stopped, we stood up and took our packs from the racks. Larry grabbed his guitar case and, as we were walking off the bus, he told me that he sometimes played in a band back in Denver.

The four of us took turns cleaning up in the bus depot's restroom while watching each other's packs. We were still a short bus ride from the Greek border, so we stayed in the depot and bought tickets for a local bus to a small village closer to the border. From there, we had to walk to the edge of the village and hitch a ride to the Yugoslavian Customs Office, where we had our passports stamped. Then we walked over to a building with the Greek flag flying out front and found the Greek Customs Office. We presented our passports and were admitted into the country.

After Mary, Larry, Ellen, and I had cleared Greek customs, we went out by the side of the building and talked. We had grown close traveling as a foursome for the last 24 hours but knew it would be hard to get rides for all four of us, plus the packs, Larry's guitar, and my bag of jeans. We decided it would be easier to catch rides as pairs, so we agreed to split up. Ellen and I said our goodbyes to Larry and Mary, telling them we hoped to see them in Athens. They started walking up the road to get some distance between us before they stuck out their thumbs to hitch a ride.

Ellen and I waited just outside the customs office door looking for cars entering Greece from Yugoslavia. The drivers of those cars or trucks, and their passengers, had to park and then walk up to the customs office to get their passports stamped. When a driver would approach the office door, I would say hello in Greek, "yassou," and ask in English if they would take two riders south toward Athens. The drivers of the first few cars that stopped looked at me and shook their heads. Ellen and I had been asking for rides for about an hour when an old, white milk truck pulled into the parking area. We saw an Asian guy get out and start heading up the path by himself. As he was walking up to the customs office, I said, "yassou," and asked him if he wanted some riders to Athens. He stopped and said in English that we could talk after he had gone through customs.

A little while later he came out, and Ellen and I introduced ourselves. We told him we were going to Athens and looking to hitch a ride. Mike, who was from Holland, said he was driving through Greece on his way to the Greek Islands and agreed to take us a little way into Greece. We grabbed our packs and my bag of Levi's and followed Mike to his van. When he opened the side door, we saw that it was equipped with a couple of beds and some camping equipment. Mike had converted an old Citroën milk truck into a camping van. Ellen and I threw our packs in the back and climbed in. I was sitting in the passenger seat when we pulled onto the road. We saw Mary and Larry standing by the side of the road with their thumbs out. As we approached, Ellen and I waved, and they waved back.

Mike immediately asked if we knew them, and I told him we had been traveling with them since meeting on the bus leaving Dubrovnik. When I said that they were good people, Mike stopped the van and picked them up. Larry and Mary were thrilled to catch a ride with us, and, when they climbed in with their packs and guitar, the van was now full. Mike spoke excellent English, and the conversation between the five of us was spontaneous and fun. We hadn't traveled more than 18 miles (30 kms) when Mike pulled off the main paved road onto a dirt side road. He explained he was in no hurry and liked to get off the main road once in a while to explore. He drove the van down the dirt road for about ten minutes until we pulled into a village that appeared to be empty. No one was around, so Mike parked the van under some trees at the edge of the village, and we opened the doors to get out and stretch. Six or seven small homes were nestled together, but there didn't seem to be any shops or activity.

Larry brought out his guitar, and, after tuning up, started playing some chords. We had hung around the van talking for about 10 minutes, when two men appeared from around the corner of a building and slowly approached us. We exchanged "yassous" and shook hands with the men. Mike brought out some booze to pass around, and, out of nowhere, more villagers appeared with cheese, bread, pickled onions, and a dozen hard boiled eggs. We hadn't been traveling with Mike for more than just a couple of hours, and we were already having a party with the local Greek villagers.

Larry, Mary, villager, Mike, villager, villager, & Ellen

After about an hour, the village men had to get back to the fields, so we thanked our hosts and continued our drive south into Greece. We drove through the city of Thessaloniki and found ourselves back in the rural countryside. Mike said that he tried to avoid spending time in big cities. The sun was going down, so we found a quiet side road and drove a little way before pulling over to stop for the night. Mike had a comfortable bed in the van. It was a beautifully clear night so the four of us found level ground near the van and unrolled our sleeping bags. I had been on the move since the bus left Dubrovnik the day before, and it felt good to crawl into my sleeping bag and get prone. Sleep came quickly in that field under the starry Greek sky.

We were very fortunate to meet Mike and catch a ride with him. He had a great attitude and was always ready to stop and meet the local people. He was in no rush, and neither were we. Mike told us that his mother was Korean, and his father was from Dallas, part Indonesian, and part African American. I figured that the Indonesian side of Mike's dad was how Mike ended up being from northern Holland. Mike owned a restaurant with his wife who was running it while he took a few weeks off to vacation in the Greek Islands.

Saturday the 27th we climbed back into the van and started out by taking a wrong turn. We eventually got back on the right road and went about 25 miles (40 kms) before stopping in a beach town on the Aegean Sea. We found a restaurant that served fish and kabob, which we ordered for lunch. The local people were curious, and suddenly a group of local folks were taking an interest in us. The white milk truck we were riding in was unusual enough, but to have a tall woman with a head full of red hair, a tall blond guy with a ponytail, Mike, Ellen, and me climb out speaking English was enough to draw a crowd. After we finished dinner, our new friends walked us around the town, and we ended up at the local discothèque. We drank beer and danced for a few hours before we made our way back to the van for the night.

The next day, we made it to the city of Farsala, about

halfway to Athens. It seemed that all we had to do was stop for something to eat or drink at an outdoor table and people would come over to us and start asking questions about where we came from and where we were going. One of the locals offered us a place to park the van for the night in a garage parking area. It was big enough to park a few cars plus it had a grassy area where we could roll out our sleeping bags. Farsala is where Achilles died from an arrow shot through his heel.

Yugoslavia had been beautiful, but the people were a little distant and didn't engage with us. Here in Greece, we found nothing but welcoming people wherever we went. We would stop at a café and people came up to us speaking German, English, or Greek. Mike spoke Dutch, German, English, and a dialect of Indonesian, so he was always ready for a conversation. I think the local people we met were mostly interested in Mike and wondered how the five of us came to be traveling together. I had never been anywhere where locals go out of their way to be so helpful. If you pull out a map in Greece, you are suddenly surrounded by people trying to help you find your destination.

We ate a lot of lamb, chicken, rice, potatoes, and drank a lot of ouzo and tsipouro, two drinks that have a strong flavor of anise. I was also trying retsina, a wine that in earlier times was sealed in clay vessels using pine resin to help seal the cork. The wine ended up having the flavor of pine resin, which the Greeks liked very much. For me, the taste took a little getting used to because it had a scent like turpentine. In recent times, the retsina was produced by fermenting the wine along with some pine resin to give it its flavor. Getting to know the various Greek alcoholic beverages was helping the conversations flow. We enjoyed the ride and each other's company as we slowly rolled along, stopping frequently to meet the local folks on our way south. As we drove through Greece in the converted milk truck, Mike, Mary, Larry, Ellen, and I became like a family in just a few days.

One night we were camping in an olive grove outside a small village. Nestled in another olive grove across the road, we saw an encampment of five or six colorful horse-drawn wagons, or vardos, pulled into a circle around a main fire. Mike explained they were Roma people who traveled around Europe. The five of us went over to the camp with a bottle of wine and Larry's guitar. The Roma were great hosts and welcomed us into their camp. They brought out booze, food, and their guitars. We sang, drank, and danced for hours, stumbling back to our camp well past midnight.

Another night we were at an outdoor restaurant in a small village when we realized that the entire village had come out of their homes and were walking up and down the main street. The waiter explained that it was the local custom for people to come to the main street after dinner to walk and talk as a village. After we finished our dinner, we got up, settled the bill, and joined the villagers as they strolled back and forth for their evening walk. Some of the locals who spoke English walked with us and asked questions about who we were and what country we were from. For a few moments, we were part of the social hour that the villagers shared every evening.

We had meandered through the back roads of Greece, stopping at restaurants and bars, meeting the locals. The people of Greece were the friendliest I'd met so far. After camping on beaches and mountainsides and in olive groves for a week, Mike dropped Ellen, Mary, Larry, and me off in Athens on Thursday the 2nd of May. It was difficult to end our ride with Mike because we had grown so close. He tried to convince us to continue with him on to the Greek Islands, but we were going in different directions. We thanked him for a great ride, wished him well, and took our packs out of the Citroën milk truck.

The four of us had never been to Athens and wanted to explore the ancient city for a few days. Mike didn't want to stay in a big city, so he took off to catch a ferry to the islands.

The four of us found a cheap hotel that had a good-sized room with four beds and a window for fresh air. It was clean and basic with the bathroom and shower down the hall. While walking around, getting to know Athens, we noticed there were many good restaurants. A meal of lamb, spanakopita, and rice was easy to find. The four of us stuck together and saw the must-see sites, including the ancient ruins of the Parthenon and Acropolis.

Ellen and I at the Acropolis, Athens, Greece

In Athens, we were just like any other tourists and not the novelty we had been in the small villages. Compared to the friendly people that we had met on our ride through Greece, the citizens of Athens were like city people everywhere and didn't have the time or curiosity to engage with us.

I had heard of an office in Athens that sold student cards to young travelers without having to see current school registration. Holding a student card reduced the price of tickets for planes, trains, or buses, both local and international. Students also got lower prices on tickets for historic sites and movie theaters. The four of us went together and found the office selling Greek student ID's. I showed my college student card, paid a few drachmas, and handed over two small photos of myself. (The BIT Guide suggested carrying two dozen small photos for countries issuing entry visas or for identification cards). After a few minutes, a man behind the counter came out with my Greek student ID. I took the card and went to the office of a local airline where I bought a ticket for a flight to Istanbul. I was ready for the next part of my travels.

For the next few days, the four of us wandered around Athens sightseeing and eating at the street stalls throughout the city. I had my ticket to Istanbul, while Ellen, Mary and Larry were headed off to the Greek Islands. They were looking at maps trying to figure out which island to go to first. Most of the travelers I had met had either been to or were going to the Greek Islands to find a warm beach. Traveling slowly through Greece was a wonderful experience, but I wasn't ready to put down my pack and relax on a beach.

On Monday, the 6th of May, it was time to say goodbye to Ellen, Mary, and Larry. The four of us had been together day and night since we met on the bus in Dubrovnik. We had hitched a ride in the converted milk truck with Mike through Greece, walked the streets of Athens, and made a lot of good memories. Ever since I'd first caught a ride with John outside the Trieste bus depot, I had found and traveled with new friends through Yugoslavia and Greece and had become a more seasoned and confident traveler.

I was eager to reach Istanbul, sell the bag of Levi's I had been lugging around for months, and start my trip across Asia.

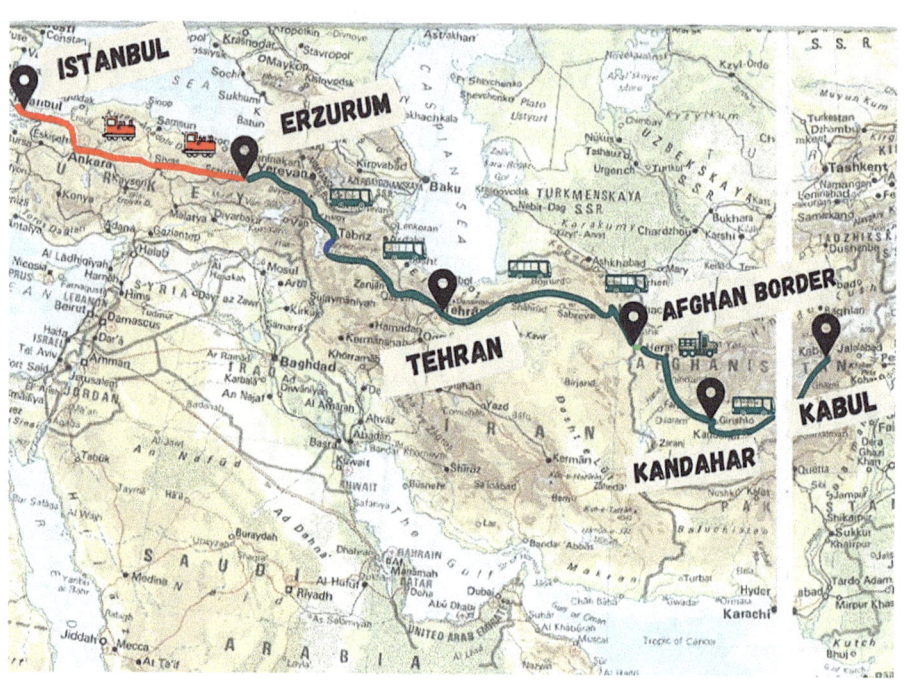

Istanbul, Turkey to Erzurum, Turkey (by train) to Afghan border through Tehran, Iran (by bus) to Kandahar, Afghanistan (by truck) to Kabul, Afghanistan (by bus)

Fifth Full Moon

The 5th full moon of the year fell on my first evening in Istanbul, and seeing it rise over the fabled city was thrilling.

The journey to Turkey was smooth, and I made another new friend. After leaving Ellen, Mary, and Larry, I loaded up my gear and took a bus to the Athens airport for the flight to Istanbul. While waiting to board the plane, I met Sue, a young woman from Australia. By now, any anxiety I had about meeting people as I traveled had faded from my mind. I had been fortunate to meet several interesting women traveling solo. Sue and I sat together on the two-hour flight and talked the whole way about the trips we were taking. She wanted to visit Istanbul as part of her travels around Europe. We decided that when we got there, we would stay in one of the hotels used by travelers in central Istanbul. Sue had heard about the Hotel Gündör, which was supposed to be clean, cheap, and well located. We shared a taxi to the hotel, which was situated just across a plaza from the Blue Mosque. We checked in, and I was shown a bed in the men's dorm, which held about 15 beds. Sue was shown to the women's dorm. The beds were no bigger than cots, but I shoved my pack and bag of jeans underneath and unrolled my sleeping bag on top. I had bought a cotton liner, which was like a sheet sewn together to make a sack that fit inside the sleeping bag. The liner had a fold of cloth at the top that could be stuffed with a shirt or towel to make a pillow. Occasionally, I would take the liner out of the bag and wash it. It was a good way to keep the sleeping bag from getting stale. The other fourteen beds were taken by travelers from all over the world, so it was a place to trade information with backpackers arriving from India. The dorm was an inside room without a window, so it tended to get stuffy. I preferred hanging out in the hotel's common room talking to other travelers when I wasn't exploring Istanbul.

On the first night in Istanbul, some of the people staying at the hotel told Sue and me about a restaurant nearby where we had a dinner of lamb kabobs, rice, and a salad. After dinner we walked around the area near the hotel with the moon rising behind the domes and minarets of the Sultan Ahmed Mosque, the Blue Mosque.

The Blue Mosque was built in the 1600s and holds 10,000 worshipers. Most mosques are built with four minarets, but the Blue Mosque is famous for having six. Some people say the extra two minarets were due to the Sultan's arrogance, but others say it was a misunderstanding between the Sultan and his architects. The Sultan asked for gold or "altin" minarets, but the architect heard the word "alti" which means six. Whatever the story, the six minarets and five domes make the Blue Mosque a unique site. At night the mosque is a spectacular structure lit up by blue lights highlighting the domes and minarets. The full moon made the exotic skyline even more dramatic, and I sensed I had truly left behind the familiar world that I knew.

The next morning, on Tuesday, May 7th, after some tea and bread to start the day, Sue and I walked around the city to get our bearings. We went to the covered bazaar which had row after row of clothing, jewelry, all kinds of trinkets, and a section with fresh fruits and vegetables. We were invited into shops to see what was being offered, such as rugs or glassware, and we were always brought a clear glass of dark black tea by boys who wandered around the bazaar. The tea boys carried metal trays that held the hot glasses and small silver bowls with lumps of sugar in all shapes and sizes. We saw many of the people drinking the tea place a piece of sugar between their teeth and then draw the hot, dark liquid across the sugar to sweeten the tea. I put a piece of sugar between my teeth to see if this method worked for me. It did work to sweeten the tea, but I felt a little clumsy holding the lump of sugar in my mouth between sips, so I went back to putting the sugar in the tea glass.

Over the next few days, I met some of the other travelers staying at the hotel, and once again, like the ants, we exchanged information. The Hotel Güngör was an excellent place to stay because Istanbul was at the starting point of the overland route for those going east and the ending point for those arriving from India and Australia. The hotel guests were a mix of travelers going both ways, and a lot of information was exchanged. I dug the BIT Guide out of my pack to check what it said about travel through Turkey and compared it to what I was hearing in the dorm room. Sometimes the travelers would confirm information in my BIT Guide, or they could update information about hotels, restaurants, and transportation in the places I might be going. I found out that each week two express trains left Istanbul bound for the city of Erzurum in eastern Turkey.

Both the express trains took 40 hours to reach their destinations, and I was told that nearly all the Western travelers took the Thursday train. It sounded like a party train, but I wasn't looking to party my way across Turkey or the rest of Asia; I was traveling across Asia on my way to Australia to experience different cultures along the way. It had been five months since I left Colorado, and I felt at ease with the people I was meeting, both the overland travelers and the local people. I didn't want to ride on a train for 40 hours with backpackers like me coming from Western countries when I could ride with Turkish passengers, so I decided to take the Monday express. I also learned from the other travelers that, if I had a Turkish student card, I would be able to purchase the train ticket to Erzurum at a reduced price. I made sure that I made a stop at the university, where, after showing my old student card from Columbia College in Chicago, I was issued a card from the Turkish National Student Union that was called "Reduction Card for Foreign Students".

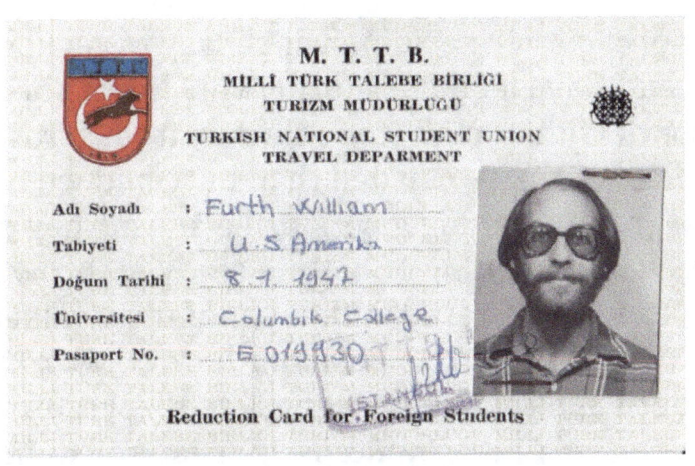

Reduction Card for Foreign Students

Thursday morning, Sue and I had tea and bread before she took a taxi to the airport and flew back to London. I went exploring with two guys I had met in the dorm room: Bill from England and Dave, an American. We decided to take a boat across the Bosphorus to see what Istanbul was like on the other side of the strait and to step onto the Asian continent for the first time. We went down to the boat dock and bought tickets that only cost us one Turkish lira, or 7¢. We boarded the boat with the other passengers and climbed some stairs to the upper deck finding a place to stand where we could watch other boats passing by. Soon, we were across the strait.

I walked off the boat and took my first steps on the Asian continent. I knew I would be spending many months exploring this part of the world before landing in Darwin and returning to a Western culture. There wasn't much to see at this point, but I knew there was much more to come. This side of the strait was a little more run down than the western side. While we were milling on a corner deciding which way to go, I heard a thump and Dave let out a short grunt. He had been hit in the back with a small stone thrown from across the street. He was more startled than hurt, and we turned to see a group of young guys staring at us. They didn't seem to be threatening or getting ready to throw more stones, so we just stared at them until they walked away. We didn't want to push our luck, so we returned to the dock and caught a boat back to the western side of the strait. My first few steps on Asian soil didn't go very well, but it was a reminder that I was in a different culture and had better pay attention.

Since arriving in Istanbul, I had been eating rice, kabobs, chicken, dolmas, and rice pudding, while drinking tea, Coke, and beer. I bought oranges, dried fruit, and nuts at the markets and was staying healthy.

One of the restaurants where travelers often ate was called Tarzan's, a small place with just a few tables. It wasn't fancy, but the food was fresh and tasted good. Tarzan, the owner, was a small, dark, strong looking but friendly guy. He always made you feel welcome in his restaurant. The backpackers liked to hang out at Tarzan's, and so did a lot of young Turkish guys. Altan, one of the young locals, was often hanging out there when we'd go for a meal. He was an easy talking guy who spoke English and would come over to chat with us. When I first went to Tarzan's with some of the guys from the hotel dorm, we were told that Altan had a brown belt in Karate and that he was also a wheeler-dealer. One of the young locals, whom we called Mike, and a few of his buddies were happy to hang out with us and practice their English.

In return, Mike and his friends tried to give us some help with the language by writing out phrases and a list of numbers in Turkish. I hoped it would help me communicate with the Turks I would meet in both Istanbul and the rest of Turkey.

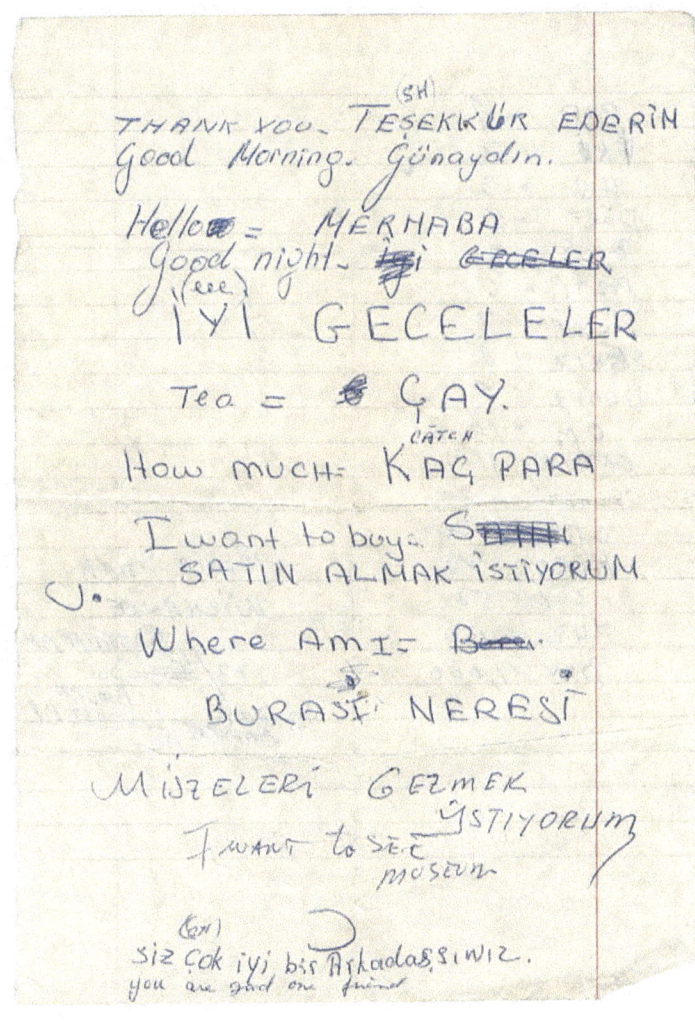

Notes on Speaking Turkish

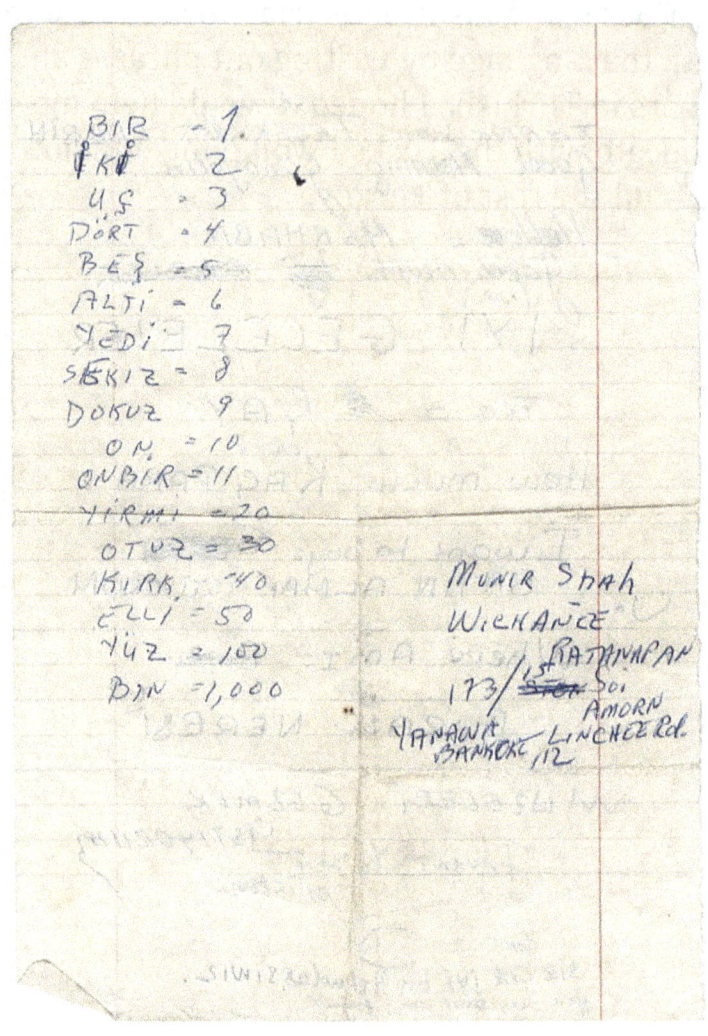

BIR = 1.
İKİ = 2
UÇ = 3
DÖRT = 4
BEŞ = 5
ALTI = 6
YEDİ = 7
SEKİZ = 8
DOKUZ = 9
ON = 10
ONBIR = 11
YIRMI = 20
OTUZ = 30
KIRK = 40
ELLI = 50
YÜZ = 100
BIN = 1,000

MUNIR Shah
WICHANCE
173/ 1st 501 RATANAPAN
AMORN
YANAWA LINCHEE Rd.
BANKOK 12

More Notes on Speaking Turkish

I asked Mike if he knew anyone who wanted to buy used Levi jeans, and he said that I should talk to Altan. I went over to Altan and told him about my bag of jeans. He said he would talk to some people and let me know the next time I stopped by Tarzan's.

Sunday the 12th, I took a fantastic Turkish bath at Cagaloglu Hamami, an 18th century public bath. I paid 30 TL ($2.15) and was treated to the same traditional bath men have had for over 200 years.

Interior of Cagaloglu Hamami
(Credit: Yadid Levy / Alamy Stock Photo)

After I paid the fee and checked in at the entrance to the Hamami, a young man took me to an individual cubicle containing a cot, a small table, and a chair. I undressed and wrapped a Turkish towel around my waist and was led to a cavernous room with a large marble slab in the middle. All around the big open room there were openings that led to smaller rooms that were heated by steam and were hotter than the main room, which was already quite warm. The attendant led me to one of the smaller, hotter, side rooms and told me to sit or lie down on the small warm marble slab there. He wanted me to stay until the steam opened the pores of my skin and I began to sweat. He came in a couple of times to touch my skin to see if there was any moisture on my arm. I was slow to break into a sweat, but eventually my body started to glisten, and the attendant led me back into the large main room with the six-sided marble slab in the center. There were a few other attendants giving massages to men around the slab, so he led me to an open section and had me lie face down on the warm marble. He then took a towel, rolled it up, and began rubbing the skin on my back. It was rough but invigorating as he turned me over and rubbed my body from top to bottom pulling the rolled towel across my skin in the same direction. I was amazed to see the dirt rolls he had rubbed out of my pores. After I was rubbed down, the attendant started pulling and pushing on my arms and legs. He took my legs and tied them in a knot and then did the same with my arms. He motioned for me to lie face down again and gave me a massage until I was loose as a goose.

My attendant had me sit up on the edge of the slab while he went over to a wall, opened a tap, and filled a bucket with hot water. He returned with the bucket and, without warning, dumped it on my head. I was surprised, but, when the hot water hit the top of my head and washed over me, it sure felt good. After I was doused, he put some liquid soap in his hands and began shampooing my hair, scalp, and beard. He went to get another bucket of hot water to dump on my head before lathering up a wet towel with more soap and using the soapy towel to wash me from head to toe. More buckets of hot water were the finishing touch. Wow! Fantastic!

I was weak from the rubbing, massaging, shampooing, soapy towel wash-up, and all that hot water. After this entire elaborate procedure, the attendant wrapped a dry towel around my head, another dry towel around my waist, and led me back to the cubicle where I had left my things. He told me to lie on the cot for as long as I wished. A hot glass of mint tea was brought to me and placed on a small table next to the bed. I lay down on the cot and relaxed after the most wonderful and invigorating experience of my life. And, I was clean!

Monday the 13th of May was my last day in Istanbul. It was also the last day I had to sell the Levi's. I had gone back to Tarzan's, had some tea with Altan, and talked about how to sell the jeans. Altan, who always had some type of deal going, told me he had talked to a student who would buy the jeans for the lira equivalent of $25 a pair. That was the best he could do. The student agreed to meet me on a corner not far from the hotel on that Monday afternoon.

I went to the corner and waited a long time in the rain, but the student never showed up, and I ended up taking the bag of jeans back to Tarzan's and selling the five pair of jeans to Altan for $4 a pair or $20 total. I felt set up by Altan, and I had no doubt he would take the jeans and make a good profit off them. I had been a mule for the clever Altan. Dragging a bag full of blue jeans for thousands of miles over the past five months, and all I had to show for it was $20, an empty bag, and a bruised ego. I would be more careful in the future when making a deal. I then took the empty bag that had carried the jeans back to the hotel and stuffed it with some winter clothing that I wouldn't need because the weather was warming up and would only get warmer as I went east. I took the bag and stuffed it into a box that Tarzan found for me. I took the box to the Post Office and filled out the necessary paperwork for sending the bag back to my parents in Illinois. The customs official wouldn't let me close the box as he said there was some further inspecting to do. I had to leave it with him and trust that it would arrive in Illinois with all the contents. I had no confidence that I would ever see that bag again. Many weeks later, my parents received the box, bag, and all the contents.

The train was scheduled to leave at 9:30 p.m. Leaving in the evening gave me enough time to have my last meal in Istanbul with Bill, the English guy I had met in the dorm. We went to dinner at a small restaurant that served a plate of hot lamb kabob, rice, and tea. After dinner we went back to the Hotel Güngör so I could pick up my bags and say goodbye to the other travelers. It had been drizzling most of the day, so, when I was ready to leave, I put on the lightweight raincoat my dad had given me, lifted the backpack onto my shoulders, and grabbed my shoulder bag and hat. For the first time since I packed my bags in Colorado, I didn't have a bag full of jeans to carry. Without five pounds of jeans, I felt lighter, more contained, and ready to start the trip across Asia. It was also a relief to have both hands free and one less bag to keep track of. I had to get to the train station on the eastern side of the Bosphorus. I said goodbye to Bill and made my way to the boat terminal, where I would catch a ferry to take me to the Anatolian/Asian side of Istanbul.

When I reached the ferry terminal, I purchased a ticket for the boat that would drop me off at Katikoy, the stop closest to the Haydarpasa Railway Station, only a quarter mile away. After the ferry reached Katikoy, I still had an hour before the train was scheduled to leave, so I put on my raincoat and backpack, slung the shoulder bag over my shoulder, put on my hat, and walked off the ferry. I started walking up the wet streets of east Istanbul in the dark drizzle. I was exactly where I wanted to be at that moment, beginning a journey through new countries, cultures, and customs, by myself. I had already been in Turkey for a week learning a few basics of the language and conversing with a few local Istanbul guys at Tarzan's. I had no reservations about taking a two-day train ride where all my fellow passengers would be Turkish. In fact, I was looking forward to it.

Express ticket to Erzurum (front and back)

When I walked into the train station, it wasn't very busy, and I purchased a ticket for the express train to Erzurum. With my Turkish student card, the cost was 73 TL ($5.10), which bought a seat and couchette, or sleeping platform, in a cabin that held six passengers. It would take 40 hours of riding from Istanbul through the middle of Turkey to reach the small city of Erzurum, 750 miles (1,200 kms) to the east.

It was after 9:00 p.m. when I found the correct platform and the train standing next to it. From the noise and smoke emanating from the engines at the front of the long train, I could tell that it was warming up and getting ready to go. A few people were looking for their assigned car, but nobody wearing a backpack like me. I walked down the platform looking for the number of my assigned car. When I found it, I climbed up a couple of steps, walked through the sliding doors, and passed several sleeping cabins with people stowing their suitcases and settling in.

When I found my cabin, it was filled with smoke, six young men, and one old man who was sitting by the window in my assigned seat. I took off my pack and said "merhaba" ("hello") to the group, and they all acknowledged me with a "merhaba" back. All the men seemed to know each other and were having a lively conversation. Some of them were smoking strong Turkish cigarettes filling the cabin with acrid smoke. The sleeper cabin had four pull-down beds, as well as benches for sitting, which would be turned into beds, providing sleeping space for six passengers. When I walked in and sat down, there were eight of us. That meant there were two more passengers than sleeping spaces available.

I was just starting my trip across Asia and facing my first tricky situation in a small, smoke-filled train cabin with Turks who spoke no English. Would I have a bed to sleep on? Suddenly, a whistle sounded, announcing that the train would be leaving shortly. Immediately some of the men started shaking hands with the old man, saying their goodbyes.

When the five relatives and friends got off the train only the old man, one of the young men in his 30s, and I were left to share the six pulldown sleeping platforms (couchettes) where we could stretch out for the night. The cabin's large window facing outside was lowered a few inches to clear the cabin of smoke and bring in some fresh air once the train picked up speed. I was saved by the whistle!

If the old man wanted to sit by the window, I was fine with that. I was just happy that there weren't eight of us sharing six spaces for 40 hours-plus and that the cigarette smokers had stayed in Istanbul. The three of us had plenty of room so I sat by my pack and read. Many English-speaking travelers carried a paperback book and traded with each other when they met at hotels or bus stations. At the Hotel Güngör, I had traded my last book for Arthur Hailey's *Airport*, which made me glad I was taking a train.

After about an hour, the train pulled into a small, quiet station. We didn't hear much activity, but a few minutes after we had stopped, a young man slid open the cabin door and entered with a suitcase in one hand and his young son in the other. They completed our cabin for the night. The train started moving again, and, when it reached a steady pace, the three other men had a quick conversation and started lowering the couchettes. The young boy looked tired and probably wanted to go to bed. There were two couchettes fixed to the wall on each side of the cabin, and I decided to use one of the lower ones to sleep on. The old man lay down on one of the seats, and the young man showed me how to lower the middle couchette. The father and son shared the other seat, and the young man climbed onto the platform opposite me. The wooden platforms were covered with leather stretched over some thin padding, but at least we weren't lying directly on hard wood. I tossed my pack onto the platform, undid the straps holding the sleeping bag, and unrolled it. I climbed onto the platform, took off my shoes, and slipped into my bag.

I was on the first of many trains, buses, boats, and planes that I would take to cross Asia on my way to Darwin. I was stretched out on a wooden platform in a cabin on a Turkish train filled with Turkish passengers and slowly heading east toward who-knows-where, unsure of what I would find. I was experiencing exactly the trip I had set out to take.

I was glad to be on the Monday express, comfortable on my couchette. This was the first night of a two-night train ride with my four cabinmates headed to Eastern Turkey. Because of the diverse makeup of Turkey, and because we were headed to the eastern part of the country, I could have been sharing the cabin with Kurds, Turks, or someone from one of a dozen other different ethnic groups. My fellow travelers spoke no English, and I had learned only enough Turkish to count to ten, say hello, thank you, and goodbye. We communicated, but it wasn't with language. We spoke with our eyes and smiles. I felt warm, secure, and confident as the rhythm of the train rocked me to sleep.

Early Tuesday morning the 14th, we slowly got up and lifted the couchettes back up into place against the walls. One by one we slipped out of the cabin to use the toilet and then came back to the cabin for the day's train ride. As we shared that spontaneous morning meal on a makeshift suitcase table, I felt a real camaraderie with the people whom I would be spending the next few hours. We passed a stark landscape as the train climbed up to the high central plateau of eastern Turkey. The countryside was getting more rugged the further east we went. For many hours we passed mountains, rivers, rolling hills, and long stretches of barren land sparsely dotted with grass, interrupted by only a few trees or the occasional farmer.

When I had been in London, I had gone to a map store that sold nothing but maps from all over the world. I looked up and down the aisles until I found a road map of southern Asia. The map would be my guide from Istanbul to Bali, and, when I studied it, I knew where I was in the world and where I was going. I had it folded so that I could see Turkey, Iran, Afghanistan, and Pakistan. My route was fairly straight until I reached India, and then I had choices to make. I liked maps, and that map would guide me over the next few months.

A field in the middle of Turkey

After spending the morning reading and looking out the window, I went in search of lunch. I walked through several sleeping cars observing cabins full of families and individuals talking, napping, reading, and eating. My fellow Turkish train passengers were like all train passengers around the world, passing the time as best they could until they reached their destination.

I eventually arrived at the dining car. All the tables were covered with white tablecloths and had places set for four diners. I was shown to one of the tables and was handed a menu that was in Turkish and English describing a fixed-price meal of soup, salad, chicken, potatoes, stuffed zucchini, a pastry, and bottled water, all for $1.50. I was hungry, and the food was fresh, hot, and tasted great. I hadn't expected the food in the dining car to be so good, but it was.

The train made occasional stops as we passed through the small villages along the route. In the middle of the first afternoon, the train pulled into a small station, and one of the men lowered the cabin window so we could purchase some food and drink from vendors standing on the station platform. There were four or five vendors selling either small packets of food or bottled soft drinks. I bought what I thought was a bottle of Fanta orange soda because the bottle had the Fanta logo on it and the liquid was orange. When I took a sip, it tasted just like Fanta. It didn't take too long to realize the bottle didn't contain real Fanta, but was just some sugary, orange-flavored carbonated drink made with local water. I had been trying to avoid drinking local water in case it wasn't healthy to drink. It wasn't!

Around 5:30 p.m. I had my first and, I hoped, my last stomach cramp and went to find the small room that held the toilet to clear out whatever bad food or drink I had consumed. I didn't realize at the time that the fake Fanta was the cause of my discomfort. When I found the small bathroom, it didn't have the Western-style toilet bowl with toilet paper I was used to. There was only a hole in the floor and places to put one's feet to squat down. Luckily, this hole was next to a wall with a grab bar to hold onto, as the train was rocking quite a bit. There was no toilet paper, but there was a small spigot for water next to the hole in the floor. Using water for cleaning after defecating was the method used by most of the world, and it would be my habit for the next few months. After finishing what I had to do, I ran the water and cleaned myself with my left hand. I had learned that cleaning was always done with the left hand so that you could safely eat with the clean right hand when knives, forks, or chopsticks were not part of the culture. I went back to the cabin and sat down hoping the bad microbes had just passed through me. I was not nauseous, and, except for a questionable belly, I felt okay.

I was lucky to be on a train with such a good dining car, so a little later that evening when I started to feel better, I made my way back for dinner. I walked into the dining car and looked around for an empty seat, when I noticed a man dressed in Western clothing having dinner at a table by himself. He looked up, and, when he saw me, he motioned for me to join him at his table. He turned out to be an American soldier named Don from San Antonio, Texas. He was a teletype operator in the U.S. Army stationed at a NATO base not far from Erzurum and only 150 miles from the Russian border. Don said that, while stationed at the base, he was helping the good guys spy on the Russians. I hadn't realized that Turkey was part of NATO or that there was a base so far into the country. I told him why I was on the train and where I was headed though, of course, he couldn't tell me anything about what he was doing at the NATO base. We chatted while having a delicious dinner of chicken, rice, and salad, with sweet rice pudding for dessert. There was plenty of rich hot tea. When I returned to my cabin, the sun had gone down, and the cabin lights were on. I had a little time to read before we lowered the couchettes for the night. I was still reading *Airport*, and the airport personnel were having a terrible time bringing the planes down to land in a fierce winter storm.

Around 11 p.m., my cabinmates and I pulled down the couchettes, said our goodnights, "iyi geceler," and climbed onto our platforms. The rhythm of the train induced sleep, and it didn't take long for me to succumb to the rocking as we rolled down the track.

The only exercise I had had since boarding the train was walking to the dining car and back. The next morning of May 15th, after eating two eggs, toast, and tea in the dining car, I figured walking up and down through the other cars was a good way to get some exercise and see who else was on the train. Not all the cabins I passed were completely full, but the people in each cabin were from this part of the world. I was expecting to see Don, the soldier I had had dinner with, but he must have been in another part of the train because I never saw him again. I was passing one cabin, and when I glanced in, I noticed a guy who didn't look Turkish.

He looked up and we nodded at each other. This tall thin guy stood up, came out into the aisle, and said, "Bonjour!" I responded, "Bonjour! Je ne parle pas français." Jean Noël switched to English; we introduced ourselves and started the usual conversation sharing why we were on this train. Jean Noël left France a week earlier and was traveling by himself with no special destination other than reaching India. We talked for a while and agreed that once the train arrived, we would go into Erzurum together and find a hotel for the night and transportation to get us to Tehran, Iran. Both of us had planned to stay in Erzurum for just one night. We agreed to meet on the platform after the train arrived at the station.

A few hours before arriving in Erzurum, the train started making stops at many of the small stations as we approached our destination. At one of those stops, the old man, the father and son, and the other young man gathered up their bags, rolled-up bundles, and prepared to get off the train. We said our goodbyes and shook hands before they left me in the cabin alone. I had a comfortable ride through Turkey and enjoyed the company of my cabinmates. Although we couldn't converse, we respected each other, and the three men and young boy made me feel welcome. Even so, I was happy to get a few minutes by myself before the train reached Erzurum.

Shortly after the train came to a stop, Jean Noël and I found each other on the platform. He traveled much lighter than I did. He carried a few belongings in a small shoulder bag and a small rolled up cotton sleeping bag. I, on the other hand, had a heavy backpack, a sleeping bag, and a shoulder bag. With his small cloth knapsack, he was able to blend in with the local surroundings better than I did with my green nylon pack. I wasn't ready for such a spartan method of travel.

We had just started walking down the platform when a young local guy came up to us. He told us, in English, that he represented the Mihan bus company and was trying to sell bus tickets for the bus from Erzurum to Tehran, Iran. Were we interested? We said, "Yes," and bought tickets to Tehran. After we purchased the tickets, the young man suggested a hotel in Erzurum that was located near the bus station we would be leaving from the next morning. One of our goals, to find bus tickets for the next day, had been met before we got out of the train station. Our other goal, a hotel for the night, was only a short walk into the city.

Jean Noël and I found the hotel and paid for a basic room with two beds. The toilet and bath were just down the hall. The two small beds had blankets, but we chose to sleep in our sleeping bags for the night. We wanted to see more of Erzurum and get some dinner, so we left the hotel and walked around the city until we found a restaurant where a few folks were already eating. The restaurant was serving a chunk of lamb on a bed of hot white rice and a pot of tea.

After dinner, we walked around the largest city in eastern Turkey and saw that, like most good-sized cities, it had a variety of shops and businesses that the nearby farmers would need when coming into town. We walked away from the center of the city until we ended up in a more rural area. The light was fading so we took a narrow dirt road that we thought would take us back to the hotel. We were about half-way down the road when we passed a group of neighborhood boys. The group was big enough to cause me a little anxiety, and, as we were passing, they shouted, "English?" and "Allemande?" Jean Noël and I kept walking, and, when we didn't respond they stopped shouting. We hadn't gone far when we heard something hitting the road just behind us. We turned to see what was happening and saw that the boys were tossing small stones at us. The stones were hitting the road well short of us and didn't come close to hitting us, but it wasn't a warm welcome. Jean Noël and I just stood there looking at the kids when a couple of adults, maybe parents, who had heard the boys taunting us, came out of their homes to chase off the kids. The tension that had built up with the boys was relieved, and Jean Noël and I continued onward to the hotel. This was the second time stones had been thrown in my direction, and I wasn't happy.

Erzurum

The evening was cool and the hills outside the city were covered with snow. Before going into the hotel, we stopped across the street at the bus depot to check with the Mihan bus company about the bus scheduled for the next morning. The agent at the desk told us the bus would be delayed for 24 hours because the driver was ill, but to check with the company early the next morning, anyway.

After dark, when the streets of Erzurum emptied, it became eerily quiet compared to the last two nights on the train. I was happy to lie down on a bed that wasn't moving, and, as a result, I slept soundly.

In the morning I heard Jean Noël moving around and, when he saw that I was awake, he told me he would go across the street to inquire about the bus. He returned after a couple of minutes and said that the bus was waiting and would leave at 8 a.m. We didn't have much time, so I quickly secured my sleeping bag, put on my pack, and followed him to the hotel desk, where we checked out. As soon as we stepped out of the hotel, we saw a vintage Greyhound-style bus sitting across the street in front of the bus depot.

We showed our tickets to the guy checking them by the door. He waved us onto the bus, and, when we climbed up, we saw that the bus was nearly full. Many of the passengers were Indians and Pakistanis going home after working in Turkey. We found a couple of empty seats near the rear and met two French guys traveling to Tehran.

Jean Noël immediately started having a conversation with them. While they were talking, I looked around the bus and confirmed what I had seen when we walked to our seats. At the back of the bus was a toilet. We were going to be on the bus for 24 hours, and I was glad there was a toilet on board in case I needed it. I wasn't quite over the fake Fanta orange drink incident and my guts were still a little rumbly. The seats turned out to be cushioned and felt like they would be comfortable for the long ride.

The terrain in eastern Turkey was flat and not very interesting until Mount Ararat came into view. This mountain, which some people think is the resting place of Noah's Ark, stands at 16,854 feet (5,137 meters), making it the tallest in Turkey. It's also a dormant volcano with another, slightly smaller cone-shaped dormant volcano, called Little Ararat, to the east. Both mountains were covered in snow insuring they stood out on the flat Turkish landscape.

The road was taking us just south of Mount Ararat when the bus stopped at a small roadside tearoom for a bathroom and tea break. I had a few minutes to walk around, look at the mountain through the morning haze, and wonder what it would mean if Noah's Ark were found up there.

In the early afternoon, the bus arrived at the Turkish border and dropped us off at the Turkish Customs Office. I took my backpack and got in line with the other bus passengers. After I was finished there, I made my way to the Iranian Customs Office and

Rest Stop near Mount Ararat

answered a few questions about my reason for entering Iran. The Iranian official looked at the visa, stamped my passport, and I was allowed in. One by one we all filed back onto the same bus, took the same seats, and continued the ride to Tehran. Compared to the rough roads we saw in Turkey, the roads in Iran appeared to have been recently paved. When the bus got rolling, the ride was smoother, and the bus driver drove a little faster.

About an hour in, the grumbling in my tummy got to the point where I needed to use the onboard toilet. I went to the back of the bus and opened the door. There might have been a toilet in this space at one time, but now the toilet was full of suitcases. I hadn't planned on that at all. The fake Fanta was still bothering me, and I really needed a toilet. I quickly grabbed my shoulder bag, which held a small roll of toilet paper, walked up to the driver, and, as we were cruising down the recently paved Iranian highway, I took out the roll of TP and held it up for him to see. No language was necessary. He took one look at the TP, almost immediately pulled off the road onto the dirt shoulder and opened the door.

We had stopped about 20 yards (18 meters) from a forest, so I jogged into the woods and found a tree where I could hide, squat, and relieve myself. I emerged from the wooded area a few minutes later a more comfortable passenger. I climbed back on board, thanked the driver who shut the door, and we continued the ride to Tehran. The necessities of the moment had me put vanity aside to take care of my needs. The bus ride continued as if nothing had happened. I was sitting next to the window, so later in the evening I pulled out the space blanket I had folded in my shoulder bag, covered myself, and tried to get some sleep leaning against the window. I managed to get about eight hours of sleep and felt rested in the morning.

Before the bus reached Tehran, we made a few stops for tea, bathroom, and morning prayers. My insides were feeling better, and the dark sweet tea seemed to calm my stomach.

During the 24-hour bus ride, I had conversations with the Pakistani and French passengers who wanted to practice their English skills. They asked me questions about America and wondered where I lived and where I was going. The travelers from Pakistan told me that it was easy to get work in Turkey, but they were going back to Pakistan to visit family. I found that English was definitely universal. Most travelers I had met knew basic English, no matter where they were from. Also, most overland travelers, regardless of nationality, carried U.S. dollars in cash or traveler's checks because U.S. dollars were the easiest currency to exchange. The dollar remained stable no matter what country you were in. Traveling was as I had hoped it would be: riding on a regional bus through Turkey and Iran with passengers from all over the world.

The bus pulled into the Tehran bus station around 10 a.m. on a sunny Friday morning, May 17th. I shook hands with Jean Noël, and we said our goodbyes and "bon voyages." He was hoping to catch a bus to the Afghan border, and I was staying in Tehran for a couple of days.

The bus station was located near the center of the city, so I put on my pack and easily found Tehran's main Post Office. I was expecting letters from my family and one letter, in particular, from friends of my parents who were living in Tehran at the time. I went up to the main desk, presented my passport, and asked, in English, if there was any mail in Poste Restante for me. *Poste Restante* is the French equivalent for General Delivery. The main post offices around the world held letters in Poste Restante until they were claimed by the recipient. The man behind the counter went to the cubby holding international letters for names starting with "F." After going through the stack, he came back with letters from my mom and dad, brother and sister, and a letter from Mr. and Mrs. Brown. If I was lucky, Mr. Brown would invite me to stay with them for a couple of days. Out of respect, I always used Mr. and Mrs. when speaking to friends of my parents.

Mr. Brown and my dad had been army buddies when they were stationed at the Panama Canal during WWII. Their mission was to defend the Panama Canal, which, fortunately, they didn't have to do. The Browns moved to Tehran after the war when Mr. Brown took a job with a company selling parts for oil production. I opened Mr. Brown's letter and, luckily, he did invite me to stay with them and gave me a number where he could be reached. I phoned him, and the first thing he told me was to call him Lloyd and invited me to meet him for lunch at his club. I had been traveling overnight and wasn't prepared to meet Lloyd at his club. I knew that Lloyd was in business in Tehran and that the club might be much nicer than what I had been used to for the past few months. I went back to the bus station and found a sink with running water at the back where I cleaned up the best I could after spending the last 24-plus hours on a bus. I had grown a beard before I left Colorado, and it saved a lot of time not shaving as I traveled. I took out my razor and shaved around the edges which were getting a little shaggy after a few days on trains and buses. I opened my pack and dug out the sage-green corduroy sport coat I had been carrying around since January. The coat was badly wrinkled, so I shook it out and pressed it the best I could with my hands to smooth out some of the bigger wrinkles. It was warm in Tehran and a little humid, and I hoped that would help relax the corduroy. That was the best I could do. Once I was halfway presentable for my father's wartime buddy, I put on my pack, went out to the street, and flagged down a taxi.

It turned out that the club was a very fancy, exclusive American club for those who spoke English. I figured most of the people there were somehow related to the oil industry. After the low-cost way I had been traveling, this club was a bit of culture shock for me. I had gone from being a backpacking traveler to wearing a coat and tie and staying with friends of my parents.

Once inside the club, I felt a disconnect from the reality of being in Iran. I had a club sandwich and a Coke while Lloyd talked about being stationed in Panama with my dad 30 years earlier. I had a light lunch because I told him my stomach was a little queasy from drinking a fake Fanta on the train from Istanbul. Lloyd gave me some great advice: if I had an upset stomach from eating bad food, the best remedy was to eat some yogurt with cucumbers much like the Indian dish, raita. He ordered a small dish of yogurt and chopped cucumber, and I was on the road to recovery. I would use that method of soothing my stomach a few times in the months to come.

After lunch, we climbed into Lloyd's chauffeured car for the ride back to his home. I was introduced to the driver, whose name was Artoosh. When we reached the house, it was a modern ranch-style home built in the suburbs of Tehran. Inside, it was like being in any American home: big kitchen and plenty of rooms. I was introduced to Lloyd's wife, Vickie, who was very kind and welcoming. She took me down a hall to a room where I found a real bed with sheets and blankets and my own bathroom. Wow! Culture shock! I was back in the American culture, only it existed in a suburb of Tehran. I knew that most people in that part of the world didn't live in that level of luxury. I had been in Asia just a few days but could see what oil could do for the people and countries connected to it.

Vickie knew my parents from the times when she and my mom would fly down to Panama for visits with their soldier husbands. She told me that, when she and Lloyd first moved to Tehran in the 1950s, the electricity was intermittent and was usually turned off at midnight. They often used oil lamps to light their home in the evenings. Things had changed in 20 years, and the Browns had a modern home filled with beautiful rugs, art, and furnishings from Iran and around the region. Staying in their home was far from low-cost travel, but I was looking forward to a shower and clean bed.

Saturday the 18th, I spent with Vickie. She had her own car and was kind enough to show me around Tehran. She first took me to the Marble Palace built in the 1930s by the Shah's father. The palace was initially used as a residence for the royal family, but in 1965, a soldier tried to assassinate the Shah, so in 1970, it was turned into a museum. Since that time, the Marble Palace had been open to the public and had become a popular tourist site. The Coronation Room had the most spectacular exhibits. It was a large, brightly lit room with mirrored walls displaying intricate silverware; copperware; and beautifully designed rugs, tiles, and glassware. I had no idea about the history and beauty of Persian arts and crafts. Iran became the official name of the region originally known as Persia, in 1935.[4]

Next, Vickie took me to a street where a lot of carpet dealers had set up outdoor stalls to display their wares. She told me that you can bargain for just about anything, and, since I would be traveling further into

------

[4] *Persia and then Iran were ruled by Shahs, or Kings, until February 1979, when the Islamic Revolution forced the Shah into exile and the Ayatollah, or "Supreme Leader," took control. In November of 1979 a group of Iranian college students stormed the American Embassy in Tehran and held 66 Americans hostage for 444 days. A few were released before the 444 days were over.*

Asia, I should learn the art of bargaining. She stopped at one stall and turned over some of the rugs to show me the difference in materials and weaves and what was considered a better rug. A rug with a tighter weave would cost more than a rug with a looser weave. Vickie had lived in Iran long enough to speak Farsi. As we passed by the stalls, she would stop and have a conversation with the merchants, but she told me she hadn't planned on buying anything, so we kept on walking.

As we walked, she explained how merchants start by offering a high price for the item expecting the prospective buyer to counter the offer with a much lower price. They go back and forth throwing out prices until either a price is agreed upon and the deal is made, or, if not, the buyer walks away.

Further down the street, we came to five outdoor stalls selling jewelry. We stopped at one of the stalls, and Vickie asked to see a ring and inquired about its price. The merchant began the bargaining by offering the ring to Vickie for 8,000 rials. The exchange rate made the Iranian rial worth about 5¢, making the merchant's offer about $400. Vickie countered by offering 3,000 rials ($150). The merchant came down a little from the initial 8,000 rials, but Vickie's top offer was 3,500 rials ($175), and she wouldn't budge from that price. Vickie thanked the merchant, returned the ring, and we started to walk away from his stall when the merchant shouted out that he would accept the offer of 3,500 rials. We turned around, and Vickie ended up buying the very nice turquoise ring because the man offered a price she couldn't walk away from. By trying to teach me how to bargain, she had ended up with a beautiful ring. Vickie told me that, sometimes, if sales were slow, the merchant will make a deal and take less profit, hoping that the one sale would precipitate more selling.

We met Lloyd for lunch at a nice Iranian restaurant. We ordered lamb kebabs, yogurt, milk, and rice. After lunch, we were discussing my travels when Lloyd asked me how I pronounced the name of the country we were in. I had been pronouncing Iran as it is spelled "I-ran." He then asked me how I would pronounce the name of the country spelled I-R-A-Q. I said that I pronounce Iraq as "E-roq." Lloyd informed me that Iran is pronounced just like Iraq only with an "n" instead of the "q." The correct pronunciation of Iran was "E-ron," not "I-ran." It was a good lesson that I would not forget.

Next, Vickie dropped me off at the Central Bank of Iran, where the Royal Jewels were on display. The Shah's father transferred the incredible collection of Royal Jewels to the State of Iran. When the present Shah took the throne, he decreed that some of the most spectacular of the jewels should be on display at the Central Bank for the people of Iran to see. I had seen fabulous collections of jewels in London and the Vatican, but this collection of Persian gems was extraordinary. The priceless emeralds, rubies, diamonds, silver, and gold had been collected over many centuries of conquest. One of the most interesting objects in the collection was a library-sized globe made of pure gold covered with over 50,000 gems. It was commissioned by Nasseridin, who was the Shah in the 1850s. The oceans and seas were created using emeralds, the continents were filled in with rubies, and only Iran and France were inlaid with diamonds. France was the center of arts and culture in the 1850s, and French was the international language at the time, which might explain why France merited the diamonds.

Sunday, May 19th, was not a day of rest in Muslim Iran but a working day. Some of the department stores in Tehran had areas where the craftspeople were creating products right in the store, so Vickie took me to see how they did their work. Later, we stopped by a pharmacy where I got an anti-hepatitis shot and bought the malaria pills I would need as I went further east.

Since meeting Lloyd and Vickie, I had learned how to sooth a grumbling tummy, pronounce "Iran" correctly, and bargain with merchants for a fair price. I had seen ornate crafts, a glittering palace, and dazzling gems all in the short time I had been in Tehran.

Iran was a modern country. With all its oil, there was nothing backward about it. Its roads and medical services were first rate. The stark contrast between modern Iranian buildings and traditional Persian crafts showed me how an ancient people evolve in a modern world. I appreciated staying with the Browns and enjoyed those few days off the road before heading to Afghanistan. I thanked them sincerely. Lloyd told me that he and Vickie would be moving back to the States in a year or two because he felt the Shah wouldn't be staying in power too much longer. He wanted to be out of the country before that happened.[5]

Before I left Lloyd and Vickie's home, I had a conversation with Artoosh, the Browns' driver. He told me to be careful of my valuables as I traveled. I thanked him and decided to repack my things so that my most personal possessions would be all in one or two places and easy to keep track of.

Lloyd and Vickie had a few paperbacks on a bookshelf and offered me one. I chose Ian Fleming's *You Only Live Twice.* James Bond's international adventures made for a perfect travel book. When it was time, I took my pack and shoulder bag out to the Brown's car. Lloyd had sent Artoosh back to the house to pick me up and take me to the bus station. Lloyd always rode in the back seat, but Artoosh let me ride shotgun on the way to the bus. He wished me well, reminded me to be careful, and dropped me off at the same bus station where I had arrived three days before.

I had plenty of time to purchase a ticket and board the 4 p.m. bus to Mashhad in eastern Iran where I would obtain my visa for Afghanistan. After this short break from the road in Tehran, I was all set to continue my travels.

I walked up to a big, shiny, Greyhound-type bus with

---

[5] *He was right. The Browns moved back to the States before the Shah was overthrown in 1979.*

wide, clear windows. The ticket to Mashhad was for a specific seat on the aisle directly behind the driver. After putting my pack in the overhead rack, I sat down next to an elderly Iranian woman who kept her face well hidden under a veil and turned toward the window. The seat was comfortable, and I had plenty of legroom with a clear view of the Iranian countryside through the windshield. I was the only Western traveler on the bus, which was fine with me.

After an hour, the bus pulled over at a tea shop by the side of the road. I climbed down from the bus and saw a big white mountain in the distance. We had stopped at a tea house with an excellent view of Mount Damavand, a dormant 18,400-foot (5,600 meter) volcano. The mountain was huge, covered with last winter's snow, and surrounded by smaller hills in the middle of a gently rolling terrain. The late afternoon sun lit up the western side of the cone-shaped mountain. After a cup of hot, dark, sweet tea, we re-boarded the bus and pulled out of the teashop and away from the imposing dormant volcano. The elderly lady sitting next to me showed her appreciation for the tea by releasing small burps. I was not accustomed to that Iranian custom, but I wanted to experience customs that were different from my own. Where better to do so than on the bus to Mashhad. The seats reclined and I could stretch out, so I covered up with the space blanket and was able to get about eight hours of sleep before we reached the ancient city.

On Tuesday, the morning of the 21st, I awoke just as we were approaching the city. I was feeling good and felt rested, so I decided that I wouldn't stay in Mashhad. Instead, I would try to reach the Afghan border by the end of the day. The first thing I needed to do was visit the Afghanistan consulate and get an entrance visa stamped into my passport.

Once the bus arrived, I got off and took a taxi to the consulate. The man behind the desk asked for two photos of me, the equivalent of $5, and my passport. Thirty minutes later, I left the consulate with a visa that allowed me to enter Afghanistan. I left the consulate and saw four backpackers standing out front, talking. Alice and Mark were from the U.S., and Eric and Bob were English. All four had their visas for Afghanistan and were deciding how to get to the Afghan border. We agreed to share one of the taxis waiting nearby. So, the five of us hopped into a cab and pooled our money to cover the equivalent of $12 for the three-hour ride to the Iranian Customs Office at the border.

We walked into the customs office, presented our passports for the exit stamp, and walked out the door on the other side expecting to see the Afghan Customs Office. Instead, we saw a stretch of dry, barren, no-man's-land separating us from the Afghan border. There were three or four taxis waiting by the road to Afghanistan ready to give us a ride across the empty no-man's-land if we were willing to pay the inflated prices they were asking. The drivers were asking double the price to go three miles (five kms) for what it had cost us for the three-hour ride from Mashhad. The five of us weren't going to pay their outrageous prices, so we shouldered our packs and headed across the arid wasteland. It was the middle of the afternoon on a hot day when we started walking, but we felt strong and were excited to be hiking our way into Afghanistan.

After a couple of kilometers, we started to slow down due to the weight of our packs and the heat. It was hotter than we expected, but it was too late to rethink the taxi option. We had walked almost two hours and knew that we had to reach the Afghan Customs Office before it closed at 5 p.m. or we wouldn't be allowed into the country. None of us thought it would be a good idea to spend the night in the middle of a no-man's-land between Iran and Afghanistan. Even so, we started looking for a potential camping site as we slowly continued east. Just about the time we thought we weren't going to make it to the border, a car approached us from the Iranian side. A couple from Philadelphia stopped to ask us if we wanted a ride for the final kilometer. Bob let out a little whoop to celebrate our good luck, and I certainly shared his feelings. We sat on each other's laps and stuffed the packs that didn't fit in the trunk into any open space around us. We made it to the border with little time to spare.

We had only been driving on the bumpy road for a few minutes when the car pulled into a compound made up of a few one-story wooden buildings, a couple of military jeeps, and an old bus. As soon as the car stopped, we opened the doors and the seven of us tumbled out. The first thing I noticed was the silence. I realized that the entire feel of this new country was vastly different from the one I had just left.

I'd had a similar feeling when I crossed the border from the U.S. into Mexico with my brother, Rich, in 1972. Iran had oil, modern cars, trucks, buses, good roads, and the noise that went with modern culture in 1974. I was now in a place that was calm and quiet.

It was still warm, but there were enough trees around the border station to provide some shade. There were soldiers at the border, but they were very laid back compared to the soldiers we had seen at other borders. The Afghan soldiers were dressed in gray, ill-fitting, baggy, unpressed uniforms. Some wore caps, and they all wore sandals. They had rifles, but they appeared to be old and were slung casually over their shoulders or hung limply by their sides. One soldier had a small yellow flower protruding from the muzzle of his rifle. Another soldier was holding a delicate wooden cage that held a small bird softly chirping. Before we even reached the customs building, we were approached by moneychangers and one bus driver who was offering tickets for a seat on his bus to Herat as well as hashish, if we needed any. Although I knew I was in the land of great hash, I declined the offer because I didn't want to get busted before I even got past customs.

Once inside the customs office, we presented our passports and visas to an official to get the stamp which would allow us into Afghanistan. After our passports were stamped, we proceeded to another building where an official checked our vaccination cards to make sure we had the proper vaccinations. We were in a world of men in turbans, hot desert sand, mountains, hashish, and the eerie quiet that was enough to let me know I was in as different a place as I had ever been. We stepped up to a window that represented a bank where we could exchange cash or traveler's checks for afghanis, the currency of Afghanistan. We didn't have much choice other than to accept their exchange rate of 53Afs to one U.S. dollar. In a larger city, I could probably have gotten a considerably better exchange rate. There was only one bus going to Herat, so we ended up buying tickets from the hashish-dealing bus driver. Even as we were boarding the bus, he again offered what he said was good hashish. I thanked him but said no. The five of us climbed onto the old bus, which was already packed with a dozen or more Afghan men in turbans. When the driver sat down and closed the bus door, the odors on the bus were heavy, earthy, and human. After walking across no-man's-land in the heat of the afternoon, I'm sure we added to the odiferous mix. Windows were lowered around the bus to let in the cool evening desert air as we drove away from the border. I didn't know how long the bus would take to reach Herat. I was just happy to be on a bus and not camping in no-man's-land. After about 45 minutes of passing nothing but darkness, a light appeared on the right side of the road and the driver slowed down, pulled over, and parked in front of a low-built adobe building. The only light was coming from an opening in the side of the building.

The driver said something to the Afghan passengers, then looked at the five of us waving his hand in front of his mouth, indicating that we had stopped for something to eat. It was dusk and we hadn't had a meal since we'd left Iran.

Alice, Mark, Eric, Bob, and I climbed off the bus with some of the other passengers and followed the driver down some stairs to a large, open, carpeted room dimly lit by oil lamps. The subterranean roadside teahouse kept cool even on the hottest days. We removed our shoes at the bottom of the stairs and left them there.

The five of us were shown to a small table in the middle of the room where we sat down, cross-legged, on the carpeted floor. No sooner had we sat down than cups of hot green tea were placed in front of us. The tea was welcome after all the dusty traveling of the past day. The room was filled with men in turbans and robes. The only woman in the room was Alice. The men were speaking in hushed tones and didn't pay us much attention. We hadn't been seated for very long before each of us had a bowl of white rice with a lump of lamb on top, yogurt, and a piece of bread placed on the table in front of us. One of the servers walked around the room with a large silver tea pot keeping the cups full, pouring more hot green tea. There were no utensils on the table, so we followed the custom of eating with our right hands. I gathered some rice and a bit of lamb in my right hand, placed it to my mouth, and used my thumb to push it in. I was in Afghanistan, sitting on the floor of an exotic, dimly lit teahouse, surrounded by locals wearing turbans, and we were all eating the same wonderful meal. I was exactly where I wanted to be.

After we paid for the meal with a few coins, we put on our shoes, and walked up the stairs. I was almost to the bus when the driver called me aside and took a piece of paper from his robe. He unfolded the paper and showed me a chunk of black hashish. The hashish looked good, and smelled even better, but, once again, I declined his offer. It just seemed too easy buying hash from the first person I had met in Afghanistan.

The bus pulled into Herat shortly after midnight on the 22nd of May. There was no moon to light the town as we entered. I had heard from a few travelers to avoid staying at a hotel called the Minerathotel. It was said to be a dump. Nevertheless, the bus pulled in front of the Minerathotel and stopped. The driver must have had a kickback arrangement with the owner. I asked him about other hotels, but he said this is the only hotel open after midnight. So, those of us who needed a place to stay grabbed our packs and checked into the dubious Minerathotel.

The hotel had two floors with several rooms on both floors. Alice, Mark, Eric, Bob, and I were given rooms on the second floor. The two couples each had their own room, and I had a room by myself. They weren't exactly rooms but cubicles with two cots, a table, and a window overlooking Herat. Oh yes, there were also no ceilings to these rooms. They were open to the main ceiling of the large room containing all these cubicles. Any conversations in the cubicles would have to be in whispers.

It wasn't till we were in our rooms that I dared to think

about the driver's offer of hashish. The driver also had a room in the hotel on the second floor, but on the other side of the staircase. Eric and Bob came over to my room, and we talked about scoring some hash. I knew that the driver was just across the hall. Since I was the one the driver had approached, I screwed up my courage and went to knock on his door. He invited me in. I walked in to see what he was selling, and he brought out a folded paper holding a nice chunk of hash and broke off a small bit for me to smell. Yes, it smelled fresh, it was soft, and easy to break up. He took some, crumbled it up, and put it into a rolling paper that already had tobacco in it. He rolled up the mixture, licked it, closed the joint, and lit up. I knew before I smoked it that it would be good, and it was. Even mixed with the tobacco it tasted great, and I quickly got a buzz. Whether it was the hash, tobacco, or the combination, I didn't care. I hadn't smoked any cannabis since I'd left Europe, and I was experiencing my first Afghan hashish high. I paid the driver his price of 100Afs ($1.75) and walked out with a nice chunk of hash.

When I got back to my room, Eric and Bob were waiting. I showed them what I had scored and immediately rolled some hash and tobacco into a joint. We smoked it by the one open window in the room and by the time we finished the joint I was totally stoned, not only from the joint but from a day that had begun in Iran and ended in Afghanistan. It was late, and I was wasted. The three of us were chatting quietly when the one single bare light bulb hanging from the ceiling suddenly went out. Shit! I was sure we were about to be busted. I grabbed the chunk of hash and ran to the open window prepared to toss it out. My heart was racing and my arm was cocked ready to throw the hash out the window as soon as someone burst through the door. The place was completely silent. No one moved. I was still waiting with my arm cocked, but nothing happened. I relaxed and went to the door. Nothing. I went into the hall, but it appeared that there were no lights on anywhere in the hotel. I walked back into my room and looked out the window. It looked like the entire village of Herat was dark. There was absolute silence. The village had just turned off the generator that powered the lights, and everyone had gone to bed except us. After the excitement, the guys returned to their room, and I went to bed stoned.

In the morning, I said goodbye to Alice, Mark, Eric, and Bob and found a man in the lobby selling bus tickets from Herat to Kandahar. I bought a bus ticket for 180Afs that would take me 350 miles (560 kms) across the Registan Desert to the city of Kandahar in southern Afghanistan. There was another old Greyhound-type bus parked in front of the hotel, and, when the few of us who were taking the eight-hour bus ride to Kandahar climbed on board, we had our choice of seats.

The passengers included six or seven Afghans, a man from Hungary, and me. I figured that the trip across the desert to Kandahar wasn't going to be too bad since the old bus had cushioned seats and might even be air-conditioned.

The bus drove away from the hotel, went a couple of blocks, turned a corner, and stopped. The driver turned to the passengers and said something in the Dari or Pashto language. The Afghans stood up, got off the bus, and started to grab their bundles and luggage from the storage under the bus. They walked across the dirt road to an old army truck outfitted with wooden benches. The older vehicle could have been a troop carrier. Above the benches were open windows, each topped with a roll of canvas that could be unrolled to cover the window protecting the passengers from bad weather or sandstorms. Our fellow passengers were handing up their bundles to a man on top of the truck to be stored for the trip. The Hungarian and I finally got the message that we were not traveling to Kandahar on the original bus but were to transfer to the troop carrier for the ride across the hot desert. There was no explanation, and we just looked at each other and figured that we had been victims of a bait-and-switch con. I got off the nice, cushy bus, walked across the road, handed my pack to the man on the roof, and found a seat on a bench next to an open window. The troop carrier drove around Herat making several stops picking up more passengers until the remaining bench space, and a lot of the floor space was filled with Afghans in turbans, a few chickens, and one woman wearing a *chadari*, sometimes called a burqa. The chadari covered the woman from head to toe with only an opening for her eyes. Seeing a woman in a chadari was new to me, and I wondered how uncomfortable she would be in the heat of the desert.

The road from Herat to Kandahar was a hot, dusty, thirsty experience but a truly memorable ride as I sat on a wooden bench next to an open window with the shimmering Afghanistan desert passing by.

Registan Desert, Afghanistan
(The landform in the above photo reminds me of
Camelback Mountain in Phoenix, Arizona.)

I had heard that there were bandits in Afghanistan who would occasionally stop a bus and rob the passengers for their money. I knew that something like that could happen, but I wasn't worried. If bandits stopped the bus, I didn't think I would be harmed, and, even if they took my pack and shoulder bag, I was confident I could deal with the consequences. There are risks when traveling, and I was ready to take some. I had been traveling with my passport and traveler's checks in my shoulder bag and knew I would have to keep those things closer to my body for the next few months. I would have to find a money belt to tie around my waist, but first, I would have to cross the Registan Desert. The truck pulled over at a small oasis in the middle of the desert.

There were stands along the road where passengers could buy soda drinks and a few other items. I found a stand selling tea in glass teacups and bought one. I could drink the tea because the water had been boiled which killed the bugs that could make me sick. The hot tea tasted strong and sweet, plus it soothed my parched throat. I was happy to have some liquid and knew I would need more for the rest of the ride. I wasn't carrying water, but I was leery of buying a drink in a bottle since my episode with the fake Fanta soda. At one of the stands, a man was selling a few pieces of fruit and vegetables. I spotted one large cucumber for sale, and quickly purchased it as a solution to my thirst. I took my seat by the window, and, when the bus was loaded and moving, I took out my knife and peeled the skin off the top of the cucumber. I took my time over the next few hours slowly nibbling the cucumber, cutting off more skin, and nibbling down the cucumber for moisture. The cucumber tasted good, stayed juicy, and I never became thirsty. I did notice that one of the Afghans on the bus undid the end of his turban, tied the tip into a small knot which he put into his mouth, and sucked on it to produce saliva. I was happy with my cucumber. (At the time, I was more interested in survival than the image of me sucking on a peeled cucumber).

The truck arrived at the Kandahar bus depot in the early afternoon. The Hungarian traveler and I shared the seat of a two-wheeled cart pulled by a swaybacked horse. We paid the driver to take us to the hotel district. Although Kandahar was the largest city in the south of Afghanistan, it still felt small. The one- and two-story buildings on either side of the dusty streets were made of a straw and clay material, just like adobe. The Hungarian had the name of a hotel where he wanted to stay, so we said our goodbyes. I had heard that the place to stay in Kandahar was the Bamiyan Hotel for only 20Afs (35¢) a night. The Bamiyan Hotel was one of the larger buildings in Kandahar with several stories. When I checked in, I received a key for a room on the third floor. The room was small and clean with one bed, a table, and a couple of chairs. After riding in an open truck through the hot dusty desert, I needed a shower. I went down the hall and took a cold shower, which was the only temperature available, since there was only one water pipe coming out of the wall. As it was late May, the air temperature was in the mid-80s° F (26+° C), which made the cold water coming out of the pipe room temperature and very refreshing.

After I got into some clean clothes, I went out and found a nearby restaurant where I ordered vegetable stew, which I ate with my right hand. I was still thirsty and drank lots of hot, sweet dark tea. Feeling better after a shower and food, I walked around Kandahar passing by rows of small shops. Each small shop was manufacturing different products. One shop had men pounding on tin sheets to make trays. In other shops, men were making charcoal or building furniture, and, in front of one shop, a man sat on the ground making wooden bowls using his foot to turn the lathe since there was no electricity on that street. He used a sharp chisel to take off the four corners of a wood block as it turned until he had a cylinder spinning smoothly on the lathe. Once he had the cylinder shape, he sharpened his chisel and started taking thin slices of wood from the center of the cylinder to begin shaping the wood into a bowl. I had made wooden bowls on an electric lathe and appreciated the effort and coordination it took to use foot-power to turn the lathe while carving the wood at the same time. I passed a few stalls selling dried fruits and nuts. I love nuts, so I bought a small paper bag of pistachios in the shell to carry in my shoulder bag for the long bus rides.

On the way back to the hotel, I was stopped at a side street by a line of camels that seemed to be in a caravan coming in from the desert. There were at least a dozen camels, all carrying packs, being led by men dressed in white robes and turbans. I might have seen a camel in the zoo, but never so close that I could smell it. These were the sights and smells of Afghanistan that I wanted to remember.

When I got back to the hotel, I recognized a backpacker I had met when I checked in. I stopped to say hello, and he told me that there was a hookah up on the roof and people were getting stoned up there. A hookah is a large water pipe that is used in that part of the world to smoke tobacco and hashish. He said that everyone took a little hash to the roof and tossed it into the bowl of the hookah. Then, they could grab a tube and take a hit. I went up to my room and took my hash up the stairs. When I walked onto the roof, there were a dozen or more travelers milling around, taking turns drawing smoke out of the hookah. The Bamiyan Hotel was a traveler's hotel with a lot of people going in both directions stopping there for a night or two. The people on the roof had all contributed a different kind of hashish into the bowl, so I broke off a corner and added a little of what I had scored from the bus driver in Herat onto the glowing coals.

I grabbed one of the tubes that connected to the hookah and inhaled a hot, smooth, and delicious toke. The mixture of hash in that bowl was very strong, but the high was clear. There was no feeling of the physical heaviness that sometimes comes with hashish. It was very trippy to be stoned on a roof in the middle of Kandahar, Afghanistan, with a bunch of travelers wearing a variety of colorful clothing picked up in the countries they had passed through. I was still wearing jeans, while most of the other guys were wearing different kinds of cotton draw-string pajama bottoms that looked cool in the bright afternoon sun. I felt like the new kid on the block, or the roof, and I was. I spoke to some of the rooftop smokers and met a few travelers who had come all the way from Australia and were on their way to Europe. There were mostly young men wearing beads, beards, plain pajama bottoms, and shirts, but there were also a few women wearing colorful skirts and vests. Many of the folks gathered around the hookah looked like seasoned travelers. Just being in a totally new environment was such a trip that I didn't need to get stoned. I was high on the exotic sights, smells, and culture of Afghanistan... but the hash was nice too!

I had a bus ticket from Kandahar to Kabul that was supposed to leave later in the morning of May 23rd, but before I boarded the bus, I wanted to walk around Kandahar one more time. I stopped at a small stand where a man was cooking eggs in a skillet over a propane burner. I ate the eggs with a little bread for breakfast and started walking up and down the dusty streets. One shop near the bus depot had beautiful handmade Kuchi clothing. The Kuchi people are a nomadic tribe who travel this part of the world in caravans and make their own clothing. Here was a shop selling shirts, pants, vests, and other things from the Kuchi people.

I was looking at some of the items hanging out front when a man came out and invited me inside. I followed him to the back of the shop and was invited to sit on a rug with the merchant and another man. The Kuchi men were dressed in traditional clothing of white cotton shirts and pants, but each man was wearing a beautiful vest. I was surrounded by piles of clothing hanging off the walls and stacked around us. I was looking for something small to buy, so that I could try my hand at bargaining. I had to get used to haggling over the next few months. This was an opportunity to buy a present for the daughter of my friend, Haruko.

Haruko and her family lived in Kabul, and I would soon be staying with them. The merchant brought out several small purses and wallets, and there was one small wallet which I decided to bargain for. He was asking 125Afs and I countered by offering 50Afs. We went back and forth a few times, but I couldn't get him any lower than 100Afs. I agreed to the 100Afs, but right away, I thought 100Afs was too much and tried to back out of the deal.

I could tell both men were not happy and became very serious. The merchant explained to me that, once a deal is agreed upon, it was considered bad form to go back on that deal. I didn't want to be in bad form, so I paid the 100Afs and bought the beautiful handmade Kuchi wallet as a present for Haruko's daughter. I also learned a lesson in the etiquette of haggling that I wouldn't forget.

I went back to the hotel, got my pack from behind the desk, and waited in the hall until I saw Tony, a guy I had met on the roof. I said hello, took him aside, and gave him the chunk of dark, tasty hashish that I'd bought from the bus driver in Herat. I didn't want to be carrying hashish into Kabul where I would be staying with a family friend, her husband, and two kids. I had already purchased the bus ticket, so, when I walked into the bus depot, I found the bus and boarded for the 8-hour ride up to Kabul. I found a seat by the window, put my shoulder bag at my feet, and waited. To prepare for the bus ride, I had gone to the market and bought a sweet melon for the moisture, two brownies, and the bag of pistachios to eat along the way. The bus stopped periodically for prayers, tea, and bathroom breaks.

When the bus pulled over for prayers, most of the passengers exited the bus, faced Mecca, unrolled their prayer rugs on the side of the road, knelt, and prayed. Even with the stops, the eight hours passed quickly on a beautiful bus ride that climbed out of the hot Registan Desert up to the milder climate of Kabul at 5,900 feet (1,800 meters).

Stopping for prayers

Bus Ticket from Kandahar to Kabul (front)

90
Roorke
150

Caution	دقت
1 Your hand bag is on your own	۱ اموال دست و بشخ خود را نگهدارید
2 The sold ticket is not transferable our enders	۲ تکت فروخته شده دوباره فروخ نمیر
3 luggage	۳ قیمت بره ... رسید ... زیرا قیمت دار اقل ...
4 kilostre otcharge overload Peshchilo till kandahar 104fs. Herat 20Afs. Than go 4p	... ۲۰ ... ۳۰ ... ۴ ... ممنوعه ... آن ... مالک برکت
4 Prohibited cargo is not allowed to be transported	۵ ...
5 please be continue at punctal Note: Insurance also of Posial bus as to ther member available we wishya... Good Tair	... وقت سیر دونیس ...

Bus Ticket from Kandahar to Kabul (back)

I first met Haruko when I was in high school and she was a student from Japan, studying Buddhist art at a U.S. university. Her roommate was a neighbor of ours, and during one visit home, she introduced Haruko to our family, and we became friends. Haruko became a specialist on the Buddhist art of Northern India and Central Asia. She married Ahmad Ali, the director of the Kabul Museum and had two children. She had been given permission to research the hundreds of artifacts being stored in various locations around Kabul and had discovered many fine pieces from Persian, Buddhist, and Islamic dynasties. The art she found had been stored in caves and back rooms and was now displayed in the Kabul Museum. Afghanistan had been a crossroads of ancient Asia, and even Alexander the Great had passed through, leaving in his path many artifacts and the blue-eyed descendants of his army.

When the bus arrived, I found a pay phone and called Haruko, who welcomed me to Kabul and told me where I could find a taxi which would take me to her home. She lived a few minutes outside the center of town, and, when I knocked on their door, they welcomed me into their beautiful home, introduced me to their children, and led me to my own room with a bathroom and a bookcase full of books on Afghanistan in many different languages.

On Saturday, Haruko showed me around Kabul, and that afternoon we stopped at the Kabul Museum where some of the artifacts she had rediscovered in storage were on display. Haruko walked me around the floors of that amazing museum covered with cases full of fascinating objects from ancient civilizations that had passed through Afghanistan over the past two millennia.

She gave me the same first-class tour of the museum that she had given to U.S. Vice President Spiro Agnew in January of 1970.[6] She had been honored to also give the same tour to the Crown Prince Akihito and Princess Michiko of Japan in 1971. I was shown amazing ivory, iron, and even wooden relics that were thousands of years old and had originated from as far away as Germany, Greece, Egypt, Rome, India, and China. The dry climate of Afghanistan helped preserve some of the treasures housed in the museum that would never have survived in a wetter climate.

Sunday the 25th, I was invited to join Haruko and Ahmad for lunch at the home of one of Ahmad's brothers. Ahmad's family gathered for lunch on most Sundays, and this Sunday, I had the opportunity to meet his family – his mother, father, sisters, and brothers. They were all highly educated and didn't require the women to wear the chadari in my presence.

A few days after arriving in Kabul, Haruko told me that Ahmad was traveling to a conference in Paris and would be gone for a month. She explained that custom would not allow for a male friend to stay in the house with the wife while the husband was away, so I could no longer stay in their home. Haruko was very sorry that I couldn't stay and apologized, but I fully

---

[6] Agnew had committed some questionable activities and resigned in 1973 and was replaced as Vice President by Gerald Ford.

understood and didn't want to make her feel uncomfortable. She solved the problem by finding a place for me to stay with two foreign women who were working in Kabul.

Mauricette was from Mauritius, the island nation in the Indian Ocean, and Sally was from England. They were sharing a home near the center of Kabul and had an extra room, which they offered to me. I thanked Haruko and Ahmad, packed up my things, and moved in with Mauricette and Sally. The two women were part of an international group of young people who worked in Kabul. I spent a week experiencing the expat life there, and I met their friends from Denmark, Spain, Sweden, Holland, and England, as well as a woman from the U.S. who worked for the U.S. Agency for International Development. The others worked for organizations such as the UN, the British Consulate, or the Peace Corps. They went to work during the day, but at night, they would get together and party. The foreign community that I partied with were not pot smokers but liked to drink beer. I was having a great time but wanted to see more of Afghanistan before moving on to Pakistan. Some of the folks I had met at a party were going into the mountains for a few days and invited me to come along.

On the morning of June 1st, I was picked up at 4 a.m. in the dark by Jan and his sister, Elizabeth, from Denmark as well as Berta, also Danish, and Eduardo from Mexico. We were going to the Kabul truck depot where we were to catch a truck to the village of Bamiyan up in the mountains of central Afghanistan. When we arrived at the depot, the truck had already left at 4 a.m., and we were too late. Jan was going to come with us, but, after missing the early bus, he decided to return home and left Elizabeth, Berta, Eduardo, and me at the truck depot. We walked outside and hired a taxi for 150Afs ($2.50) each, for a ride to Bamiyan.

Bamiyan is only a little over 80 miles (130 kms) northwest of Kabul, but between driving over twisting dirt roads and making stops for repairs, we averaged about 12 miles per hour (20 kms per hour). It was a fantastic drive through the mountains and valleys of central Afghanistan up to Bamiyan, which sits in the Bamiyan Valley at an elevation of 8,200 feet (2,500 meters). It reminded me of driving through the Rocky Mountains. After three flat tires and a carburetor repair, we arrived in Bamiyan seven hours later. Luckily, we had a taxi driver who was also a mechanic and an expert tire changer. As soon as the taxi dropped us off in the small village, we saw two huge Buddhas carved out of the face of a tall sandstone cliff. Elizabeth, Berta, Eduardo, and I were directed to a one-story adobe building that had a few empty rooms where we could stay for the night.

The man who answered the door showed us a room that slept four, which was just right for us. It was a small, empty room with a nice carpet and very little else. We each took a corner and unrolled our sleeping bags on the carpet. Very content to have a roof over our heads for the night, we shared the bathroom just down the hall. There weren't many people in the village and only a couple of places for visitors to stay.

Nearby our lodging was a small restaurant, where we ordered vegetables, rice, and tea. We saw that there was meat available, but we weren't sure how fresh it would be, so we stuck with veggies and rice.

The Bamiyan Valley was part of the ancient Silk Road, a route that connected China with the Western world. Caravans would pass through the Hindu Kush Mountain region as they followed the well-worn road back and forth between the Eastern and Western worlds. Those caravans had carried the artifacts I had just seen in the Kabul Museum. Bamiyan itself was an important site for Buddhist religious activity starting in the second century CE. Buddhist monks would live as hermits in small caves carved in the side of the Bamiyan cliffs, and monasteries served as centers for religion, philosophy, and art.

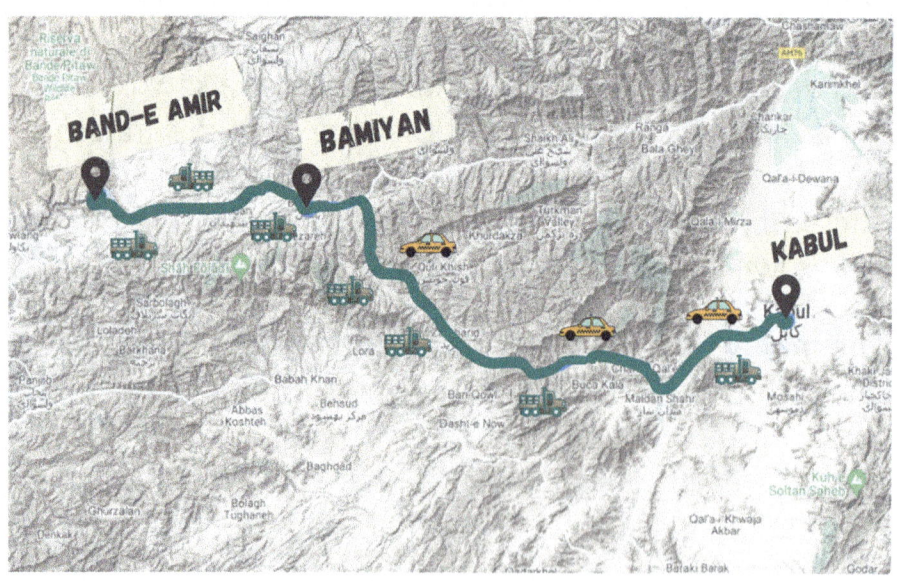

Kabul, Afghanistan to Bamiyan, Afghanistan (by taxi)
to Band-e-Amir, Afghanistan (by truck) back to Kabul (by truck)

Photobombed in Bamiyan

Both Buddhism and Islam played a strong role in Afghanistan's history, but, after the final Islamic conquest by the Turkic Ghaznavid dynasty in the ninth century, the region that is now Afghanistan would remain Muslim. Many of the Islamic emperors over the years wanted to destroy the standing Buddhas, believing they were forbidden images of God. Some even fired cannon balls at the Buddhas in an attempt to bring them down. The artillery fire only managed to knock off a leg of the tallest Buddha.[7]

Over the centuries, monks had lived in the carved-out caves where they would meditate. No monks lived in the caves in 1974, but wild Kuchi dogs had populated the lower caves and formed packs. Kuchi dogs were bred and trained by the same nomadic Kuchi people I had dealt with when purchasing a present for Haruko's daughter in Kandahar. The dogs were originally bred to protect caravans and the flocks of goats, sheep, camels, and other livestock that traveled with them. Wolves, big cats, and thieves would have preyed on the caravans were it not for the Kuchi dogs. I was familiar with the crafts of the Kuchi people but not their ferocious dogs.

Elizabeth, Berta, Eduardo, and I wanted a closer look at the standing Buddhas and bought tickets to walk around the base of the larger of the two Buddhas. The taller or "Western" Buddha stood about 180 feet (55 meters) high and was created around 618 CE,

---

[7] *Much later, in March 2001, the Taliban, a militant Islamic movement, succeeded where the various emperors had failed and destroyed the two standing Buddhas. Their loss is a huge cultural and historical loss for Afghanistan and the world.*

while the smaller "Eastern" Buddha was about 125 feet (38 meters) tall and was built around 570 CE.

Ticket for the Bamiyan Monument

The Afghans called the taller Buddha "Salsal" ("light shines through the universe"), and they called the smaller statue "Shamama" ("Queen Mother"). Looking up at the massive figures, I was amazed just thinking about the effort it must have taken to carve the Buddhas out of the cliff more than a millennium earlier.

We walked away from the larger Buddha and were going along the bottom of the cliff not realizing that there were wild Kuchi dogs living in the caves just a short way up from the path.

Berta was curious about the caves and started walking toward the entrance to the closest one. When she got near the entrance, a pack of five or six big brown dogs came running out of the cave barking, growling, snarling, and nipping at Berta's bottom. The quiet afternoon turned dangerous with those angry, charging dogs, easily weighing 100 pounds (45 kgs) each. I was pumped with adrenaline at the sound of the ferocious animals. Berta started running toward us, and the three of us started to yell and throw stones at the pack of dogs to scare them off. Most of them stopped, but one of the dogs got close enough to give Berta a small nip on the left buttock. We kept on yelling and throwing stones until we finally succeeded in forcing the dogs back into their cave.

As soon as it was safe, Berta quickly pulled down her pants to reveal the area where she felt the dog's teeth grip her pants and perhaps her skin. It would have been serious if the nip had broken the skin, but it looked as though the nip had just scraped the skin a little and hadn't drawn blood. Berta and Elizabeth immediately went back to the village to find a medical clinic and have a doctor inspect her to see if she needed any rabies shots.

We had heard that a Peace Corps worker in another part of the country had died from the bite of a rabid dog. Berta never had a reaction to the bite and didn't need the painful shots, but it was a very scary experience for all of us, especially, of course, for Berta.

We stayed only one night in Bamiyan, and, on the morning of June 2nd, the four of us got up at 6 a.m. and caught an early truck for a dusty, cold, four-hour ride west to Band-e-Amir.

Band-e-Amir is a high desert valley where there is a series of six sapphire-blue lakes, each contained in its own natural walls made from a mineral deposit called travertine. As the truck climbed out of the Bamiyan valley, we saw beautiful plateaus, high desert, and alpine peaks. The bumpy ride was like driving through Western Colorado and Eastern Utah with sandstone cliff faces and canyons around every turn. As we approached the Band-e-Amir valley and wound our way down from the surrounding mountains, we could see a few of the lakes below. The water was so clear that we could see huge fish swimming beneath the surface of the blue lakes. Band-e-Amir is a unique place, well worth the four-hour truck ride on another windy troop truck with hard wooden benches.

When the truck reached the small village of Band-e-Amir, we found a teahouse near one of the lakes that had a few empty guest rooms with Afghan rugs covering the floors. We each paid the owner of the teahouse 10Afs (17¢) so that the four of us could stay in one of the vacant guest rooms. Again, we each picked a corner of the room, put our packs down, and unrolled our sleeping bags on the carpet. The teahouse served a breakfast of eggs, potatoes, and tea for 25Afs (40¢). Lunches were a plate of rice, spinach with yogurt, and tea. If the meat of the day looked and smelled fresh, we could add it to the plate.

On June 3rd, Berta, Elizabeth, Eduardo, and I rented horses from some farmers and followed a winding shepherd's trail around the side of the closest mesa that eventually led us up to the flat top. From the top, we rode near the edge so that we could look down on the clear, blue lakes and up and down the valley. We were in the middle of Afghanistan, and the sky was so clear we could see a long way down the valley. We watched as hawks, eagles, and other birds hunted or just rode the updrafts.

Making whistles by the river

The higher elevation made it possible to see the 16,000 foot (5,000 meter), snow-covered mountains of the Koh-i-Baba range south of us. The Koh-i-Baba range is an extension of the even taller Hindu Kush range that sits to the north. The name Hindu Kush seems to come from a time when slaves were being transported from the tropical climate of India to the colder climate of Turkistan in western Asia. To reach Turkistan, the slaves had to endure the cold and snow while crossing the mountains on their journey through Afghanistan. Many of the slaves didn't survive, hence the name Hindu Kush, or Hindu Killer.

To get down from the mesa, we followed a trail that took us to the river on the valley floor. We followed another trail and rode down a canyon where we

A lake at Band-e-Amir

passed the remains of an old rock dwelling leaning against the canyon wall, charred by fires that must have once warmed the inhabitants on cold winter nights. We had reached the bottom of the canyon and were walking the horses slowly along the river when we saw three boys sitting on the bank by the water. When we got closer, we saw that they were making something out of the clay from the riverbank. It turned out they were making clay whistles. Each boy would take a small ball of clay from the riverbank and mold the moist lump around his thumb to make the shape of the whistle. Then, they removed the hollow piece of clay off the thumb and sealed the open end. With a small stick, they made holes in just the right places so that the musician could blow into the whistle and make a note or two. After they completed the whistle, they placed the still moist instrument on a warm stone on the riverbank to dry for a few hours. The boys had a whistle that was already dry, so I bargained with them until we reached an agreed price. I had a fresh new whistle made by one of the boys.

The next day, Tuesday, the 4th of June, I met Eduardo in the common room and had eggs; naan, a tortilla-like bread; and hot tea for breakfast. I had packed some dried fruit and nuts into my shoulder bag because Eduardo and I were going to walk to one of the lakes not far from the teahouse. I wanted to get a closer look at the lakes and the travertine walls that contained the water like a raised swimming pool. The water was crystal clear, and, with a perfectly windless and calm morning, the surface was glassy smooth. It looked as if the ground level had once been at the same level as the lake, but over time the dry wind had blown a certain amount of the surface away leaving only the travertine walls to hold the water. To see elevated lakes in the middle of the desert was surreal.

When Eduardo and I returned to the teahouse, he went to our shared room and packed his things. He wanted to catch the daily truck back to Kabul with Elizabeth and Berta. All three had to get back to their jobs, but I decided to stay at the teahouse one more night. We said our goodbyes, and I wished them a good trip.

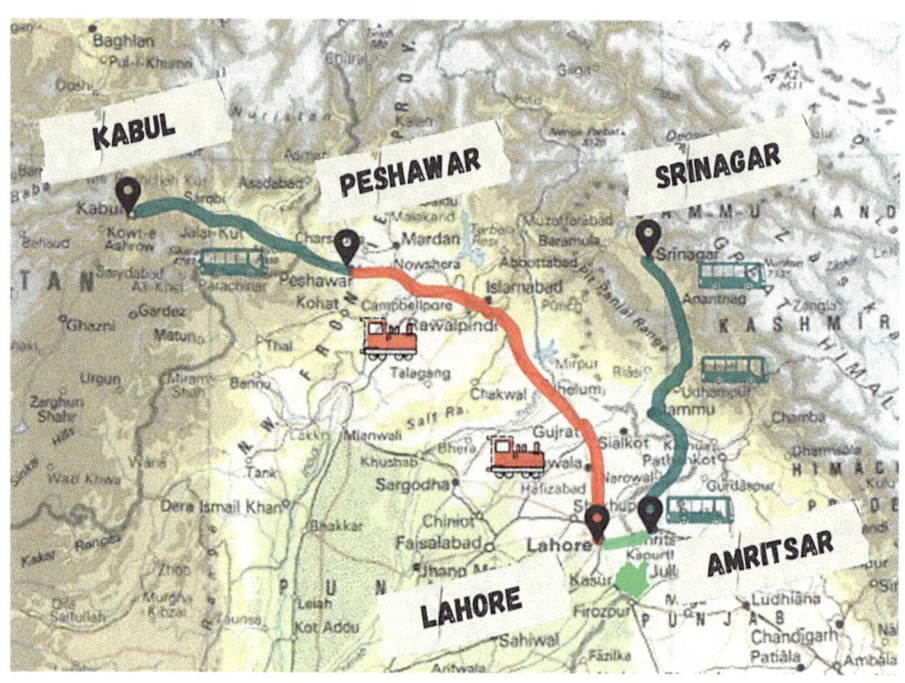

Kabul, Afghanistan to Peshawar, Pakistan (by bus)
to Lahore, Pakistan (by train) to Amritsar, India (by hitchhiking)
to Srinagar, India (by bus)

Sixth Full Moon

The sixth full moon found me deep in the mountains of Afghanistan. I was traveling by myself again and liked the feeling of being on my own and making decisions that only affected me. I was having tea by myself in the tearoom when three guys walked in. Woody, ex-U.S. Navy; Dave #1 from England; and Dave #2 from Colorado sat down and introduced themselves. We were like the ants and started exchanging travel information when a truck rolled into the compound. We saw a few more travelers with backpacks climb off the back of the truck and head our way. I was just getting to know Woody and the two Daves, when Tina and Todd joined us, and we started introductions again. Then five Japanese backpackers entered the tearoom, and my quiet teatime turned into a lively international gathering of 11 travelers.

Kenichi spoke a little English and introduced himself, two other young men, and two young women. Hiroshi also spoke some English, so with Kenichi and Hiroshi translating, the 11 of us sat around drinking tea and swapping stories about where we had come from and where we were going.

It was great meeting Japanese travelers and hearing about their travels coming from Japan. It looked like we would all be taking tomorrow's truck back to Kabul with a stop for one night in Bamiyan. We had a few minutes before dinner, so we all went behind the teahouse and found some low walls to sit on while passing around a joint.

No sooner had I said goodbye to my friends from Kabul than I found myself in the company of travelers telling stories of new places I had yet to visit.

When it was time for dinner, we strolled back to the teahouse and went to the kitchen for our bowls of rice, vegetables, and a little bit of lamb on top. All 11 of us sat on the floor of the teahouse and used our right hands to shovel the tasty meal into our mouths. After dinner, a few of us walked around the lake closest to the village. It was a clear night when both the barren landscape and the still lake seemed to light up due to the brightness of the perfectly round moon reflecting off the surface of the water. I was on my own but sharing June's full moon with new friends in the mountains of Afghanistan.

Early Thursday morning, Woody, the two Daves, the five Japanese travelers, and I met for morning tea before we headed back to Bamiyan. We left the teahouse and walked over to find a place on one of the wooden benches in the back of the truck, which was covered with a canvas canopy to protect us from the wind and sun. A few locals climbed on, but the truck sat silent in the cool morning air until there were enough passengers aboard to justify starting the engine for the bumpy four-hour ride. When there were enough paying passengers, the truck started the lumbering climb out of the Band-e-Amir valley.

After a beautiful ride through the mountains, the truck arrived back in Bamiyan. Woody, the two Daves, and I found the small Landi Hotel to stay in for the night. Kenichi, Hiroshi, and their friends had heard of another hotel and left to go find it. The Landi Hotel had dorm rooms containing six cots each. We checked in and were shown an empty dorm room where I put my pack down on a cot in the corner. We were the only people in the room, so we had plenty of space. As usual, the toilet and shower room were just down the hall. The hotel was clean and comfortable.

A few days ago, when I first arrived in Bamiyan with Elizabeth, Berta, and Eduardo, we had only walked up to the base of the large Buddha and along the sandstone cliff to the right when the pack of Kuchi dogs had burst from a cave nipping at Berta. I didn't want to go near the lower caves again but remembered hearing that it was possible to take a trail behind the larger Buddha and enter the cave on top of the massive head. I told Woody and the two Daves about the possibility of sitting on the Buddha's head, and they were interested in exploring, so once we were settled in the Landi Hotel, the four of us went in search of a trail. We left the hotel and walked up to the Buddha, turned left, and not long after the cliff face ended, we found a path through some brush that led up and around a hill until we were behind the cliff face. The trail ended at what looked like a cave in the hillside, but when we walked through the opening, we were standing on the Buddha's huge head, 180 feet (55 meters) up, looking out across the wide valley at snow-capped mountains on the horizon. The four of us walked further out onto the head, where there was plenty of room, and sat down. Our small group was quiet as we gazed at the distant Koh-i-Baba Mountains.

I looked up at the ceiling above the Buddha's head and saw faded, pockmarked images painted centuries ago. The images and designs had been painted by artists traveling the Silk Road sometime during the seventh century CE and are the earliest oil paintings using different colored pigments mixed with drying oils. The images above the Buddha's head might be characters from Buddhism's long history and mythology, but it was hard to tell due to the poor condition of the ceiling.

That was one of those moments when, by being far from what was familiar, it became clear to me that I was in another world where the expanse of history had been playing out for thousands of years and that my time on Buddha's head was just an infinitesimal moment. If I may paraphrase Ralph Waldo Emerson, "It's not about the destination, it's about the journey," and, quoting Buddha, "Happiness is a journey, not a destination; work like you don't need money, love like you've never been hurt, and dance like no one's watching."

I had set out on a journey that brought me, happily, to the top of Buddha's head. I felt good about my travels so far and was confident and eager to continue onward to Pakistan and India.

On Thursday, June 6th, the five Japanese travelers, Woody, the two Daves, four other Western travelers from the Landi Hotel, and I grabbed our packs and climbed onto an old military truck bound for Kabul. This troop transport truck with wooden benches had no canvas top and was completely open to the elements. Once we took our places on the benches, we were joined by an old man who carried a large cloth-wrapped bundle and was leading a goat on a leash. Another 10 local Afghans piled on for the bumpy 10-hour ride back to Kabul.

We started early in the morning while it was quite chilly, but the air warmed up at the lower elevations where it became hot and dusty. The goat peed and dropped little pellets which we lived with until the truck stopped for tea and our own toilet breaks. The ride in the open truck was again a beautiful journey through the middle of mountainous Afghanistan, but the wooden bench was hard on my ass, and I was happy when we pulled into Kabul.

Over the weekend, I took time to explore Kabul. On Saturday, I went to Chicken Street, which was the main shopping street in the city for all travelers and visitors. At the corners along Chicken Street were stalls grilling lamb kabobs. The kabobs were grilled on grates over a bed of glowing charcoal spread on the bottom of long metal trays. The air was filled with a smoky, appetizing aroma that drew me to a stall where I ordered a kabob before continuing down the street. Each side of Chicken Street was lined with small shops, one after the next, selling a variety of goods. You could find

Afghan carpets, antiques, gems, silver, gold, onyx chess boards, brassware, Afghan coats, clothing, and lapis lazuli.

Lapis lazuli is a beautiful, blue, semi-precious stone that has been mined in northeast Afghanistan for centuries. The beautiful intense blue color has made lapis a much-desired stone since 7,500 BCE. It has been made into jewelry, boxes, chess boards and pieces, small statues, and vases. It's also been used in architecture. When the blue stone appeared in Europe during the Renaissance and Baroque periods, it was ground up to create ultramarine pigment to be used in frescos and oil paintings by artists such as Raphael and Vermeer.

On Monday the 10th, I found my way to the area in Kabul where the black market was thriving. The black market was a place where items were sold or traded illegally, outside the established economy of the city. The black market in Kabul sat next to the traditional market, which sold fruit, vegetables, meat, live animals, kitchen utensils, clothing, and a variety of other goods, whereas the black market traded in illegal items, such as weapons, drugs, and foreign currencies. I was searching for the section where the moneychangers were offering foreign currencies. I was hoping to purchase Indian rupees at a lower rate than what I could get in India.

I walked around the edge of the main market until I found the area where the black-market dealers had set up stalls and were doing their business. I passed tables covered with a variety of rifles, pistols, knives, swords, and other weapons. I even passed by a few machine guns.

The group of moneychangers had gathered at one end of the street so that, as I approached the group, one of the men came up to me and offered a variety of currencies. There were a few serious looking men holding rifles, milling around the moneychangers, offering security. If I waited to exchange my dollars in India, I would only get 8 rupees to the U.S. dollar. I haggled with the moneychanger who had approached me and eventually bought seven Indian 100-rupee notes at a rate of 9.25 rupees to the dollar. It was illegal to take Indian rupees in or out of India, so I would have to smuggle the rupees across the border at Lahore. I wasn't worried about being caught because I figured that the border guards would be more interested in the hashish smugglers.

When I finished the transaction, I started bargaining with the man for some Pakistani rupees. I would be passing through Pakistan in a few days on my way to Srinagar in Kashmir and wanted some Pakistani currency. I didn't save much money buying the few rupee notes, but the adventure of purchasing something illegal on the black market excited me.

Sally and Mauricette had been generous enough to offer me a place to stay when I left Haruko's home because her husband went out of town. So, on my last night in Kabul, Sally, Mauricette, and I walked to Chicken Street for some good pizza and beer. At dinner, Sally told a disturbing story about a young woman she worked with. She said that her friend was not wearing a chadari as she was bicycling to work that morning. Suddenly, an old man grabbed her arm, pulled her off the bike, and threw her to the ground because she was wearing Western clothing, which was considered immodest by the more conservative members of the Muslim faith. Some young women in Kabul wanted to be free to wear Western clothing, but the religious men lashed out when they did. It wasn't safe for an Afghan woman to leave her head uncovered.[8]

We walked slowly back to Mauricette and Sally's house, which gave me the chance to thank them for introducing me to their international group of friends. Their kindness provided me the opportunity to experience how expats were living in Afghanistan. We said goodnight and went to bed.

For the three weeks since I had crossed into the calm atmosphere of Afghanistan from the more modern, oil-producing, 20th century Iran, it felt like I had entered a totally different world – and I had. Wherever I traveled in Afghanistan, I found the same tranquility I had experienced at the border. I felt comfortable traveling on public transportation, staying in dorm rooms or cheap hotels, and eating with my hands in small restaurants or street stalls. Crossing into Pakistan would mark the beginning of my travels through the

---

[8] *More recently, in 2021, the U.S. Army withdrew from Afghanistan, and the Taliban quickly overran the Afghan Army, taking control of the country. In May of 2022 the Taliban officially required women to wear the chadari or burqa in public.*

Indian subcontinent and South Asia, and I was relaxed and ready.

As a parting gift, I gave Sally and Mauricette a small vase holding a flower. I thanked them, put on my pack and hiked to the same bus station where I had arrived. The ticket window had a few people waiting, so I got in line and bought a ticket for 100Afs for the bus going from Kabul to Peshawar, Pakistan. I was looking forward to going through the fabled Khyber Pass, a strategic point on the Silk Road. I boarded a bus that resembled a school bus, found a seat next to a window, and settled in for the five-hour ride to the border of Pakistan. The open windows plus the warm weather and clear skies made for a pleasant ride across the sparse woodlands of eastern Afghanistan. When the bus reached the border, it pulled to a stop in front of a small, wood-framed building that held the Afghanistan Customs Office.

Without the Afghanistan flag flying in front, I wouldn't have known that the rundown building was the official customs office. The old customs buildings had the same rundown feeling as the customs buildings I had passed through when I first arrived in Afghanistan a few weeks before. I followed my fellow passengers off the bus and went into the customs office where we took our turns presenting passports to a young man in a faded uniform who sat behind an old school desk.

He took my passport, stamped it with an exit visa, and signed and dated it with a Bic pen. From there, I walked a short distance to the Pakistan border.

Outside one of the white buildings flew the flag of Pakistan, indicating the customs office. One by one the bus passengers left Afghanistan and went inside the Pakistan Customs Office. This office was a bit more official looking than the Afghanistan office. The customs officials wore crisp army uniforms, and a prominent photograph of Prime Minister Bhutto hung on the wall behind the main desk. I presented my passport which held the visa allowing me into Pakistan. I also presented my medical card showing which vaccines I had received, and when. Smallpox was still a threat in parts of the Indian subcontinent, and the effort to eradicate it required that all travelers entering Pakistan, India, and Nepal be vaccinated. Vaccines were also required to guard against Hepatitis A, Hepatitis B, and Typhoid fever. It was still possible to catch malaria in the countries I would be traveling through, so when I was in Tehran, I had purchased a supply of pills to protect me. I had been taking one pill daily for a few weeks to build up the protection I would need against any malaria-carrying mosquitos I might meet on my way to Darwin. As long as I was in Asia, I had to continue taking malaria pills. The BIT Guide said just about any pharmacy in a big city would carry the pills, so I could get more when needed along the way. I was directed to continue taking them for 10 days after leaving the malaria zone, which meant my first 10 days in Australia.

Since all my papers were in good order, the official stamped my passport, and I was allowed into Pakistan. I followed the other passengers and climbed back onto the same bus we had been riding since leaving Kabul. Peshawar was only 25 miles (40 kms) away, but the bus had to climb about 5 miles (8 kms) to the top of the Khyber Pass at 3,500 feet (1,070 meters) and then descend into the Peshawar valley, which was nearly at sea level.

The Spin Ghar Mountains separate Afghanistan from Pakistan, and the Khyber Pass was the only way over the mountains to and from Kabul. For centuries, the Khyber Pass was a strategic part of the Silk Road that connected Shanghai, China in the East to the port of Cadiz, Spain in the West. Many battles were fought to control the pass because whoever controlled the Khyber Pass controlled the flow of goods and armies. Genghis Khan and other Mongols used the pass when they wanted to expand their territory.

As the jostling bus descended from the summit, I thought about all the armies, people, camels, trade goods, and history that had tramped over the same route that I was traveling. Winding down the mountain, turban-covered men were standing by the side of the road, many of them holding long, ancient-looking rifles.

It didn't take long before I could feel the air temperature start to rise as the bus left the cool of the mountains and dropped into the heat of Pakistan and the subcontinent. The roads in Pakistan were good, and the bus quickly reached Peshawar, which was much warmer than Kabul. I had been wearing a jacket in the cooler weather of Afghanistan, but now I would have to find a place for it in my pack. I got off the bus and walked over to the nearby train station looking for a hotel. I found a small hotel offering a simple room with two cots and the toilet and shower down the hall. I was finding that the cheap little hotels were clean and provided a bed and bathroom for very little money.

I put down my pack, sat down on the bed, and pulled out the map of southern Asia. I refolded it to show Pakistan, India, and Nepal. I was heading into the hot summer weather of Pakistan and India. I had met many travelers who had gone up to the Swat Valley In northern Pakistan to avoid the heat and smoke good hashish, but I decided to just travel through Pakistan and cross into India before heading north to the cooler weather in the Indian state of Kashmir. Over the next few months, I would be spending many days in the heat, but first I wanted to visit the freshwater lakes of Srinagar. The problem was that there wasn't a direct route to Srinagar, India from Peshawar, Pakistan. The border between the Pakistan part of Kashmir and the Indian part of Kashmir was closed due to the unresolved border Issues between the two countries.[9]

The only way to reach Srinagar, the summer capital of Kashmir, would be to make a big loop starting with a

---

[9] *Dating back to 1947, India was divided by Partition, and a new country called the Dominion of Pakistan was created. Although Kashmir remained part of India, the population was at least 70% Muslim and related to Muslim Pakistan more than to Hindu India. A few weeks after Partition, the First Kashmir War was fought over the Kashmir-Jammu region between India and Pakistan, resulting in two-thirds of the region being controlled by India and one-third by Pakistan. In 1974, the border between the two countries was still in dispute and remains closed in 2023. In 2019, India repealed the status of Kashmir as a "state" and reorganized it, along with Jammu and Ladakh, into a "union territory".*

15-hour train ride southeast from Peshawar to Lahore Pakistan, where I would cross the border into India, and then travel for two days back north to Srinagar, by bus, where backpackers were staying on houseboats. I could see on the map that although the train would pass within 100 miles (167 kms) of Srinagar it would take me three days to get there.

Having plotted my next move, I left my pack in the room, went back over to the train station, and bought a ticket to Lahore. I knew from the BIT Guide and from other travelers that trains were the best way to get around Pakistan and India. I would be leaving early the next morning.

Outside the Peshawar train station early Wednesday, June 12th, I found a few food stands and bought a bag of roasted peanuts and a few dried apricots for the trip. I was hoping there would be vendors selling hot food at some of the stations we were sure to stop at. I boarded the train for the 15-hour ride to Lahore and met four backpackers sitting in one of the cars. Paul and Mark were from San Francisco and Chris and John were from England. I introduced myself, stowed my pack, and made myself comfortable for the long ride. We exchanged travel Information, and then, I was happy to sit quietly and look out the window, nap and read.

It didn't matter to me that it would take a few more days and a circuitous route to reach Kashmir. I enjoyed traveling and waking up each morning knowing I would be experiencing something new that day. Before I left Kabul, one of the expats had given me Hermann

Hesse's *The Glass Bead Game*, and I would have all day to see what the game was all about.

The western Himalayas run through Kashmir giving that part of India a cooler climate due to the higher elevation. June was still early enough so that it would be possible to hike into the mountains before the monsoons set in.

The open windows on the moving train kept the passenger car comfortable, but, whenever the train stopped at a station, the car quickly warmed up to the temperature outside.

At each station I could smell the aromas of Pakistan: cooking foods, smoke, and the smell of dense vegetation roasting under the sun and heat. It must have been 100° F (38° C) when the train arrived in Lahore, and that kind of heat was a new experience for me. I walked off the train into a wall of hot air, or maybe it was more like a pillow of hot air. It hit me, then enveloped me completely.

Waiting on the platform were a group of boys and young men trying to convince us that their hotel was the best place to stay. Paul, Mark, and Chris followed a young guy to a nice hotel while John from Bristol and I went with the boy who offered a room with two beds in the Swat Hotel for 4 rupees each, or 40¢. The hotel was made up of separate little units that each had a small table with two chairs and two rickety cots made up with dirty sheets. Very basic, but that was all we needed. I had never been in 100-degree heat before, and it was oppressive. Once in the room, I stripped down to shorts and stretched out on one of the cots. John and I rested for a while and then walked around the dusty grounds searching for the communal shower. We found a bare pipe, about six feet up, coming out of the middle of a white tiled wall. The single faucet turned on a thin stream of tepid water, which was enough to rinse me off and cool me down.

On June 13th, John and I decided to stay at the Hotel Swat for another day before crossing into India. Back in Chicago, my brother, Richard, was celebrating his birthday, but I was walking around Lahore to see what the shops and streets were like. It was so hot and bright, the air seemed to come over me in waves. I kept stepping into shops just to get out of the heat. One of the shops was selling auto parts, but I just looked around until I had cooled down enough to go back out into the heat for a few more minutes. When I got back to the room, I read, slept, and stood under the stream of tepid water every couple of hours.

On one trip to the shower, I passed a couple of guys sitting in front of a room. I said hello and was greeted by Ira from New York City and Cesar from Venice, Italy. A third guy came out of the room and introduced himself as Marco from Zagreb, Yugoslavia. They all spoke English, and we fell into easy conversation about our travels. After a few minutes they invited me to join them for a smoke. Marco brought out a clay cylinder, called a *chillum*, which was around four inches long with one end shaped like the bowl of a small pipe. He bent down, picked up a small stone, and dropped it into the bowl of the chillum. The stone would cover the small hole at the bottom of the bowl and block the hash from falling through, while still allowing the smoke to be drawn into the lungs. Marco then crumbled some nice-looking dark hash into the bowl, added a pinch of tobacco, and lit it up.

He held the pipe between the first and second fingers of his right hand and made a loose fist around the bottom of the pipe. His left hand closed around his right hand to fully enclose the pipe. Marco put his lips to the space made by the thumb and first finger, and, after Ira held a match to the bowl, Marco drew in the sweet smoke. Ira told me that they had pooled their money and were driving Marco's Fiat from Europe to Goa, on the west coast of central India. They were stopping for the night but would be crossing into India the next day. Once the hash and tobacco started to glow, they passed the chillum around. After a few hits from the chillum, I thanked them and continued to the shower, pleasantly stoned.

It was already 100° F (38° C) when I woke up at six in the morning on June 14th. I was sweaty and groggy from a fitful night of sleep in a hot stuffy room. I was thirsty, and the juicy slice of watermelon I had bought the night before sounded good. The melon would be warm, but at least it would be wet and sweet. I raised myself on one elbow to make sure it was still on the corner table where I had left it when I went to bed. The melon was there, but something was wrong. It was not bright red, as it had been when I went to bed. The fruit now had a black coating moving over it.

I reached for my glasses and put them on to get a clearer picture of the problem. The problem was that the watermelon was now covered by a mass of black ants that were feasting on my breakfast. I hopped out of bed, grabbed the infested fruit, and ran outside to find a place to dump it. I went back to the room and swept out the few ants left in the corner. John was still asleep, so I grabbed my towel and headed off for a rinse down. At that early hour, the water was cooler than it would be later in the day. It was June, and the heat and humidity had been building toward the monsoon rains, which would start in July. Living at a comfortable 7,000 feet (2,100 meters) in the foothills of the Colorado Rocky Mountains last winter had not prepared me for the blanket of humid heat I was experiencing.

After standing under the pipe for a few minutes, I started back to my room and passed by Cesar, Marco, and Ira, who were already smoking a chillum. They offered me a hit, and I gladly accepted. Cesar started the conversation by asking whether John and I were going to cross the border into India that day. I told him that we were going to take a bus to the border later that morning.

Cesar said that they were also crossing the border, and, since they had a car, they would be happy to give us a ride to save us the hassle of using the local bus system. I thanked them but told them that, since I had been traveling in Asia, it was my self-imposed policy to cross borders using only public transportation to avoid getting busted in someone's private vehicle.

Just before I left the States, I had read a news article about two young American women who had hitched a ride in Greece. They were picked up in a van that was crossing the border from Greece into Turkey, and, when the Turkish border guards found hash hidden in the van, everyone in the van was arrested as smugglers. The futures of the two women did not look bright sitting in a Turkish jail, and I was not going to echo their fate by crossing the border with people I didn't know.

Marco assured me that they weren't smuggling anything across the border because of the psychic Indian border guard. "What psychic border guard?", I asked. They couldn't believe that I hadn't heard of the woman who had psychic powers and knew if there was anything illegal being smuggled into India.

I did have something illegal to smuggle into India, but it wasn't hash: The Indian rupee notes I'd bought on the black market in Kabul. I didn't think anyone would look for rupee notes, but I wanted to hide them the best I could. So before leaving Colorado, I had a friend sew a hidden pocket onto the inside beltline of my jeans. I could hide a few extra dollars in the hidden pocket so that if my shoulder bag and backpack should get ripped off, I would still have money on me. My plan for crossing the border was to stick three of the rupee notes in the hidden pocket, a couple between photos in my wallet, and two under a loose piece of leather in the sole of my shoe. I was confident that I would pass through Indian customs with no problem. I was skeptical of the psychic border guard's supposed powers. I thanked Marco for the offer, but still declined the invitation to ride with them across the border in their Fiat.

As the morning progressed, John and I went to a nearby food stand for a breakfast of eggs and naan. It just seemed to get hotter and hotter, and the thought of dragging our packs and ourselves through the dusty streets of Lahore was not appealing to either of us. My policy of crossing borders on public transportation was weakening.

When we got back to the lodging, we found out that Ira had gone to the airport to catch a plane to Goa and would meet up with Cesar and Marco later. Marco told us that they really needed us to cross the border with them because they were short on cash. They explained that each car needed a certain amount of cash between the passengers to enter India. The additional foreign currency that John and I carried on us added up to the amount that the Indian government felt necessary. Marco said that he and Cesar would drive us to Amritsar in the Punjab. John and I finally relented and agreed to accept a ride across the border.

It didn't take long to stuff our belongings into our packs and load them into the trunk of the Fiat. Before we started for the border, I again asked them to promise that they weren't carrying any dope across the border. Cesar pulled out a little piece of hash and said that it was the last of their dope. They dropped it into their chillum, and we smoked it right there in the courtyard of the Swat Hotel before leaving for the border, slightly stoned.

We arrived first at the Pakistani side, and, with very little effort, had our passports stamped with exit visas. John and I again climbed into the back seat of the two-door Fiat to cross the short distance to the Indian border station. When we arrived at the station, a guard in uniform directed Marco to park the car. We grabbed our packs and walked into the customs building. The first room we entered was completely empty, but an open door led us through a series of mostly empty rooms until we came to a room where three Indian soldiers were sitting behind a desk. John, Marco, and Cesar passed through the room with no problem, but, when I passed the desk, one of the soldiers detained me and started asking me questions about military buildup in Pakistan. Had I seen any tanks, and if so, which way were they facing?

It was a casual conversation, and I explained that I hadn't really noticed any military buildup on the Pakistan/India border. After a couple of minutes, the officer in charge said that I was free to move into the next room. I went through a door to catch up with the others and arrived at the final room where our bags would be checked, and our passports stamped with entrance visas.

When I walked into the final room, Cesar, Marco, and John were just finishing up and getting their passports stamped. As I entered the room, I came to a long, wooden, beat-up platform where the border officials inspected packs, luggage, and bags. At the far end of the platform, two men and a woman in uniform turned as I entered the room.

The woman said, "I'll take this one," and started walking slowly toward where I was standing with my pack. She had me put down the pack on the wooden rack and took my passport. She matter-of-factly asked me how many U.S. dollars I was bringing into the country. I told her I had about $300 between cash and traveler's checks. She then asked me how many Indian rupees I was bringing into the country. That was a trick question, since I knew it was illegal to bring rupees into India.

I told her I was not bringing any rupees into the country. She looked at me and told me that if I had any rupees on me that I should tell her since she would find them eventually. It was at this point that I realized that I was facing the psychic border guard whom I had heard about. I once again stated that I had no Indian rupees. I knew that she knew that I did have rupees hidden on me, but I looked her square in the eye and told her that I didn't have any. She held my gaze and said that if I didn't tell her where the rupees were hidden, she would have a male guard take me into a back room and have me searched. I told her again I didn't have any rupees, and with that she called a male guard over and gave him instructions in Hindi.

Just then Cesar came up to me clearly agitated saying that he had told me not to try anything like this because it would get them all into trouble. I just stared at him until he turned and went back to wait with

Marco and John. The guard led me to a small room just off the main room, and, when he opened the door, the interior looked like a storage closet. The walls had shelves stacked with supplies, leaving barely enough room for a small table, the guard, and me. He asked me to empty my pockets onto the table. I was just putting some things on the table when the psychic guard burst through the door.

There wasn't enough room in the storeroom for her to join us, so she just leaned in and demanded that I take down my pants. I did what she said, and, as soon as my jeans were down around my ankles, she reached down to where the hidden pocket was located and pulled out three 100-rupee notes. She stood up, and we were face-to-face in that tiny space when she reminded me that she had warned me to tell the truth. She demanded to see my wallet and proceeded to pull two more 100-rupee notes from between my family photos. She then directed me to pull my pants back up and had me follow her to where my pack was sitting. I was told to unload the entire pack because, she said, if there was any hashish, she would find it.

Luckily, I didn't have any hash. She never did find the two 100-rupee notes hidden in my shoe. She knew, because of her psychic abilities, that I didn't have any hashish on me, so as soon as she had finished a cursory search of my bag, she said she was going to check with her supervisor to ask what she should do with me. I could see Cesar and Marco giving me the evil eye, and John was just blankly staring at me. The psychic guard came back and asked me when I would be returning to this border to leave India. I told her I would be flying out of Calcutta on my way to Burma in about two months. She again left me to confer with her supervisor. When she returned, she said that she would be sending the five 100-rupee notes to the customs agent at the Calcutta airport and that, when I was leaving, I could pick them up from the agent there. She handed me a receipt for the rupee notes, which I was to present to the agent in Calcutta. I was dumbfounded to think that these rupees would not just be confiscated but would be sent on to Calcutta.

When I finally got my passport stamped, I walked out of the Indian border station where Cesar, Marco, and John were waiting for me. I had to stop by the currency exchange window and cash in one of my traveler's checks to replace the rupees just taken from me. I threw my pack into the trunk of the Fiat, and there was a bit of grumbling about how stupid I was to go up against the psychic border guard.

I was still in a little bit of shock about what had just happened and didn't have much to say. After a couple of miles, we passed the last checkpoint, showed our passports, and were really in India. We hadn't gone much more than a mile or two when Cesar and Marco started laughing. John and I exchanged glances; we couldn't figure out what was so funny.

Marco reached under the passenger side dashboard and pulled out a kilo, or 2.2 pounds, of fresh, dark Afghan hashish wrapped in plastic. The dark brown brick was about 10 inches (25 cm) square and about one inch (2.5 cm) thick. When he tore open the plastic wrapping, the car filled with the smell of fresh hashish. Marco turned and looked at us and said they had 30 kilos, or 66 pounds, of hash hidden under the seats and behind the dashboard. I couldn't believe it and had no idea how they had gotten by the guards.

I was furious. These guys had used John and me to help get them into the country while they were smuggling in a huge amount of hash. If we had been caught, I'm sure we would probably still be languishing in an Indian jail. John and I couldn't believe what had just happened. Had we really been in a car with two guys smuggling hash into India? I was caught smuggling Indian rupees by the psychic border guard who said she would know if I had any hashish on me, but these guys had just smuggled in over 60 pounds of hashish. I had no problem asking Marco to break off a chunk of the hash for both of us. He obliged by breaking off some soft fresh hash from the corners of the brick. I stuffed the chunk into a plastic 35mm film holder I was carrying. It filled the canister. I wanted something for being used and for being put in so much danger. I also wanted to smoke some of their excellent smelling hash.

Amritsar was about 30 miles (50 kms) from Lahore. The roads were good, and it didn't take long to get there, which was fine with me since the friendliness between the four of us was gone and there wasn't much to talk about for the last few miles. As soon as we pulled into Amritsar, Marco and Cesar dropped us off at the bus station in the center of the city. John and

I were going to catch a bus to Jammu that afternoon. We grabbed our bags out of the trunk, turned, and watched the Fiat, full of hashish, head off to Goa. I had thought those guys were going to Goa to hang out on the beach and smoke hash, but I had unknowingly assisted in providing the latest supply of fresh Afghan hashish to the beach town.

We were now in the Indian state of Punjab. The city of Amritsar is the second largest city in Punjab and home to the Sikh religion. We purchased our bus tickets but still had some time before leaving for Jammu, which was only a five-hour ride and would put us halfway to the city of Srinagar, Kashmir.

Amritsar was very hot, and I was wearing jeans. John and I walked around the center of the city and saw the beautiful Golden Temple, which is one of the holiest sites of the Sikh religion. The Golden Temple is open 24 hours a day to people of all faiths, both for worship and as a place to gather. When the temple was built in the 1580s, it was called Harmandir Sahib, but, during a reconstruction in 1830, it was covered in gold foil and became known as the Golden Temple. The Temple had been rebuilt many times after Mughal and Afghan armies had overrun and destroyed the city.

Once the bus for Jammu started moving, I tried to relax and absorb what had happened on my first day in India. I still couldn't believe that I had faced the psychic border guard and had been busted, then crossed the Indian border in a car packed with hashish without getting busted, and, nonetheless, remained free to ride a comfortable bus onward to my next destination.

The beautiful five-hour ride into the green foothills of the Himalayas went quickly, and we reached the city of Jammu in the late afternoon. John and I put on our packs and walked around the bus station until we found a decent hotel with an available room for 6 rupees each, or 60¢. It was a clean room with two cots, clean sheets, and a ceiling fan that turned just enough to move the air around. The bathroom and shower were down the hall. It wasn't hard to find a good meal at one of the many food stands scattered around the bus station. We ended up at one stand that served a variety of hot curried vegetable dishes with rice. That was all we needed before walking back to the room to spend a hot, humid night being lulled to sleep by the whoosh of the ceiling fan softly turning.

The next morning, June 15th was already hot. We left the hotel early and made our way back to the bus station, where we bought tickets to Srinagar for 15 rupees each, or $1.50. We found some seats near an open window just as the bus pulled out of Jammu and started climbing out of the valley. We progressed slowly, going back and forth up the switchbacks into the snow-covered mountains. Occasionally the bus would stop by a mountain stream. John and I would follow our fellow passengers down to the shore where I'd scoop up cold water with my hands and drink directly from the fast-moving stream. Other passengers had cups or a vessel to hold the water, but I was happy to use my hands. I was drinking pure mountain water that had originated high in the Himalayas. It was a memorable ride around snow covered peaks; past fast-moving, turquoise-colored rivers; and over rocky passes to reach the next valley. I was glad to be climbing to higher altitudes and could feel the temperature getting progressively cooler as we approached Srinagar. The route into the Kashmir Valley ran through the Jawahar Tunnel, which runs under the mountain for nearly two miles, connecting the two valleys. When we exited the tunnel, the panoramic views of the Kashmir Valley below were fantastic. We started the descent into the rich air of the green valley dotted with lakes. What a relief to be out of the heat!

The trip took 11 hours to go 165 miles (270 kms), stopping at most of the villages and towns along the way. I had assumed that because it took five hours to go 125 miles (200 kms) from Amritsar to Jammu that it would take longer to go the 165 miles (270 kms) from Jammu to Srinagar, but not twice as long. I was learning that each ride had a life of its own; sometimes the schedules displayed at the stations were just... suggestions.

When the bus finally pulled into Srinagar, we were at an elevation of 5,200 feet (1,600 meters), which is just under a mile. Denver is the "mile high" city in the U.S., and I had been living at nearly 2,000 feet (610 meters) higher in Evergreen, Colorado, which had an elevation of 7,000 feet (2,100 meters). The air was fresh and cool, and I could understand why Kashmir was the place many Indians and Europeans flocked to during the summer months to avoid the intense heat baking the rest of India.

It was early evening when John and I stepped off the bus. Just one man was waiting with an offer of lodging. Usually, there were several men waiting to offer a variety of places to stay. The soft-spoken man represented the owner of a houseboat on one of the lakes around Srinagar and offered us a room with two beds for 5 rupees (50¢) each. Without any other choices, we agreed to go with him and stay on the houseboat he represented. We lifted our packs and followed the quiet man to a houseboat on a river that feeds into Dal Lake.

Dal Lake was one of the bigger lakes in the middle of Srinagar with many houseboats lining its shores. During the 1840s, the Dogra Maharaja of Kashmir restricted the building of houses in the Kashmir Valley. The British, who needed a place to cool off in the summer, got around the Maharaja's rule by building big houseboats moored on Dal Lake.

When we arrived at the houseboat, we were introduced to Mohammed, the owner. Mohammed promptly took out some papers written in English and handed them to John and me. The papers were testimonials by British and Australian travelers attesting to the fact that Mohammed provided a friendly and safe houseboat and that it was a good place to stay. Mohammed and his wife lived in the lower level of the two-level houseboat where there were sleeping quarters and a kitchen.

John and I were shown to a room at one end of the boat and were told that the room on the other end was occupied by another traveler. Between the two rooms was an open communal area where we were served meals, tea, and had an open view of Dal Lake. We walked into a clean room containing two small beds made up with sheets and blankets. The room had its own bathroom with a sink, shower, and toilet. Mohammed's houseboat was on a river near the downtown area of Srinagar and had a nice view of the sun setting over a nearby bridge. We could see other houseboats moored around the shoreline with people living on them.

Mohammed's wooden houseboat was beautifully crafted with a lot of intricate detail above the doorways, on the railings, and throughout the boat. We learned that this houseboat, like most of the others, was made from cedar trees that grew in the north of Kashmir. They used older cedar trees which had a tight grain. The hull could supposedly sit in the water for up to one hundred years before needing to be replaced with fresh timber.

John and I shared a room, and we soon met the other houseboat guest, Mark from Perth. As a single, he was paying 10 rupees ($1.00) for a room just like ours at the other end of the boat.

On June 16th, Mark, John, and I took a local bus to Nageen Lake, another lake in Srinagar. It was smaller than Dal but still had several houseboats of all sizes moored along its green shores. The bus dropped us off at a country club right on the lake that catered to wealthy Indians and a few Europeans. There were tennis courts, a swimming area in the lake, plus a small restaurant serving tea. We went to the changing room and put on the swimsuits we had brought along just for this occasion. We had heard Nageen was a clean lake and a good place to swim. This freshwater lake reminded me of the small pristine lakes in northern Wisconsin and Minnesota. After a refreshing swim in the clear, fresh mountain water, we got dressed and walked around the lake before finding a bus to take us back to Dal Lake and Mohammed's houseboat.

We were sitting in the comfortable chairs in the common area when Mohammed's wife brought us some freshly brewed, dark tea. Mark had some hash which he put in a pipe with a little bit of tobacco, and we passed it around. We got stoned and relaxed on the lightly rocking boat. When it started to get dark, Mohammed's wife lit the oil lamps and brought out an excellent dinner of curried vegetables, rice, and more tea. She placed it on the table in the middle of the common area where the meals were served. John, Mark, and I ate the delicious food with our right hands and chatted into the evening.

On the cool morning of the 17th, Mohammed's wife brought up a breakfast of eggs, toast, and tea for the three of us. Later that morning, John went to the main post office in Srinagar to mail some letters. While at the post office, he met a local man who offered him an entire house to live in, not far from Dal Lake, for less than 5 rupees (50¢) a day. When John returned to the houseboat, he asked if I would go to the house with him and check it out.

We boarded a bus and went to look at a ratty house with a small kitchen and no furniture. It sat in a quiet neighborhood. Since John wanted to hang out in Srinagar for a while, he agreed to take the house and moved in that night. I kept the room on the houseboat for myself and happily paid the additional 5 rupees.

Several wooden boats moved slowly around Dal Lake. These were the shikara boats, the main transportation used on the lake. A shikara is pointed at the bow, widening to about five feet (1.5 meters), before ending with a flat stern. Many were 25 feet (7.6 meters) long, or longer. Some were decked out with a canopy over part of the boat, while others were left open to the elements. Men were paddling around the lake in their shikaras filled with fruit and vegetables, jewelry, tin boxes, carved walnut wood figurines, and a variety of other items. Many of these shikara boats would make stops at Mohammed's houseboat offering their goods for sale. I did purchase some mangos from one of the boats.

On June 18th, a Tuesday afternoon, a shikara pulled up alongside our houseboat, steered by a man who introduced himself as Rafiq. He told me he was a tailor. He offered to make me a shirt and a pair of pants out of the lightweight cotton cloth of my choosing. I knew from experience that, once I left the higher altitude of Kashmir and descended into the 100° F (38° C) heat in New Delhi, the jeans and shirts I had been wearing for the last few months would be too warm.

I invited Rafiq onto the houseboat where he showed me samples of clothing that he had made and the different fabrics from which I could choose. After he displayed two or three styles of pants and shirts, I chose the pajama style pants with a drawstring and a lightweight collarless Indian shirt with long sleeves. Rafiq said he would sew a hidden pocket inside the left side of the shirt where I could hide things. I thought about the hidden pocket in my blue jeans that didn't fool the psychic border guard. Nonetheless, I thought that an inside shirt pocket might be a good idea. Next, Rafiq laid out a variety of fabrics in different weights and colors. I asked him to make both the shirt and pants out of a lightweight white cotton cloth. He pulled out his tape measure and had me stand up so he could take my measurements. He charged me 20 rupees ($2.00) for the pants and 33 rupees ($3.30) for the shirt. Rafiq climbed back into his shikara and paddled off, promising to bring the finished clothing back to the houseboat the next day.

On Wednesday June 19th, Mark and I took an hour-and-a-half bus ride into the mountains up to a hill station called Gulmarg, which sat at an altitude of 8,600 feet (2,600 meters) and was even cooler than Srinagar. Gulmarg was another popular retreat for the Indian population and the British who could afford to spend the summer months in the mountains of Kashmir. It was a clear day, and at that elevation, I had great views of the horizon filled with huge snowcapped mountains. The open fields were covered in a variety of blooming wildflowers, and the forests were green with trees of pine, fir, and cedar. In the heat the trees gave off a vivid scent of cedar and pine.

Mark and I walked around but mostly sat under trees. Even at that altitude, it was too hot to spend much time in the sun. Kashmir had the altitude, mountains, and trees that reminded me of my home in Colorado. After experiencing the intense heat in Pakistan, the mild temperature in the Himalayan foothills was refreshing. I would have to learn to live with the heat. My new pants and shirt were a good start in preparing for the heat and humidity that I would be experiencing soon.

When we returned to the houseboat, Mohammed's wife brought a nice pot of hot tea and crackers to the common room. While we were having tea, Rafiq paddled up to the houseboat and tied up his shikara. He climbed on board and presented me with the finished clothing, nicely folded. I took the shirt and pants to my room and tried them on. They fit perfectly. Rafiq had sewn an inside pocket in the shirt with just enough room to put a few rupee notes. The pajama pants were lightweight and cool and would be just what I needed for the next few months. I went out to show Rafiq, and I could see that he was pleased with the fit. We shook hands, then he stepped into his shikara and paddled off.

On Thursday, June 20th, I put on my backpack and said goodbye to Mark, Mohammed, and his wife before leaving for the bus depot, where I bought a ticket for Pahalgam, a hill station four hours east of Srinagar at an altitude of 7,200 feet (2,200 meters).

Over the past month, I had listened to travelers who suggested I visit the beautiful Pahalgam region. I wasn't going to hold the bus company to their four-hour schedule as we slowly crawled up the mountain taking several switchbacks before reaching Pahalgam, situated high in the Lidder Valley. The hill station was surrounded by pine forests and snow-covered peaks. At that altitude, the air was thin and fresh with clouds crossing the sky, sometimes allowing the sun to peak through, and sometimes bringing a light drizzle.

When the bus arrived, a few men were waiting at the bus depot and tried to convince me that the hotels they represented were the best. Most were offering rooms for 20 rupees ($2.00) a night, but one man was offering a tent for 10 rupees ($1.00), and I decided to go with him. I followed Ahmed Bhat, a local guide, who informed me, in English, of his services as we walked to the tent. Just about everyone in India, from the border guards to the bus drivers, spoke English. When the British were in control of India from 1858 until 1947, a great many Indians were hired as civil servants to help run the British bureaucracy. This period was called the British Raj, and during that time, English was adopted as the common language throughout India. In a huge and diverse country like India that has dozens of regional languages and even more local dialects, English became the one language everyone used to communicate making travel a little easier for me and other Anglophones.

One of the services Ahmed was offering was a three-day trek to the Kolahoi Glacier at 11,200 feet (3,400 meters). It would cost me about 120 rupees ($12.00) for the trip. I decided to hire him as a guide and take the trek up to the glacier. I paid him a little in advance so he could purchase the supplies we would need for the three days. He would carry the supplies and be the cook on our trek. Ahmed was an easygoing, middle-aged man who walked me to the tent at a pretty good pace. I had the feeling that he would be a very good guide and companion in the mountains.

The tent was situated in an open area that gave me a panoramic view of the surrounding mountains and valleys. The large canvas structure was sitting next to a creek that flowed slowly over rocks making a soft gurgling sound. It was owned by a hotel that wasn't far, but I was happy with my spacious canvas housing which held a bed, a chest of drawers, plus a table and chairs. I had put my pack down and was getting familiar with the tent, when a young man, about seventeen years old, showed up at the tent's door introducing himself as Hakim. He spoke enough English to explain that the hotel had sent him to attend to my needs. The hotel must have been worried that I was sleeping in a tent on the side of a mountain all by myself. For 10 rupees, I had my own tent with a cot, a local guide, and a protector. I did not feel that I was in any danger but welcomed the company. He walked me around the village and pointed out the good restaurants and food stalls and where I could find the toilet in the hotel just up the hill. At the end of his introduction, he offered to get me "number 1 chars," or hashish, if that was what I wanted.

Hakim wore a long wool brown cloak that hung down to his knees and reminded me of a big Mexican sarape with sleeves. Under the cloak, he carried a wicker basket woven around a clay pot containing hot ash and coals, which he called a *kangri*. The wicker basket insulated the warm clay from resting directly on the body while giving off a warmth held in by the wool cloak. It was a good way to ward off the cold on those cool Kashmir nights.

There was a large clay pot inside the tent, which Hakim kept fueled with slow burning walnut wood to keep the tent warm at night. When I turned in for the night, Hakim curled up around his kangri and slept just outside the tent. On one side of the tent was a gurgling creek, and on the other, was Hakim. I climbed into my sleeping bag and slept very well.

Ahmed had purchased the rice, vegetables, and other items we would need for our trek. Early on Saturday morning, the 22nd, he came by with all the supplies in a pack, ready to go. I put on my backpack, and we left Pahalgam to begin the climb up to the glacier. It had rained the previous night, so the going was slow due to the mud. Ahmed kept a good pace, but I managed to keep up with him. By noon, we had hiked the 7 miles (11 kms) into the tree-covered Aru Valley, reaching the village of Aru. We stopped at a small shop for tea and chapati, the unleavened flat bread that was essential to this part of the world.

By the time we finished our tea, the clouds started to clear, and the sun came out, making the hike that afternoon much easier as we climbed another eight miles (13 kms) to reach Lidderwat by 4 p.m. Lidderwat was just a single tourist guest house in the Lidder Valley nestled high in the Kashmiri Alps. The guest house had several rooms and served as the base camp for treks up to the Kolahoi Glacier and other sites in the mountains. The rooms were available for the night on a first-come, first-served basis. The Lidder Valley is surrounded by snowcapped peaks with pine trees covering the mountains up to the tree line. There were a few farmers in the valley raising goats, sheep, water buffalo, horses, chickens, and children.

Ahmed went out and bought eggs, milk, butter, and cheese from the farmers. When he got back, he went into the kitchen, which was available to whomever wanted to build a wood fire and cook. He prepared a fine dhal, vegetable curry, and rice dinner. It was early in the season, and, except for a couple of hikers, we had the small dining area and the rest of the guest house to ourselves. Ahmed and I each took a room for the night. My room held a couple of beds with bare mattresses, so I put my pack down on one mattress and my sleeping bag on the other. The room had a window with a wonderful view of the snowcapped mountains. A toilet and cold shower were down the hall.

Sunday the 23rd of June, we were awakened by the sound of rain. I looked out the window and saw gray clouds low over the mountains. We decided to eat breakfast and see if the rain would pass before continuing up to the glacier. Ahmed made two omelets with onions and fried cheese, served with chapati and hot tea. The rain stopped before we finished, so we packed for what Ahmed said would be a four-hour walk up to the Kolahoi Glacier.

It started drizzling shortly after we left, so I threw my raincoat over my pack and myself, and we continued to climb through incredibly beautiful country. We passed waterfalls, snowy patches, and boulders the size of a house. The clouds were low; it was chilly, and everything was wet.

We stepped on rocks to ford small streams and crossed larger streams using bridges built by the local farmers. As we climbed higher, the drizzle turned to a steady cold rain. Thankfully, I had a good hat. The parts of me that were covered by the raincoat stayed dry, but the bottom of my pants were completely soaked. The combination of cold, rainy weather, wet pants, and blisters I could feel forming on my heels started to dampen my spirits.

After an hour of steady cold rain, we sought out the shelter of a dry space under the overhang of a large rock. After we sat for 20 minutes under the frigid rock looking out at the beautiful green mountainside, I knew I didn't want to continue up to the glacier. Ahmed said that we still had a couple hours to climb. He said it would get colder, and he wasn't sure if the rain would stop. We agreed to abandon the climb and retraced our steps back down to the valley.

On the way down, we came to a farmer's mud and stone house that we had passed on the way up. We could see that there was smoke coming out of a hole in the middle of the roof, so we walked to the house and Ahmed called out. The farmer came out of his home and spoke to Ahmed for a few seconds before we were invited in. We were greeted by the farmer's wife, holding a baby, and five more children. They were gathered around a small fire in the middle of a large open room. We were invited to join them sitting around the fire on local wool carpets placed on the dirt floor.

Between two of the children lay a 20-day-old baby water buffalo edging close to the fire for warmth. Ahmed gave me a dry blanket, which I wrapped around myself and then took off the wet pants. I sat down cross-legged, in front of the fire, holding the pants up to the heat to dry and angling to feel some of the heat myself.

The room smelled moist and earthy from the smoky fire, buffalo milk warming in a pot, the baby water buffalo, the wet gear that we were trying to dry, and our own human odors. How do you capture in words the smells and aromas of the places you visit?

I was keenly aware of the rare experience I was having high in the Kashmiri alps. I was sitting in a circle with a buffalo farmer's family and a baby buffalo, all warming ourselves by a slow-burning, smoky fire. The wife was dressed in ornate headgear with a beaded piece hanging down her back and wore her dark hair in braids. She was wearing shiny necklaces and bracelets made of silver and stones. While breastfeeding the baby, she continued to prepare and serve warm buffalo milk to her children. When she finished feeding her children, she made a few buffalo milk chapatis and Kashmiri tea for Ahmed and me. The chapatis tasted musky from the buffalo milk but were warm and filling. I sipped the hot tea expecting it to be sweet but was surprised that it was salty. The mountain people who live in that part of Kashmir used buffalo milk and put salt in their tea, instead of sugar. Still, the pungent salty tea was hot and much appreciated.

A shout from outside sent the father and a couple of the older boys scurrying out of the hut. A few minutes later, they returned, leading four huge, lumbering water buffalo into the barn side of the hut. The low mud and stone hut had thick logs spanning the ceiling covered by a thatched roof with a hole in the middle to vent the smoke. The family and their water buffalo shared the same roof when the weather turned bad and had welcomed even me into their shelter.

It was still raining and cold, but I was eating freshly made chapatis surrounded by four huge, wet steaming beasts and a family of smiling Kashmiri mountain people kind enough to share their food and fire.

After my pants dried, I put them on, and Ahmed and I thanked the farmer and his family and started back to Lidderwat in the rain. It was hard to leave the warmth of the smoky hut, but the fresh air smelled good.

Ahmed ran down the steep terrain over rocks, puddles, streams, and mounds of buffalo pies, trying to find the easiest and safest path off the mountain. Even though I tried to follow his footsteps, he was moving faster than I could, and I ended up stepping into a few streams. Going downhill is harder on the legs than going uphill, and I was feeling the weight of my pack with every step. I was glad to be approaching Lidderwat.

We finally reached Lidderwat, and, once we were inside the guest house, Ahmed got a fire going and brewed some tea. He brought out cow's milk and sugar to flavor the tea, and the hot milky sweet tea was refreshing after the trot down the valley. I stepped outside to smoke some chars and was able to mellow out and relax, even though my legs were so stiff I could hardly walk. I felt out of shape and disappointed in the shoes that caused my feet to blister. It had been nearly six months since I'd left Evergreen, and I thought that, having lived at a high altitude, I would have been able to handle a trek in these mountains with no problem.

I was chilled, and the only place in the guest house that offered some warmth was the kitchen. Ahmed and I sat close to the wood-burning stove. After we dried off, Ahmed made some dhal, vegetable curry, tomato curry, and rice for dinner. I was very tired from the day's climb and descent, so after dinner I thanked Ahmed and went back to my unheated room. I crawled into my sleeping bag, covered myself with a gray wool blanket provided by the guest house, and spread out my space blanket over the wool blanket to hold in the heat. Just a few days before, I had been overwhelmed by the heat of Pakistan, and now, I was trying to stay warm in the cold Kashmiri Himalayas.

It rained all night, and, when I awoke at 6:30 a.m. on the morning of June 24th, there was still a steady rain coming down. I couldn't get back to sleep, so I got up, got dressed, and went to the kitchen hoping to sit by the fire and drink tea. I walked into the kitchen and saw a woman and three children gathered by the fire for warmth, drinking hot tea. I took my position against a wall and took my turn with the warm kangri that was passed around by those of us in the kitchen. When the kangri was passed to me, I held the warm wicker basket under my jacket to feel the heat. It felt good. Ahmed came into the kitchen and started to make tea, an onion omelet, and chapatis. It was a good breakfast for a cold rainy day, and the food lifted my spirits.

The low clouds started to clear a little and revealed fresh snow not only on the higher peaks in the distance, but also just 100 feet (30.5 meters) above the guest house where I was waiting for the rain to stop. Except for a few breaks, it rained all day on the 24th, and the temperature barely stayed above freezing. To keep warm, I either sat by the fire or lay in my sleeping bag and read. Somewhere along the way I ended up with a copy of Frank Herbert's *Dune*, a story which took me to a desert world that was much warmer than cold, rainy Lidderwat.

On Tuesday the 25th, it was still raining, but Ahmed and I decided we couldn't stay in Lidderwat any longer. We packed up our things and left the guest house in a drizzle, practically running the seven miles down to Aru. I think it was on that stretch of the trek that I ripped the silver dollar-sized blister on my left heel. I stopped and took out a couple of Band-Aids from the small first aid packet I had with me. I cleaned up the blister, applied the Band-Aid, and tried to keep up with Ahmed.

We reached Aru and stopped to have a rest and some tea. We sat down and met two couples in the tea shop who had just hiked up from Pahalgam in the rain. They were hiking without a guide and didn't want to go any further up the mountain. They were cold and wet and wanted to go down to Pahalgam. After tea, Ahmed led all five of us down the mountain to Pahalgam, and once again, I went back to my tent by the stream for 10 rupees ($1.00) a night. That night, the management put Hakim in the tent with me armed with a knife. I didn't ask him why he needed the knife, but I figured that the hotel management knew best. On my last day in the canvas tent, I traded Hakim a pair of my leather shoes for some hashish. In a few days I was headed into the heat of India and didn't need the leather shoes or their weight in my pack.

Early Saturday morning the 29th, I boarded a bus in Srinagar and rode for 12 hours back down the mountains to Jammu. We had one flat tire, which only slowed us down for an hour. The bus pulled into Jammu around 7 p.m. and, together with two Indian guys I had met on the bus, I jumped into a taxi at the bus depot. They told the driver that we wanted to go to the train station. My fellow travelers wanted to take a train to Bombay, and I was hoping to catch an overnight train from Jammu to New Delhi.

I found the ticket window at the train station and asked for a reserved 1st class seat to New Delhi. With a reserved 1st class seat, I would be assured a seat on the train. The man at the window shook his head and said the reserved seats were sold out. He had seats in the 2nd class car, but they filled quickly due to the first-come-first-seated policy. I knew I might have to stand most of the way to New Delhi, but I bought a 2nd class ticket anyway. I had time to look around several food stalls gathered just outside the station and found one with pots of simmering hot vegetable curry.

A plate of curry, dhal, and five chapatis cost one rupee. I stood near the food stall and tore off pieces of chapati to grab the curry and dhal and then used my thumb to push the food into my mouth. Street food like this was the best way to eat. When I had finished the satisfying meal, I handed the metal bowl back to the cook and thanked him.

Just as I was about to board the train, I was approached by a man dressed like a porter. The man offered me an actual place to lie down for 10 rupees, in addition to the 22 rupees I had paid for the original ticket. The catch was that I would have to stand in the reserved 1st class car for an hour-and-a-half before a place to lie down became available in 2nd class. I followed the porter onto the train to a place where I could stand near one of the doors at the end of the car. I rested against the wall when the train left the station, waiting for a bench to open in 2nd class. I was standing in a corner of a train car with my pack between my legs. The train was overfilled with Indian passengers and me, sitting and standing everywhere, traveling to one of the most populated cities in one of the most populous countries in the world. I was traveling on public transportation completely by myself, but not alone. Most of the people on the train were strangers to each other, and I was just one of the strangers, but I was wearing jeans and carrying a backpack, while they were dressed in comfortable lightweight clothing carrying bundles and suitcases.

I had been traveling in Asia for six weeks by train and bus, sleeping wherever space was available, and eating food when and where I could get it. I had gained enough travel experience and was ready for the heat of New Delhi in July.

The porter eventually came back and showed me to the empty bench where I could stretch out and get some sleep. I put down my pack to use as a pillow and curled up around my shoulder bag which held the things I didn't want to lose. As the night progressed, the train car added a few passengers at every stop. People started to sit on the edges of my bench until I was in the fetal position. Eventually I had to sit up and share the bench with my fellow passengers bound for New Delhi. Out of the 13 hours on the train I was able to sleep for about six.

After the sun came up, a tea merchant appeared at one

end of the train, and for a few cents, I was able to buy a nice warm cup of sweet, milky tea. When I finished the tea, I returned the metal cup to him which he washed and set aside for a future customer. The train was just a few hours from New Delhi. When I looked out the open window, I noticed a change in terrain. We had descended from the green mountains and hills of Jammu to the flat, baked earth of Punjab. It was early morning and already starting to heat up.

At 10:30 a.m. on Sunday morning the 30th, the train pulled into New Delhi station. When I walked out, I saw a row of rickshaws with their drivers standing next to, or sitting on, their bicycles. The rickshaws had a flat seat big enough for two passengers, who would be protected from the sun and rain by a canopy. Other than walking or taxi cabs, the rickshaws were a good, cheap way to get around New Delhi.

Over the last few months, I had spoken to many travelers who had spent time in New Delhi, and I had written down the names of a few cheap places to stay. Several people had mentioned a guesthouse called Mrs. Caloco's, which was also listed in the BIT Guide, so I decided to stay there. I negotiated a price with one of the rickshaw drivers for a ride to Mrs. Caloco's Guesthouse at No. 3 Janpath Lane, but I had no idea what a fair price was and probably paid too much.

The bicycle rickshaw stopped in front of the guesthouse, so I put on my pack and went to check in. Mrs. Caloco wanted to see my passport and wrote down the numbers before assigning me a cot in one of her dorm rooms for 7 rupees a night. My assigned room had four cots and a large slow-turning fan hanging from the ceiling. The three other cots were occupied by two guys from Thailand and one from England. The guesthouse had a few separate dorms for men and women with men's and women's showers and toilets down the hall. There was a communal area to meet other travelers and exchange stories. My dorm mates told me the tap water was drinkable, which I was glad to hear.

The monsoons were to start any day, but, until they did, each day would be getting hotter and more humid. As soon as I put my pack down on the cot, I unpacked my flip-flops and the pajama pants and shirt that Rafiq had made for me in Srinagar. I took off my jeans and second pair of leather shoes and changed into my new, loose-fitting shirt, pants, and flip-flops. I would be more comfortable wearing clothing that was better suited to the heat and didn't make me stand out as a backpacker passing through.

I grabbed my shoulder bag and went out to see what was within walking distance from the guesthouse. Mrs. Caloco's Guesthouse was located on a small lane that ran between busy Janpath Road and the quiet grounds of the Jantar Mantar observatory, which contained 13 architectural astronomy instruments designed and built by Maharaja Jai Singh II in 1724. *Jantar Mantar* means "instruments for measuring the harmony of the heavens." The park had the world's largest sundial that sits 114 feet (35 meters) long at the base, stands 70 feet (21 meters) high and is 10 feet (3 meters) thick.

The other instruments in the observatory were very large and looked like modern architecture but could measure time, predict eclipses, and track stars.

Also, not far from Mrs. Caloco's, I passed a tea stand under a canvas roof large enough to cover the counter and a dozen or more tables. Under one end of the overhead covering was a long table with two men behind it preparing and serving hot dark tea and fresh coffee. On a hot day, people would duck out of the sun or a rain shower to stop, take a break, and drink their choice of hot or iced tea or coffee. I had been drinking so much tea for the past few months that I treated myself to a nice tall, iced coffee with milk and sugar, which reminded me of my mother. She enjoyed iced coffee during the hot Chicago summers. The rest of Sunday I took it easy because I had traveled over 24 hours from Srinagar and needed the day to adjust to my new surroundings.

I discovered that the guesthouse was not very far from Connaught Place, so I was well situated in New Delhi. Connaught Place is one of the main financial, commercial, and business centers in New Delhi. Many of the countries I would be passing through on my way to Australia had embassies or consulates near Connaught Place, so it would be easy to obtain the visas I needed to enter Nepal and Thailand.

I wanted to take care of some business that could only be done in a large city like New Delhi. I went to the main post office and retrieved my mail from Poste Restante. Once again, it provided a reliable mailing address and helped me stay in touch with my family. I stopped by the American Express office in Connaught Place and exchanged some U.S. traveler's checks for Indian rupees. I located the consulate for Nepal and applied for a visa to enter that country. The staff at the consulate required three photos, 30 rupees, and told me to return the next day. It was already heating up, so I returned to my room to wait out the middle of the day when the heat would be most intense. When I got back to the guesthouse, the guys from Thailand were gone and two guys from New Jersey had taken their cots.

Charlie and Steve had just arrived in India that morning. They had flown directly from New York and seemed dazed from the heat and the abrupt change of cultures. I was thankful that I had been traveling overland and had gradually adjusted to the strangeness of waking up in new and different places every day. The late afternoon temperature was reaching about 100° F (38° C), and the humidity was building up and forming a thick cloud cover.

On July 2nd, I left the guesthouse early to beat the heat. As I was walking to Connaught Place, I noticed people eating something out of small terracotta cups. There was a line of people leading up to a walkup window where they were buying fresh milk yogurt that had been made in the clay cups. I got in line, and, when I got up to the window, I purchased a cup of yogurt and a glass of fresh milk. The man at the window handed me a small flat wooden stick to dig the yogurt out of the cup. When I finished the milk and yogurt, I handed the glass back to the man and tossed the clay cup on the ground. The area around the yogurt shop was littered with broken terracotta and wooden sticks. I was told that because the yogurt cures in the unglazed terra cotta, some of the moisture is absorbed into the clay making the yogurt creamier and richer. The yogurt was a fresh, new taste that I would like to try again. It was delicious!

I continued to the Nepalese Consulate and picked up my passport with the visa stamped on one of the pages. The Thai consulate was nearby, so I went there to apply for their entry visa. They also wanted three photos and a few rupees, but they stamped my passport page immediately. My last stop for the morning was the main railway station to buy a train ticket to the city of Agra where the Taj Mahal sits.

When I got back to Mrs. Caloco's another traveler I'd met in the community room asked if I wanted to share a chillum. We went out the back door onto a covered porch to light up the chillum, and, just as we got the hash glowing, raindrops started to hit the ground, and then, it began to pour. The sky opened up, and the temperature dropped about 20° F (11° C). The relief was instant! The monsoon had reached New Delhi, and we ran out into the street with a lot of other happy people to get drenched under the first rainfall of the season.

The rain had cooled off the city and taken a lot of tension out of the air. I had been feeling the strain like everyone else, and the heat had been getting to me. Everything was a hustle and a hassle from navigating train schedules to haggling with the taxi drivers. Everything was a negotiation, which got to be wearing. When a driver and I agreed on a price, I always felt that I could have done better to keep the price down. There was an unwritten code that encouraged all travelers to bargain and get the best price possible, keeping prices low for the next guy. I did my best, but it was trying.

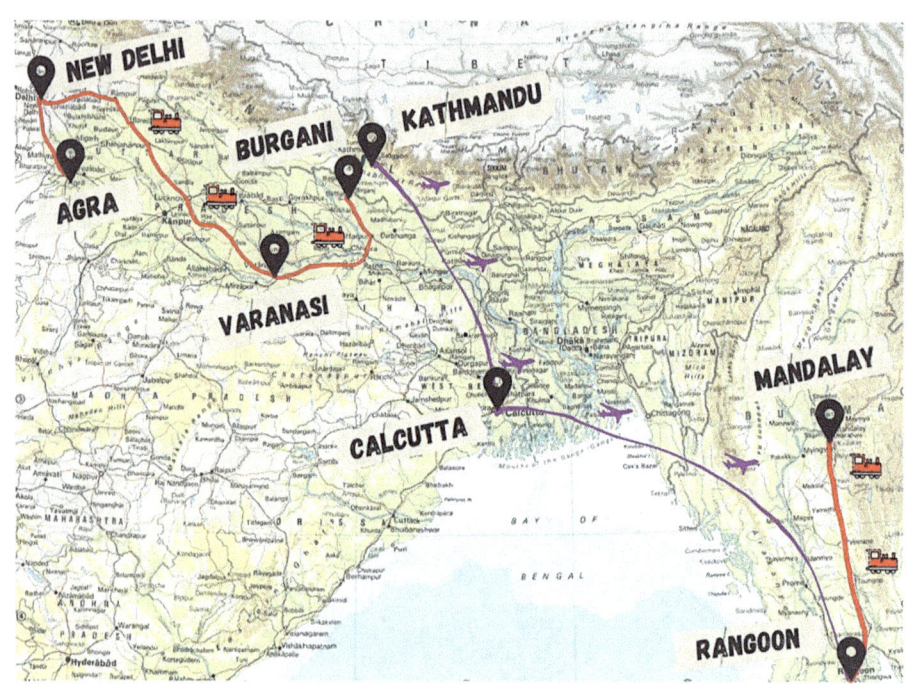

New Delhi, India to Agra, India and back (by train)
New Delhi, India to Varanasi, India to Burgani, India (by train)
to Kathmandu, Nepal (by bus) to Calcutta, India (by plane)
to Rangoon, Burma (by plane) to Mandalay, Burma (by train)

Seventh Full Moon

On Wednesday morning, the 3rd of July, the Taj Express left at 7:15 a.m. I had a comfortable seat, and, in a little over three hours, the train arrived in Agra. I was glad to be out of New Delhi for the day, and when the train stopped, I threw my pack over my shoulder, stepped down to the platform, and walked out of the station to the area where the bicycle rickshaw drivers were gathered. An older man came up to me and asked where I wanted to go, and I told him that I was looking for a hotel for one night. He said that he knew a good clean hotel with reasonable rates, so I agreed to go with him. We agreed on a price for the ride to the hotel, and he got on the bike and started peddling to the Hotel Jaggi. On the way there, the rickshaw driver said that after I was checked in he would take me to the Taj Mahal, plus give me a tour of Agra for 13 rupees. In addition to visiting the Taj, he promised that he would take me to a good lunch stand and then to a gemstone store where he knew the owner.

A tour sounded like a good way to spend my time in Agra, so I agreed to do it. We arrived at the Hotel Jaggi, and I left my pack in a room which was clean, with two beds and a small bathroom. My tour started at the Taj Mahal. I was standing in front one of most iconic structures in the world. In the heat of the day, its size and bright white marble were mesmerizing, making it hard to look away.

The Taj Mahal

I was glad we started at the Taj, but the temperature was rising. Now that the monsoon rains had started, it wasn't as hot, but it was still warm for me, and now very humid too. I knew that I would be returning that night to see the Taj by the light of the nearly full moon, so I left with the driver to continue the tour. He took me to a street stand for a curry and chapati lunch and then to the gem store.

When we arrived at the gem store, the merchant had me sit down across from him while he showed me beautiful rubies of all sizes. I ended up buying a small one. I had heard that there were good silversmiths in Bali, and I hoped to have the ruby put into a silver ring once I reached the island. After the merchant and I agreed on a price for the ruby, we shook hands, and he pulled out a small clay pipe. He put some hash in the bowl, offered the pipe to me, and we smoked a bit of hashish to celebrate the exchange. After I was nicely stoned, the driver took me to Agra Fort, a massive stone fort that had once been the residence of the emperors of the Mughal Dynasty. The fortress was huge and very ornate, but the thought of exploring on a hot day didn't feel like something I wanted to do, so the driver took me back to the hotel. I spent the afternoon lying in bed wearing only the pajama bottoms Rafiq had made for me. I was reading a book about the French painter, Paul Gauguin, called *The Moon and Sixpence* by Somerset Maugham. Gauguin traveled to Panama and Martinique before landing in French Polynesia, where he painted and sculpted his best-known art. Traveling though Asia in 1974 was basic and rough. I tried to imagine what travel might have been like for Gauguin in the 1890s.

I ate a late dinner at a Chinese restaurant near the hotel before returning to the room to light up a bowl of hash, preparing to go out into the hot, humid Indian night. I had no trouble finding an empty rickshaw on the busy street outside the hotel. I climbed into the seat and told the driver I wanted to go the Taj Mahal.

He started peddling, and I sat back for the ride of a lifetime. The streets were even more crowded at night than they had been during the day, and they were alive with bright lights, street sounds, and the cooking odors of India as we glided toward the Taj Mahal. The rickshaw driver was moving quickly through the busy streets of Agra past wandering cows, chickens, people, and open stores, all under the light of the bright moon. The streets of Agra were vibrant with an atmosphere almost like that of a carnival. It was a cloudless night lit by the moon high over Agra.

I had been told by many travelers that seeing the Taj Mahal in the light of a full moon was an incredible experience, so I had planned my travel schedule over the past few months with an eye on the moon's cycles. My plan was to arrive in India in early July, which would be just in time for the full moon on the 4th. I was in Agra one day short of the full moon, but it was full enough for me.

The driver let me off at the main gateway to the Taj Mahal. I walked through the gateway and saw the beautiful white marble building glowing in the moonlight. I took a few minutes to take in the entirety of the Taj Mahal with its minarets, small domes, and the large dome before I started heading down the walkway beside the reflecting pool. The dome seemed to get brighter and more beautiful the closer I got to the mausoleum. After entering through one of the arches, I could see that the marble floor and the dome overhead came alive in the moonlight. I walked around until I came to the tomb of Shah Jahan, who had built the mausoleum in 1632 to hold the tomb of his favorite wife, Mumtaz Mahal. Their tombs sat side by side under the magnificent dome.

I stayed an hour with my eyes glued to either the Taj or the moon. It was a mesmerizing evening. The hot night air was filled with the scents of people's perfumes and the incense being burned around the grounds. The exotic sights and sounds plus the mixture of scents and aromas created an intense moment of sensory overload. That moment was truly one of the highlights of my trip.

For the past six months, I had traveled solo over 9,000 miles (14,500 kms) to experience the most incredible evening at the Taj Mahal in the middle of India. When I was in the luminous white mausoleum surrounded by people from all over the world, I felt that I was part of that world.

***

A good thing about having a bathroom in the hotel room is not having to go down the hall to use the facilities. A bad thing is a faucet with a slow drip interrupting the hum of the city with its constant, rhythmical ping. After a sleepless night in Agra, I took the train back to New Delhi on the morning of July 4th.

That afternoon I was hanging out at Mrs. Caloco's thinking about how I was going to celebrate the 4th of July. At just that moment, Charlie, one of the guys from New Jersey, walked into the room and asked if I wanted to go to a club for a swim and dinner that evening. He had met an Indian man, Samir, on the train ride down to Agra, and, after they had talked for a while, Samir invited Charlie to be his guest at the Roshanara Club in Old Delhi. He'd asked Charlie to invite some friends along for an evening of swimming and dinner. This was the perfect way to celebrate the

4th of July, so I changed into my one, clean pair of pants rolled up in the bottom of my pack for special occasions and a shirt with a collar. I grabbed my swimsuit and was ready to go. Charlie and Steve were waiting with Steve's new Vietnamese friend, Chim, whom he had recently met at Mrs. Caloco's. Steve introduced me to Chim, and we went outside where Samir was waiting.

We piled into his comfortable black car with air conditioning and drove about 15 minutes from New Delhi into Old Delhi. It was a little surreal to be observing the steamy street life that we were usually a part of from the comfort of a cooled car.

Samir turned off the busy street into a suddenly lush area, driving through a variety of shade trees and green hedges, which, Samir explained, was the entrance to the Roshanara Garden, where the club building and cricket pitch were situated. The Roshanara Garden was built in the 1600s by Roshanara Bega, the daughter of Shah Jahan, the shah who had built the Taj Mahal. The large park-like garden spanned many acres in the center of Old Delhi, displaying a variety of beautiful plants from all over the world. The tomb of Roshanara, the garden's creator, was in the park as well. Though she died in 1671 and the tomb shows the wear of time, its elegance and ornate detail were still apparent despite the deterioration. In 1922, the British, some bureaucrats, and the emerging Indian elite came together and decided it was a good idea to take a portion of the garden grounds and build a cricket pitch and a club house. In addition to the cricket pitch, there were also tennis courts, a swimming pool, a bar, and, of course, the beautiful club house.

After Samir parked the car, Charlie, Steve, and I were shown to the men's changing room and Chim to the women's. We put on our swimsuits, locked our clothes and valuables in a locker, and dove into the big pool. The water was the perfect temperature for the hot humid night. The four of us splashed around the pool for a while before we got out and joined Samir, who was waiting at a poolside table. He invited us to join him for dinner but knew we would enjoy the large swimming pool. He was right. I certainly hadn't planned on swimming in a pool while passing through Delhi. It was an unexpected treat.

When we were all settled at the table, Samir motioned to a waiter, and we ordered drinks. Everyone else ordered hard liquor, but I ordered a beer and was glad I did, because nothing is better than a cold beer on a warm summer night. We sat on the veranda overlooking the green grass of the empty cricket pitch. Who would have thought that, in the middle of overpopulated, overheated Delhi, sits this quiet, cool oasis?[10]

While we waited for our drinks, I had a chance to look at the old British club and saw that it had been well maintained. All the grounds were manicured and the waitstaff wore crisp white shirts. Our drinks came

---

[10] *In August of 2022, the Roshanara Club celebrated its 100th year.*

with tasty vegetarian snacks and potato chips, so we snacked and drank by the pool.

After we'd had a couple of rounds and loosened up, we went back to the changing room, took showers, and got dressed. Once dressed, we walked about 25 yards from the pool to the outdoor dining area and sat down at a table with a tablecloth. The waiter came over and we ordered some grilled chicken pieces, a vegetable dish, some yogurt raita, and more drinks. We took our time eating a delicious meal. I had been traveling inexpensively to make my funds last, but this unexpected glimpse of well-to-do India was a nice change, and it gave me a better perspective on the huge divide between the haves and have-nots.

The full moon came into sight as it slowly rose over our 4th of July celebration. It lit up the club grounds while we ate, drank, and relaxed, thanks to our generous host. I drank more beer that evening than I had in several months, and I was ready to go when Samir drove us home at midnight. There was less traffic going back to Mrs. Caloco's, but there was still a lot of activity for midnight. We thanked Samir again, went to our dorm rooms, found our cots, crawled into our sleeping bags, and immediately fell asleep.

I got up early on the 5th because Charlie and Steve were leaving for Kathmandu, and I wanted to say goodbye. They pushed off, and I went looking for something to eat. I found a small stand not far from the hotel and ordered a couple of eggs.

They must have been bad because I felt nauseous shortly after I ate them and quickly returned to the hotel toilet to vomit. I had been fortunate with my health over the past few months. The few times that I ate or drank something that did not agree with me, I would either regurgitate it quickly, as with the eggs, or pass it through my system in a few days. I had seen a few guys with dysentery and wanted to avoid that horrible bug, or any other kind of illness, as I traveled. One of the fears I had when traveling alone was getting sick and not being able to get the help I would need. As soon as my stomach rejected the rotten eggs, I felt better and washed out my mouth.

Now that I was feeling better, I ventured out and went to an international telephone office to find out how to make a long-distance telephone call from New Delhi to my parents in the suburbs of Chicago. I walked into the office and stood at the main counter. I spoke to a bored clerk who assured me the process was simple. He would write down the telephone number and name of the country to be called and then assign me one of the small booths lining the walls. Each booth had a chair and small table with a black telephone sitting on it. I would wait in the booth until the international connection had been made, and then the phone in my booth would ring. I thanked the man for the explanation and scheduled a call to my parents for the next day. I hadn't spoken with them since leaving Europe, and I was looking forward to hearing their voices and catching up on news from back home. My next errand was finding a bank to exchange some U.S.

traveler's checks into rupees. I was hoping to get at least 10 rupees to the dollar.

I started back to Mrs. Caloco's and was walking along a hedge when a man, dressed all in white including his turban, popped out from behind the hedge and beckoned me to stop. For some curious reason I was intrigued by this man and wanted to hear what he had to say. He was a little shorter than me and carried a little extra weight under the white sash that secured his white tunic. He asked me to follow him through the tall hedge into a grove of trees. We hadn't gone more than about ten feet into the grove when he stopped abruptly and turned toward me. We were in a quiet area surrounded by the hedge with no one in sight. He explained that he was a swami and could tell my future. He requested 2 rupees to do a reading and held open what he called a small book of prayers. I dropped the 2 rupees onto the open book. Placing coins or paper bills onto his open book was the only way he would accept payment. I was very skeptical of fortune tellers, but for 2 rupees, I figured I could stand in the grove and have a swami predict my future. I was traveling for experiences just like this.

He began by telling me he could tell me my mother's name and the name of a girlfriend that I had once almost married. He asked if I had a relative with the initial "D". It took me a little bit to remember that I did have a cousin named Danny Delson. He said he would also tell me my age and the number of brothers and sisters I had. He would also tell me something about my future and gave me a choice of paying him 30, 60, or 90 rupees. He indicated that the amount of information he provided would be in direct proportion to the amount of money I surrendered. I told him I didn't like any of those prices, but eventually he convinced me to put 10 rupees on the prayer book with a promise to add 20 rupees if he performed some magic. The meeting with the swami was getting more interesting, so I put one of my newly acquired 10-rupee notes onto his open prayer book. After he closed the prayer book on the rupee note, he took out a square piece of white paper, placed it on the cover of the book, and took out a pencil. He tilted his book in such a way that I couldn't see what he was scribbling, but he seemed to be reading me and sizing me up while making little notations. He folded the paper twice, handed it to me, and told me to hold it in my right hand.

The swami then took out a second small square of white paper and asked me a series of personal questions. He asked for the day, month, and year of my birth and wanted to know how many brothers and sisters I had. Next, he asked for the name of an old girlfriend, and I told him Cheryl. Cheryl was my high school girlfriend, who wrote me a Dear John letter when I was a freshman in college. After I answered his questions, he stated that he would write down a number that represented the amount of money I would inherit. Again, he tilted his book so I couldn't see what he was writing.

He took this second piece of paper with the information I had just given him and said, "I am going to throw this information away." He turned his back to me and appeared to crush the piece of paper with my personal information into a ball and throw it into the bushes behind him. But actually, he pocketed the paper with my personal information and crushed a third blank piece of paper he had secretly reserved for this purpose and threw that instead. He then told me to take the original folded paper with his predictions that I had been holding all this time and tap my head with it three times. I was then to drop this original folded paper onto his open book. I did as I was instructed and dropped it onto the open book, but, as it landed, the swami slightly tilted the book, and the paper bounced and fell to the ground. He chided me that I had dropped it the wrong way. He bent over to pick up the fallen paper. While bending down he must have quickly replaced the fallen paper holding his supposed predictions with the paper containing my personal information. I couldn't see the switch because he had turned his back to me when he picked up the fallen paper. He explained that he would demonstrate the proper way to drop the folded paper onto the book, which he did and handed the paper back to me to try again. Once more, I tapped the folded paper to my head three times and dropped it onto his open book. This time the folded paper stayed on the book. He unfolded the scrap, and like magic, it had written on it:

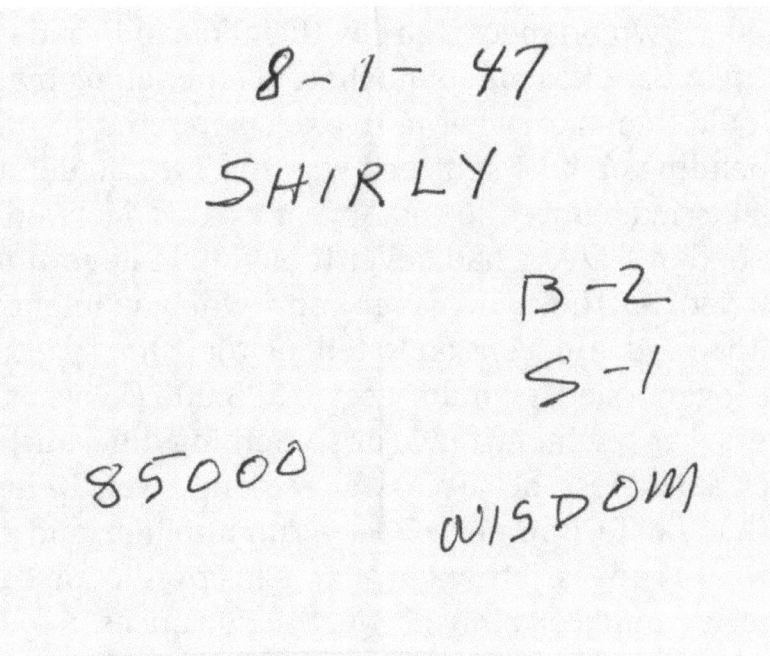

This is a copy of what the folded paper looked like.

Due to his "clairvoyance," he claimed to have foreseen the answers, but certainly the words and numbers I was looking at were my responses to his questions. He then asked for 30 rupees since he had performed a magic trick, as he said he would. Although I knew there was no magic involved, I paid him only 20 rupees, reminding him that I had already put down 10 rupees to initiate his display of talent. The swami was working all the angles trying to get as many rupees from me as possible. So far, he was doing a pretty good job. I had paid the agreed-upon 30 rupees, and it was his turn to tell me 30 rupees worth of my future.

The swami proceeded to tell me I would live more than 75 years and then die suddenly. He said that I'd had some good luck and that more was on the way. In

August, I would meet a girl by the name of Brenda or Betty in Bangkok, or somewhere further along my trip. I would then marry her in two to six months, depending on how smitten I was, but I would definitely be married before the end of year. Wow! Married by the end of 1974? I had never thought about getting married, but, hey, you never know who you might meet on the road. He went on to tell me that shortly after getting married, I would receive $85,000 (I wasn't sure if this was the inheritance or something different), start a business, be successful, return to New Delhi with my wife, Bonnie or Becky, run into him, and give him 100 rupees. I thought that, if his prediction came true, it would certainly be worth 100 rupees.

He said I'd receive a telegram or urgent message about my mother's illness, but by the time I reached home, she would be all right. Although I wasn't taking the swami's predictions seriously, I was glad I'd be calling home the next day and talking to my mom, even though I knew she was in very good health.

The swami told me that we were in the month of July and the fourth sign of the zodiac, meaning that I was under the sign of Jupiter. Therefore, I should avoid making male and female friends and avoid a person with a name that contained the letter R. His prediction for the month of July was a lonely one with no friends. Maybe that was the price to pay for marriage before the end of the year.

He added that my worst fault was that I told secrets, which I emphatically denied. He finally warned me that, if I ever said one word about this meeting to anyone, none of his predictions would come true. This was our secret, and he was daring me to keep it. Then he took out a picture of his swami brothers who were not as fortunate as he was and asked for a little baksheesh to help feed them. I put one rupee on his book and found my way out of the grove before he conned another rupee out of me.

I think the swami saw me coming out of the bank, or perhaps he had a man working in the bank who told him how much I had exchanged, so he knew how much he could ask for. He then stopped me, led me to the grove, and ran through his sleight-of-hand act while I handed over rupees, a few at a time, until he had relieved me of 34 rupees in exchange for his performance and the promise of a bright future. Thirty-four rupees was close to the amount I was spending every day on food and lodging, so it was an expensive experience, which felt like a rip-off at the time.

From the rickshaw drivers to the swami fortune teller, I felt I wasn't very good at haggling, and I was starting to feel frustrated. If I couldn't get better at bargaining, I would be spending too much of my money.

If just one prediction came true, I'd be amazed and convinced that he was clairvoyant. I hoped it was the one in which he predicted that I would live to be 75.[11] Of course, by sharing the details of the meeting I have

---

[11] *Now that I am writing this memoir at the age of 75 years, I am hoping that his foretelling of my future is short by about 20 to 30 years.*

not kept the secret and ended the power of his predictions.

On the night of the 5th, I went to a discothèque with Steve's friend, Chim, and Marylan, a girl from Germany whom I had met at Mrs. Caloco's. We wanted to get out of the heat, and I always liked to dance. The discothèque, called The Cellar, was air conditioned and had loud music and a dance floor. Cokes cost 2 rupees instead of the usual 80 paise, (there are 100 paise to one rupee), so I didn't drink a lot of Coke. The food was pretty good, and they had several Western dishes on the menu, which were overpriced. Air conditioning was a nice change, and I had fun dancing with Chim and Marylan.

Saturday morning the 6th was quiet, and I couldn't find a rickshaw driver. When the business week was over, the demand for rickshaws dwindled. I found a driver with a horse cart and did my best to bargain for a good price. He finally agreed to take me to the Old Delhi train station for 3 rupees. I planned on leaving for Varanasi, on the Ganges River, in a few days, and I wanted to buy a ticket for the overnight train. It would be good to have a place to stretch out for the 16-hour train ride.

The ride to the train station was a slow one. The closer we got to the station, the more crowded the streets became. The horse was in no hurry and clip-clopped along, winding through a maze of ox carts, horse carts, bicycles, bicycle rickshaws, cars, people, and stray animals going every which way. Yes, just as you've heard, cows wander wherever they want and must be shooed away from food stalls. The horse cart ride filled my senses with an orchestra of the sights, sounds, and smells of the old city.

Along one narrow street, we passed a large white bull lying dead by the side of the road next to a smaller cow, also dead. The bull was huge, bloated, and had its feet propped up on a cart. Everyone was passing by the sad sight, getting on with their day as if this was an ordinary scene, which it probably was, but not for me. Once I arrived at the old station, I bought a 3rd class ticket with a reserved sleeper on the Upper India Express to Varanasi and managed to find a rickshaw back to Mrs. Caloco's. After a little bargaining, I paid 3 rupees. For once, I knew the appropriate price for a ride.

I had been eating a lot of curries, dhal, rice, and chapatis since arriving in India, and most of the food I found was in street stalls and was served straight from the pot. The Indian diet was a nice change from some of the meat dishes I had been eating in the Muslim countries. I was fine with the vegetarian diet and enjoyed the different small dishes that made up a meal. There was no haggling when it came to street food or restaurants; they listed their prices. It was a relief not having to dicker for food. The haggling for everything was starting to wear on me. I didn't think I came out very well on most of the negotiating, and in the 105°F (40°C) heat, my patience was being tried. Bargaining was the way business was done, and if I wanted to hang onto my rupees, I had to at least try to make better deals. Meanwhile, it seemed as if I was spending a lot more than I had expected.

Up until I reached New Delhi, I had been eager to explore the cultures I was passing through. The heat and crowded streets of New Delhi subdued that interest, and, instead of the curiosity that drove me to explore, I found myself hesitant to venture out. Wherever I went, I was constantly being asked questions about where I was from, if I had money to exchange, or something to sell. Quite often men approached me seeking something that they thought I had or could provide, or they just wanted to practice their English. Fending off the curious was getting to me.

I had grown a beard before leaving Colorado, and a few times young men would come up and ask me if they could touch my beard. I usually said yes, but occasionally a guy would be walking by and just reach out and touch it, which was shocking. Men did grow beards in India, but the young men were obviously curious about mine.

While I felt like a foreigner in the countries I passed through, I had always felt a camaraderie with the travelers I met along the way. That seemed to change in New Delhi. The travelers I met here were different. I had lived in big cities before, and in New Delhi, as in most big cities, people tend to insulate themselves from the mass of other people and become more withdrawn. The travelers who had been in India for three months or more didn't interact at all. They had packed away their Western clothing; dressed in Indian shirts, pants, and sandals, carrying only a light shoulder bag. They were in their own world and had tuned out everything and everyone. Travelers and locals seemed to get more into their own trip and weren't open to making contact or friends. Until I reached New Delhi, almost everyone I had met on the road had been open to sharing a story or at least to engaging in some conversation. It seemed that I'd either gotten off that track, or perhaps people just acted differently in India. It wasn't exactly loneliness, but I felt more isolated in New Delhi than I had been since I left the States. It didn't help that the Australian visa I had applied for was in question, and I wouldn't be able to straighten out the problem until I reached Bangkok in August.

On Monday the 8th, I went down to the market where I found the stalls selling beautiful cloth. When I was in Barcelona, I had promised Marta that I would send her a few yards of cloth from India. She made her own dresses and was looking for something different from the fabric she could get in Spain. I found some colorful fabric that I thought Marta would like, had it wrapped up for mailing to Barcelona, and carried the bundle to the Post Office. I had to get back to the guesthouse to pack for the Upper India Express to Varanasi, which was scheduled to leave Old Delhi at 8:10 p.m. that evening. I would have time for dinner and still arrive at the station in plenty of time to find my spot on the train before it left the station.

Once I was on the train, I spent the hot night on a

reserved bench in 3rd class and managed to sleep about nine hours using my backpack as a pillow while wrapping the strap of my shoulder bag around my arm. When I awoke, I pulled a book from my shoulder bag and started reading *Papillon* by Henri Charrière. Sometime in the early afternoon, the train arrived in Varanasi ahead of schedule, which was most unusual and unexpected.

There were plenty of rickshaws waiting when I exited the station, and I hired a young driver who said he would help me find a hotel close to the river Ganges. He took me to a couple of options which were farther from the river than I wanted to be before dropping me off at the Hotel Chandra. The man behind the desk told me the hotel was only a 10- to 15-minute walk from the Ganges.

Once I was settled in my room, I decided to walk down to the sacred river, but, after walking for 15 minutes through the hot dusty streets of Varanasi, I realized that I was nowhere near the Ganges. I continued onward when a young man came up to me and explained that he was a university student on break. He offered to show me a sitar factory where Baba Ram Das had bought his sitar. I knew who Ram Das was. He was born Richard Alpert and, along with Timothy Leary, did research at Harvard with psychedelic drugs in the 1960s. After continuing his experiments off campus, Alpert went to India in 1967 where he met his guru and studied yoga and meditation. His spiritual teacher gave him a new name, Ram Das. I didn't know that he played the sitar. I was familiar with the long-stringed instrument popular in India and used in Hindustani classical music because Ravi Shankar was a well-known sitar player, and George Harrison had used the sitar in some of his music, too.

The young guy offered to show me around his hometown, so I followed him through a maze of small streets until we came to the door of the sitar factory. The student knocked on an unmarked door and we were greeted by a middle-aged man who would be our guide through the factory. I followed the guide slowly through several rooms where different parts of the sitar were being hand-crafted, assembled, and finally displayed in the last room. Some of the rooms smelled of fresh cut wood, while the others further along in the process smelled of the oils that were used to seal the wood creating its final glossy finish. When the tour was over, the young man showed me two or three of the finished sitars and asked which sitar I would like to buy. I told him the sitars were beautiful, but I was traveling and wouldn't be able to travel with a sitar. Without another word, I was led to a back door and found myself out in some dark alley with no idea of how to get to the river or back to my hotel. I kept weaving through the back alleys, hoping I was headed in the right direction, until I found a larger avenue and followed the road downhill toward the river.

I hadn't gone far when another university student approached me with an offer to visit a brocade factory that was owned by his uncle. I could get a special deal, which the public was not offered, but I was under no obligation to purchase any material. I followed him through a maze of alleys until we found the factory. After taking the factory tour, I was offered some beautiful material but declined to purchase anything, so, once again, I was quickly shown the door to some back alley and had to find my way back to a main road. I felt as if I was being used like a pinball, bounced around from one player to the next with the goal of extracting rupees from me.

I knew I was getting close to the river when the roads started filling up with people, and the small shops lining the roads became more numerous. Just before I reached the river, I passed a side street that had over a dozen colorful carts lined up, six carts to a side. I turned up the side street and saw that each cart was piled high with mangos in all shapes and colors; there were shades of green, yellow, and gold, and one cart was full of bright red mangos.

I noticed the people who purchased the mangos had different ways of eating the fruit. Some people used knives to cut the skin off and held the ends while eating around the pit. Other people cut off parts of the fruit and then ate it off the skin.

Yet another way to eat the mango appeared to me to be the most efficient and the least messy. The person would start softening the fruit by gently squeezing the mango with both hands until the fruit was reduced to juice and pulp inside the leathery skin. Lucky squeezers then bit off the stem end of the mango just enough to open the skin and gently squeeze the mushy contents into their mouth.

After the fruit was drained from the skin, all that was left was the pit. The skin with the pit still inside was tossed to the side of the road. It was a very neat and simple way to eat a mango. I finally bought a couple of familiar gold-colored mangos that were ripe and ready to eat. I put one in my shoulder bag and started to gently squeeze the riper mango into pulp. A juicy mango was the perfect treat after the winding journey I had taken to reach the river.

The crowded road ended at the Ganges, where a road ran parallel and above the water. All along the river were ramshackle buildings and a series of stairs, called ghats, that led down to the water. I walked up and down observing the people in the water below. They were using the ghats to reach the holy river for bathing, washing clothing, praying, and cremation. In the harsh heat of the day, the scene, the smells, and the throng of people was overwhelming. I didn't want to intrude on this holy place, so I decided to return to the river the next morning and hire a boat to take me to see the shoreline in the early morning light.

When I was ready to return to the Hotel Chandra, I realized I had no idea how to get back there. Wherever I walked kids of all ages came up to me asking questions, so for 50 paise I hired one of the kids to take me back to the hotel. It took us 45 minutes to get there, instead of the 10 to 15 minutes I had been told.

Luckily, walking through Varanasi - or through any part of India - was a fascinating experience, so it was probably good that the hotel wasn't too close to the river, after all. The scene near the river was frenetic, but by the time I reached the hotel, the streets were calmer.

Early the next morning, Wednesday the 10th, I hired a rickshaw driver to take me down to the river. On the way, he offered to give me a tour around Varanasi after my boat trip. That sounded like a good idea, and I agreed to the tour. He dropped me near a pier where I found a boatman who I hired to take me out on the water. He slowly paddled up and down the river so that I could observe the rituals of bathing, praying, and cremation from a different perspective. The boatman wanted 10 rupees, but I managed to get him down to seven. I was starting to feel more confident in my haggling abilities and thought that I might be saving a rupee or two.

Once back on shore, the rickshaw driver began his tour by peddling me to a small kiosk where I could start the day with tea and fresh yogurt. He then took me to a temple dedicated to Hanuman, the Hindu monkey god and companion to god Rama. The temple was a little rundown, so we didn't stay long. The next stop on his tour was unexpected. It was the only animated temple in all of India and was housed in a beautiful building of white marble that had six or seven Walt Disney-type animatronic robot figures throughout the building. Each figure resembled and was dressed like the god it represented.

Krishna was a blue-skinned figure wearing a golden robe. His lips moved while a recorded voice recounted, in Hindi, the well-known stories associated with him. Shiva, Hanuman, Ganesh, and other Hindu gods had their own robotic likenesses telling stories. I thought it was a little strange, but the Hindu gods were fantastical enough that they were rather convincing in their animated bodies.

Throughout the day, I was constantly tossing 10, 25, or 40p into a cup to buy flowers and incense or to have someone watch my sandals. There was a constant outflow of cash everywhere I went.

That evening, I left the Hotel Chandra and took a rickshaw to the Varanasi train station. I was heading north to Nepal. I bought a ticket for the overnight train that would take me to Raxaul, close to the Indian/Nepalese border. I was told that it was necessary to make two connections to reach Raxaul. While waiting to board the train, I saw another guy with a backpack and met Jean from Holland.

After we introduced ourselves and engaged in a little travel talk, I realized we were both trying to get to Raxaul and eventually to Kathmandu. Once we found our seats, we started talking to two other travelers in the same car. Christophe from Germany and Patrick from France were also headed north to Nepal. We settled in for the slow ride to Mazaffarpur, located in the northeast Indian state of Bihar, bordering on Nepal. We were scheduled to make the first connection there before switching to a train going to Sugauli. From Sugauli, we would change to another train going to Raxaul on the Indian/Nepalese border. Unfortunately, when we arrived in Mazaffarpur, we had missed the connection and had to wait five hours for the next train. At least I had some other travelers to share the time with.

Jean, Christophe, Patrick, and I went over to some food stands near the station and ate dhal and chapati. We found some shade and stayed out of the sun waiting for the train. It finally arrived, and after a slow ride to Sugauli, we learned that there would be no train for the final leg to Raxaul until the next morning. We had no choice but to spend the night on the station platform.

Sugauli was a small station, so once the last train left, the station master turned off the platform lights and locked up the station, leaving the four of us and dozens of stranded Indian passengers outside on the platform in the dark. The only light came from the brightly lit street next to the station. It looked as if there were a dozen or more food stands lining each side of the street.

With our packs on, the four of us made our way to the brightly lit area and walked up and down past the small kitchens trying to discover which foods were creating the terrific aromas that filled the night air making me hungry. Each stand was serving similar dishes of vegetable curry and rice, and they were charging only 2 rupees for all you could eat. We picked one stand, and, when our food was ready, we sat around a table and talked about our travels. We had all night. Having enjoyed a tasty meal, we were ready to spend the night at the train station in Sugauli.

After dinner, we went back to the station and found enough room on the platform to throw down our sleeping bags as a cushion on the brick surface. We stretched out on the hard platform with the other passengers waiting in the heat and mosquitoes for the next day's train. I slept till midnight, then got up and stood under cool water coming out of a pipe in the wall. I finally got back to sleep for a few more hours, and around 4:30 a.m., I sensed movement around me. Passengers sleeping on the station platform had started to rustle, waking up in time to catch the 5 a.m. train to Raxaul.

In the early morning light, the train arrived, and a few passengers exited before all the passengers with tickets for Raxaul, including me, scrambled aboard to find seats on the already crowded train. Luckily, I found an empty seat and sat down with my pack to wait for the train to pull out. I wasn't sure where Jean or the other two guys ended up. I waited for the train to start moving, but it just sat at the station. Around 6 a.m. dozens of farm workers walked up to the train and scrambled on top of the train cars. The conductors eventually arrived and kicked the farm workers off the top of train, but, once the farm workers were off the train, they quickly gathered in front of the train and sat down in a non-violent protest. After a few hours, the local police called for reinforcements and the protesters were dispersed. I think the farm workers wanted to get to Raxaul for work, but the police didn't want them on top of the train and wouldn't let them get close to it.

At 10:00 a.m., five hours after the scheduled departure, on Friday morning, July 12th, the train finally pulled out of Sugauli. Two hours later, we arrived in Raxaul. When I stepped off the train, I saw Jean waiting on the platform. Not far from the train station we found a room at the Tourist Lodge with two beds and a shower room down the hall. We took turns washing off the thirty-six hours of train travel before lying down for a rest.

We got up as the sun was going down and walked around Raxaul just as the sky lit up with streaks of red and orange. We found a restaurant that served a spicy goat curry and then went back to the lodge for an early night.

Saturday morning, Jean and I didn't wait long to grab our packs, leave the Tourist Lodge, and hop on a horse-drawn cart. I asked the driver to take us to the customs office at the Indian border. When we arrived, we saw it wasn't open for business yet. There was a restaurant next door, so we went over and ordered fried eggs and tea while we waited. It felt like the owner of the restaurant might have been related to the customs officer, and the customs office wouldn't open until the restaurant had a few customers. By the time I had finished the breakfast of questionably fresh eggs, the Indian Customs Office had opened, and Jean and I went in to have our passports stamped with an exit stamp. We walked out of Indian customs and made our way over to the Nepalese Customs Office, where we presented our passports with the proper visas and vaccination cards. While the customs agents were looking over our passports, I glanced up and saw a picture of King Birendra hanging on the wall behind the customs agents. I realized I was leaving the democracy of India and entering a country ruled by a King. We were handed back our passports and cards allowing us into the country.

Although we were in Nepal, we were still a few miles from Birganj, the closest village with bus service to Kathmandu. We looked around for a bicycle rickshaw, but the only transportation we saw was a horse-drawn, six-seater rickshaw. Jean and I had plenty of room in the six-seater and spread out for the slow ride to the bus depot. After about thirty minutes, we reached the bus depot and walked up to the ticket window. We were told the express bus to Kathmandu with reserved seats had already left. For 15 rupees we purchased tickets for a bus leaving later that morning. The later bus had a first-come-first-seated policy, so after it pulled in and allowed passengers to get off, we found seats in different parts of the bus.

Shortly after I had stowed my pack and settled in, we began the 13½-hour bus ride into the Himalayas, climbing up the foothills through rain and clouds to reach Kathmandu at 4,600 feet (1,400 meters). It wasn't long before the scenery started to change from the dry flatlands to the green rolling hills. The heat and humidity of India was behind us, and the higher elevation and cooler temperature forced the passengers to close the breezy windows.

During the day-long bus ride, the police stopped the

bus four times to inspect for bombs they suspected were being smuggled into Nepal. Apparently, the King's life was in danger, and police were checking all passengers coming into the country. The bus stopped at the last checkpoint at 8:30 p.m., and officials had us open our bags one last time.

The bus finally arrived in Kathmandu, and Jean and I met up when we got off the bus. A group of boys were trying to convince us to choose the hotel they represented. We chose to go with one boy to a hotel called the Green Valley Lodge. For 4 Nepalese rupees each per night, we were assured the lodge was clean, quiet, cheap, and supposedly had hot water for showers. When I woke up Sunday morning, I was in no hurry to get up and explore Kathmandu. Since leaving Varanasi, I had been traveling for 72 hours, day and night, and had been sitting on a bus for the last 13½ hours of the trip. I was happy to stay on my cot and continue reading *Papillon*. Would Papi ever escape from his island prison?

Jean had places he wanted to see, so we agreed to explore Kathmandu on our own. Later that morning, when I had some energy, I got up and walked over to a place called, "Freak Street." Freak Street was populated with pie shops, hotels, restaurants, and legal hashish shops. Kathmandu was one of the few places in the world where hashish was sold legally, and, therefore, was a popular destination for travelers passing through that part of the world. The pie shops served very good fruit pies filled with apples, peaches, or cherries. A variety of other Western-style pies were offered, complete with beautifully browned crusts.

Since I had left Europe, I had heard about the pie shops of Kathmandu, and I was ready to try some. I picked one of the shops and ordered a slice of cherry pie with a cup of tea. It was delicious and every bit as good as I had heard it would be. The pie shops all played rock n' roll music, so it was like being in a Western environment. Freak Street was a familiar oasis from the strangeness of traveling through foreign countries and cultures where I found everything new and different. Traveling was very stimulating, and I was always alert trying to navigate the different languages, customs, and foods. But on Freak Street in Kathmandu, suddenly there were Western foods and music, and the Nepalese waiters spoke English, French, and German. Apple pie and rock n' roll! It was a welcome change to eat familiar foods and listen to familiar music, but that wasn't the real Nepal that I was traveling to see.

On Monday the 15th, I got up and decided to visit the nearby Charumati Stupa, which was located on a hill about a mile-and-a-half from the center of Kathmandu. The original Buddhist stupas were constructed to contain the earthly remains of Buddha and his closest followers. Over time, the stupas were built to contain relics of Buddhist monks or nuns. Walking through the narrow streets, I passed calm, peaceful people and a few Buddhist and Hindu temples.

Before I arrived in Nepal, I had thought the Nepalese people were mainly Buddhists, but, actually, only about 9% are Buddhists. Over 80% of the Nepalese people consider themselves Hindu. In fact, Buddhist and Hindu religions seem to blend into a Nepalese form of religion.

I heard chanting and the gentle beat of a drum coming from one of the Buddhist temples. As I approached, I could see a procession of monks, following each other clockwise while spinning several large cylindrical prayer wheels made from embossed metal. Each monk was chanting in a tone that blended with the other monks, creating a calming resonance. Out of nowhere, a young Nepali guy appeared right next to me and asked if I wanted to smoke some marijuana. He introduced himself as Anish and said that he had recently picked flowers from plants growing in his mountain village. He had hiked three days from his small village to Pokhara and then rode a bus for 120 miles (190 kms) to reach Kathmandu. I had heard that, when the skies were clear, the views from Pokhara of the Annapurna mountain range, which included three of the ten highest peaks in the world, were supposedly spectacular. I wouldn't be visiting Pokhara this trip because the rain clouds were low, obscuring any view of the mountain tops.

I couldn't pass up the opportunity to smoke Nepalese flower, so I agreed. We walked to his brother's souvenir shop, not far from the stupas, and headed to the back of the shop where he rolled two joints using some green flower tops. The buds were young but flavorful. The fresh flower was not as strong as the hash I had scored on Freak Street the day before, but that was hashish and this was young bud. We sat in the back of the souvenir shop surrounded by trinkets, when my new friend started to explain Buddha, Shiva, Kali, and Siddhartha to me. Anish told me the story about Siddhartha sacrificing himself to a hungry tigress to spare the big cat from eating her own newborn cubs. Siddhartha, or the Buddha, had many lives before he reached Nirvana. The tale about the tigress was about sacrificing oneself for the greater good. After telling me about Buddhist and Hindu gods and goddesses, Anish sang some Nepalese songs. He had a beautiful voice, and the songs were simple and melodic with a pleasant rhythm. He pulled out a wooden flute and played some Nepalese tunes to introduce me to the music he liked. I wished that I had a tape recorder to record his beautiful voice and gentle songs.

The time I spent with Anish really lifted my spirits. While I had been in India, the people who approached me usually wanted to know where I was from, or they wanted to touch my beard, or they were looking for some coins. People were always wanting something, and I got tired from the barrage of questions; even though they were just asking for information, it was always the same information.

Boys gather around a shrine to Hanuman, the monkey god

From the moment I met Anish, he was sharing with me. He shared his homegrown pot; stories of his gods; his songs, both sung and played on the flute; and his friendship. The difference I felt from the previous weeks in India where people were constantly demanding something from me definitely changed my attitude. I did buy a small carving of Ganesh from his brother to remember the afternoon.

On Tuesday the 16th, I said goodbye to my temporary roommate, Jean, and moved from the Green Valley Lodge to the Annapurna Lodge, which was just off Freak Street. We were doing different things, and I wanted to get my own room, which was fine with Jean. I found a hotel that had a room with four windows and good ventilation for 10 rupees, or $1.00. It was comfortable and clean, and I liked the toilet down the hall with the squat-style hole in the floor because I had been using it so much. Some of the food I had been eating was going through me. I had been using the water method for cleaning myself, and it was much easier on my bottom than TP would have been.

The morning of the 17th I woke up determined to clear up what had been causing my bad stomach. I started the day with a big bowl of curd, which is different from yogurt in that the milk is curdled with lemon juice or vinegar, while yogurt is fermented with bacteria. I followed up the curd with a mango and bananas. I was hoping that whatever was in my gut would be flushed out by the curd and fresh fruit.

After breakfast, I walked to the post office to check Poste Restante. I wanted to see if there was mail being held for me and I wanted to buy postcards, stamps, and an aerogramme.

Aerogrammes were a cheap way to send a letter internationally and were available in most countries around the world. It's a sheet of thin, pale blue paper designed to be an all-in-one letter and pre-stamped envelope. One side of the aerogramme is blank for letter writing, while the other side has a place for the address, return address, and stamp, plus additional space for a few more sentences. There are lines on the paper indicating the proper way to fold the aerogramme. After that, it is obvious where to lick it shut. Since it's pre-stamped, it can be dropped into any mailbox within the country. It was the cheapest way to send a letter abroad, and I mailed one or two aerogrammes from every country I passed through.

I wanted to stay in touch with my family and let them know I was okay. The international telephone call I had made to my parents from New Delhi was full of static and was frustrating because the conversation was so fragmented. After that, I decided to send aerogrammes instead of calling internationally.[12]

It was drizzling when I came out of the post office, so I went back to my room at the Annapurna Lodge and lay down to read a book that someone passed on to me. *Untouchable* by Mulk Raj Anand helped me to better understand the Indian culture. I would be passing through Calcutta, the most populated city in India (nearly 8,000,000 residents) before continuing my travels and wanted to be able to handle some of the things that had frustrated me about the country.[13] I was hoping that the book would give me some insight to help improve my attitude toward the people I would meet.

Sitting in the pie shops on Freak Street gave me time to think about where I wanted to go. I was in Nepal, halfway around the world from home, eating cherry pie and listening to Led Zeppelin. And yet, it felt like I could have been in any American pie shop, and I knew I wouldn't connect with the local people of Nepal while only hanging out with other travelers. Plus, listening to

---

[12] *My father saved all the aerogrammes I sent and kept them in a 3-ring binder for me. I still have those aerogrammes, and they have helped me tell this story.*
[13] *Calcutta, the capital of West Bengal, was renamed Kolkata in 2001.*

western music on a tourist street made me think of home too much. I was comfortable in Kathmandu, and it would be easy to stay there. I could find a remote village to stay in because the people were friendly and the atmosphere was so relaxing compared to India, but it wasn't time to kick back in a small village. And, trekking was out of the question, too. Nepal is usually socked in by clouds most of the summer months, and the sky doesn't clear up enough for trekking. My timing for visiting Nepal was off by a few months, so I would just have to return some future autumn when the weather would be cold and clear. I knew that it was time to keep moving.

Smiling young villagers outside Kathmandu

To reach Calcutta, I could take another grueling bus ride through the mountains of Nepal followed by overcrowded, unpredictable train rides through the heat of India, or I could just fly there. I would have to take planes to Rangoon and Bangkok anyway, so I opted to add a flight from Kathmandu to Calcutta.

After breakfast on Monday the 22nd, I went to the Union of Burma Airways office and bought a ticket from Kathmandu to Bangkok, with stops in Calcutta and Rangoon, for a student rate of $130.50. Thankfully, I still had my student card and saved $44.00 off the regular fare of $174.50. Once I had the plane ticket to Rangoon, I went to the Burmese embassy to apply for a seven-day visa. Seven days was the maximum number of days I was permitted to stay in Burma.[14] The President of Burma was a military dictator named Ne Win, who limited travelers to seven days in Burma so that they wouldn't get too comfortable or cause trouble. I handed over four pictures of myself plus $5.70 to the embassy staff before they would stamp the visa into my passport.

While waiting at the Union of Burmese Airways office, I'd met David, an American from D.C. We chatted for a few minutes and agreed to find a place to eat after finishing our business with the airline. Over lunch, David told me that he was a lawyer taking three months off to see some of the world. He had been flying from city to city, staying at nice hotels in rooms by himself. He was eating at good restaurants, also by himself.

---

[14] *Since 1989, Burma has been called The Republic of the Union of Myanmar and Rangoon has been called Yangon.*

Staying in a hotel room is a lot more isolating than staying in a dorm room with other backpackers or sharing a hotel room with another traveler. He spent at least twice as much money as I did and didn't have the opportunity to meet many people as he flew from city to city. David reminded me of my travels through Scandinavia before I met Walter, the world traveler.

Traveling meant that every day was filled with new experiences, new sights, new people, new challenges, and new decisions to make. Unlike the routine days at home, where having a job regulates practically every hour of the day, traveling presents a succession of choices to be made throughout the day. Every morning, I would wake up faced with the freedom to select what I wanted to do that day. I was happy with the decisions that led me to Kathmandu, and I was confident that I would get myself to Australia.

On Saturday, July 27th, I left Nepal and flew Union of Burma Airways to Calcutta. It was an easy, hour-long flight on an old noisy prop engine plane. After the plane landed, I passed through customs and walked out of the airport back into the heat and humidity of India. It was easy finding a local bus that went to the center of the city. When we reached the center of Calcutta, teeming with people, I stepped off the bus and found my way to the Salvation Army. Like the ants passing information, another traveler had told me that, when passing through Calcutta, the best place to stay was the Salvation Army. For the equivalent of $1.35, a traveler could get a cot in a dorm room plus a breakfast of cereal, omelet, bread, and tea.

Calcutta was the largest, most populated city I had ever visited. Eight million people trying to live in a place that was only meant to be home to one million. The Salvation Army was a haven from the overheated streets. There were fans hanging from the ceiling moving the heavy air, keeping the darkened interior a little more comfortable.

On Sunday the 28th, there was a line of people outside the Salvation Army that went on for blocks. I had heard that a million people without homes lived on the streets of Calcutta, and the Salvation Army served breakfast to a few thousand of those people every Sunday morning. The Salvation Army also served me breakfast that morning, and, soon after, I left the dorm room and went out into the heat to explore Calcutta.

I walked over to the Indian Museum, which turned out to be an overwhelming experience. The huge museum had six large sections comprising 35 galleries displaying an incredible collection of cultural and scientific artifacts from all over Asia. Contained in the long, tall halls were collections of armor and ornaments, fossil skeletons, mummies, and Mughal paintings. One hall contained weathered wooden sections from buildings that were once part of ancient villages, while other halls contained sculptures, paintings, and coins representing countries and kingdoms throughout Asia. The armor from battles long ago was displayed in one gallery, and I couldn't help but think about the warriors who put on protective gear and went to war. Whether a soldier was a professional or a conscript, he or she would wear metal plates or chain mail as protection from the thrust or slash of a sword, pike, or knife. Armed with similar weapons, the soldiers came face-to-face with other soldiers, each intent on killing as many people as possible.[15]

There was a tremendous amount of information and visual stimuli in the Indian Museum, but the air inside this big old building was a little stale, so, after a couple of hours, I needed to get my body outside, breathe some fresh air, and shake off the fatigue.

While walking around Calcutta I passed a sign that read:

Calcutta: A City of Palaces?
A City of Slums?

Calcutta was once known as the City of Palaces due to a population of rich British and wealthy Bengalis who built large residences in the city. Calcutta was designed to be the center of British government in the late 1700s, but the government was moved from Calcutta to New Delhi in 1911.

By 1974, the most populated city in India had outgrown its intended population and could not provide for the number of people who lived there. It was common to pass people sleeping on the streets

---

[15] *In 1970, I was lucky to avoid being drafted. Out of 366 possible lottery numbers, my birthday, January 8th, drew number 199. The government stopped drafting young men when the last lottery number, 196, was called. I missed being drafted to fight the war in Viet Nam by three numbers and can only guess what I would have done if my number had been called.*

with nothing but a sarong wrapped around them. To keep clean, some people living on the street would stand by the side of the road washing themselves using a pail of water. With the sarong loosely wrapped around their bodies, they splashed themselves under the sarong to wash away the dirt and sweat. The people without homes practiced hygiene as best they could.

On my way to the post office to check Poste Restante for mail, I was approached by a beggar who had only one arm. He held out his good hand and was very persistent, demanding that I give him a few paisa or coins. I kept walking trying to ignore him, but he followed me down the street waving the stump of his other arm at me until I relented and put a few coins in his cup. I had seen a lot of begging both here and in New Delhi. When I first arrived in New Delhi, I would toss a few coins on the cloth the beggars sat on or in their cups. After seeing a number of terribly disfigured children and adults, I had become callous, and the stumps didn't seem to move me. I had heard that some of the infants with twisted bodies were purposely deformed because a deformed baby brought in more money. I couldn't believe that that was true. Also, leprosy was still infecting people, and the way the disease affected the skin and disfigured the face, hands, and feet was always disturbing to see. At some point, the number of people living on the street begging for a few coins blended into the fabric of Indian life, and I was forced to accept that the fabric hadn't changed much over time. I don't think I had ever seen such a wide divide between wealth and poverty. For a middle-class boy from the suburbs of Chicago, the divide was part of the culture shock.

Reincarnation plays a big part in the belief system of many of the religions of India. People who lead a good life may be reborn into a caste that is higher than their present caste, and their next life can be better. People who don't lead a good life may be reborn into a lower caste, and their next life would be harder. It seemed that everyone was responsible for their own karma. As I traveled, and in life, I had the philosophy of treating everyone as I would like to be treated. I felt that my karma was in good shape so far.

Although the heat and the press of people were the same as in New Delhi, in some ways Calcutta was easier to maneuver around. It didn't seem that people were as confrontational here as in New Delhi, or maybe I was a little more seasoned as a traveler and knew how to get through my day less affected by the stress of heat, the monsoon rain, and the number of people I encountered every day.

I had heard the Tiretta Bazaar was a good place to check out, so on the 29th I left my dorm room at the Salvation Army and wandered along the road leading to the bazaar. I tried to take in what life must be like for those living in Calcutta. The bazaar consisted of dozens of stalls selling clothing, kitchen items, food, and all kinds of dry goods. Young men were carrying car parts on their heads, and there were several carts overflowing with a variety of goods being pulled through the streets by horses and men. There were rickshaws powered by bicycles, and for the first time, I saw rickshaws being pulled by men on foot. I had heard that a few years earlier the government tried to ban human-powered rickshaws, but the drivers themselves protested and won the right to continue pulling their rickshaws through the streets on foot.

Shortly after noon the next day, on Tuesday, July 30th, I took a taxi to the Calcutta Airport. When I presented my ticket to the woman behind the counter at Union of Burmese Airways, I was informed that the scheduled flight to Rangoon would be leaving four hours late. She handed me a coupon for a free meal at the airport restaurant, so I thanked her and looked around for a place to settle down and wait.

That's when I remembered the psychic customs lady from the India/Pakistan border. She had said she would send the five 100-rupee notes she had found on me to the customs office at the Calcutta airport. With the four-hour delay, I had the time to go to the customs office and see if she had really sent those notes to Calcutta. I presented my passport and the receipt for the five notes to the customs agent. The agent found my name on a piece of paper, then directed me to another customs office where they were holding my notes.

When I found the second office, I presented my passport and receipt to the agent who went into the room behind his desk. A few minutes later, he returned with the same five notes that were taken from me a few months before. The notes were folded and sewn together with saffron-colored thread. He presented me with a paper showing there were charges of 27.30 rupees to get the notes back, which, I guess, was a handling charge. I had already converted my remaining Indian rupees into Burmese kyat, thinking that I wouldn't need any more rupees, so I had to exchange some dollars into rupees so I could pay off the 27.30 rupees and collect the five notes. The agent handed me the five notes, which I would take to Bangkok and sell to a traveler headed to India. I hoped he would have better luck than I did smuggling the rupee notes into India.

The plane scheduled for Rangoon finally arrived in Calcutta. It would take a few minutes to unload and reload passengers and baggage, giving me time to go to the duty-free shop. I bought a gold carton of British 555 cigarettes for $3.75. The travelers I had met who had been through Burma told me that once in Burma I could take an unopened carton of cigarettes and a bottle of whisky to the black market and sell them for enough kyat to cover expenses for the week. I decided not to buy a bottle of whisky, mainly because I had no place to put it. My backpack and shoulder bag were completely full. As it was, I would have to carry the carton of 555s in my free hand.

I then waited for the "Fokker Friendship" two-prop airplane to be refueled for our flight. The plane lifted off on a beautiful, slow take-off and climbed through the clouds emerging into a clear blue sky. Below us, I could see a sky full of monsoon storm clouds. Flying in a slow-moving two-engine plane was a very nice way to fly. The prop plane never got very high and, after it left the dark clouds behind, I had a bird's-eye view of the land and water passing below.

The flight took 2½ hours and we landed in Rangoon at 8:30 p.m. When we were passing through customs, one of the armed soldiers who was standing around asked me if I would sell him one of the cigarette packs from the unopened carton. I shook my head and told him no, with a smile. He knew I needed the carton intact to be able to sell it on the black market. He knew and I knew how the game was played, and he was just letting me know that he knew.

To get through customs, I had to fill out forms stating what items I had brought into the country, the exact amount of money I was carrying, and whether I had a camera or not. I had shared a dorm room with a few travelers in Calcutta who were headed in the same direction I was and three of them had been on my flight. David, the American I had met in Kathmandu in the Union of Burma Airways office; Yossi, an Israeli; Charlie, a Briton; and I met outside of the customs office. We located a window to exchange money and I exchanged a U.S. 10-dollar bill for 45 Burmese kyat, so I was getting 4.5 kyat for one U.S. dollar.

We went out to the street and found a driver who would take us into Rangoon for 4 kyat. We checked into the YMCA for 3 kyat a night each and were shown a dorm room with wooden platforms to sleep on. I unrolled my sleeping bag on one of the platforms and was happy to get in the bag and read awhile before I fell asleep. Luckily for me, I was able to sleep almost anywhere.

Early Wednesday morning the 31st, David, Yossi, and I got up early and caught the 7 a.m. express train to Mandalay. As soon as the train left the station, we all went to the dining car, where there were comfortable seats, bad music, and seven other Western travelers who had come to Burma from Bangkok. They were exploring Burma like me but were flying on to India at the end of their seven-day visa. Larry from the U.S.; Jim, Robin, Phil, and Rose from various Australian cities; and Murray from New Zealand, along with the three of us, started a very pleasant ride. Around noon, the train pulled into a station, and vendors came up to the windows carrying baskets with rolled-up banana leaves filled with rice and chicken curry. We bought the curry lunch and cold Mandalay beer for 5 kyat ($1.10).

We arrived in Mandalay at 6:30 p.m. When we got off the train, an official came up to our group of backpackers and directed us toward two Chinese hotels not far from the station. One hotel had a room for two costing 8.80 kyat ($1.95) per night; the second had a room that cost 7.70 kyat ($1.70) per night. The difference was that for an extra kyat there was a shower using cold water, while for 7.70 kyat you had a bucket of cold water and a cup to bathe with. Yossi and I opted for the 7.70 kyat per night at the Man San Win Dar Hotel, and the others went across the street. The Man San Dar Win Hotel was clean, comfortable, and had a mosquito net over the bed, plus a fan in the ceiling to keep the air moving.

Business card for hotel in Mandalay (front and back)

I had been carrying the 555 cigarette carton since I had flown out of Calcutta, and on Thursday, the 1st of August, I went looking for the local black market. I had met a traveler in Rangoon who explained to me how to get there. He told me to look for the square that was set up as a food market. There would be the usual stalls selling a variety of fresh fruit, vegetables, and some dry goods, and, if I walked around the market carrying the 555s, someone would approach me with an offer to buy the carton.

Within a minute after I entered the market square, a young Burmese guy waved me down and offered a price that I knew was low for a carton of 555s. We traded prices back and forth, but I had heard that the going price for a carton of cigarettes was 85 kyat, and that's what he paid me in the end. After exchanging cigarettes for kyat, we shook hands and parted. I now had nearly enough to pay for the rest of my stay in Burma, and my confidence in my haggling ability was increasing.

I went back to the hotel and joined some of the travelers walking to the Union of Burmese Airways' office to check on flights to Pagan, an abandoned ancient city that sat 100 miles (160 kms) southwest of Mandalay. The Pagan Empire ruled over the Irrawaddy valley, considered the heart of Burma, for 250 years beginning in the 1050s CE. The empire was the birthplace of the language and culture of the region that was to become Myanmar in 1989.

Pagan has over 5,000 pagodas and I'm sure would be an amazing site to visit, but I decided not to go. I had already seen many old historical sites and structures, so I decided to stay in Mandalay and experience the Burma of today. I didn't want to keep moving from spot to spot without taking the time to see how the people in each part of the world lived. Mandalay was a lively and bustling city, whereas Pagan offered the crumbling ruins of a once-vibrant civilization.

Yossi and I met up with David and the five other folks in front of their hotel across the street. We found a pony cart that could take all of us to the bottom of Mandalay Hill situated on the northern edge of the city. Mandalay Hill has over 1,725 well-worn steps leading from street level to the top of the hill. As I climbed the stairs, I passed many pagodas and shrines placed just off the stone steps. It seemed that at every holy spot we would have to remove our shoes, so we all decided to climb barefoot up and down the hill. As we walked up the hill, we passed stalls selling flowers, paper streamers, food, and drink.

Once at the top, we found a food stall where I bought a nice rice curry on a banana leaf. We sat on a bench enjoying the wonderful view of Mandalay and the wide Irrawaddy River below, which flows from the north, moves south through the middle of Burma, and empties into the Andaman Sea 1,400 miles (2,200 kms) later.

After lunch, I decided that traveling in a large group was getting to be too much for me. Traveling in a group was fun for a while, but making group decisions became cumbersome. It was nice to travel with one person who shared the joys and occasional tough moments, but even two people traveling together insulated them from direct contact with the locals. A group of six or seven looked and felt like a tour group, so I went back down the hill and caught a bus back to Mandalay, alone.

Once I got back to the center of the city, I walked to the market area and went to a shop belonging to Aung Cho, whom I'd heard knew about Burmese jade and other stones. When I arrived at his shop, he handed me his card, and I could see he was also a philatelist – a collector of stamps – but I didn't need any stamps at the moment. I told him I was interested in jade, and he showed me some Burmese jade which had a nice green color. I was familiar with Japanese jade, which can be a light green, but I didn't know what good Burmese jade was supposed to look like. I was just hoping that Aung Cho was selling me the real thing. I wasn't ready to buy yet, so I told him I would think about the jade and come back the next day.

Giant White Cinthe at base of Mandalay Hill

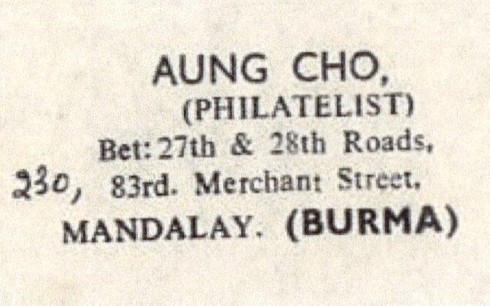

Card from Aung Cho's shop

Friday morning the 2nd, most of the backpackers staying at the hotel across the street packed up and took a cart down to the Irrawaddy and caught a boat downriver to the ancient city of Pagan. From Pagan, they would continue to Rangoon by boat. I would be on my own for a while, and that was fine with me. One of my concerns leading up to this trip was whether I would be lonely or not, yet here I was, once again, happy to be a solo traveler.

Early that afternoon I went back to see Aung Cho, and we talked over tea for a couple of hours. Much like India, the British Empire held power over Burma from the early 19th century until 1948. At times, English was taught as a second language, and it had been the primary language of instruction in universities. We chatted about gems, sapphires, rubies, smoke stones, and jade. I was carrying two Mexican gold half-pesos that I had bought in Mexico in 1971. I traded one of the gold half-pesos for 18 pieces of Burmese jade. The gold was worth about $20, and Aung Cho was offering 17 pieces of jade that were just the right size for rings for

$1 each and one larger stone perfect for a necklace that he valued at $3. It seemed like a good deal to me, so we shook hands and made our trade. I hoped the stones were real and not synthetic because I had heard from other travelers that if the stones were real I could get $3 to $5 for each stone if I chose to sell them. I was thinking that I would have four of the ring-sized stones set into rings by a silversmith when I reached Bali. I planned to give one ring to each of my three siblings when I returned to the States. Trading a Mexican gold coin for the Burmese jade felt like a good deal and would always be a good memory of Mandalay.

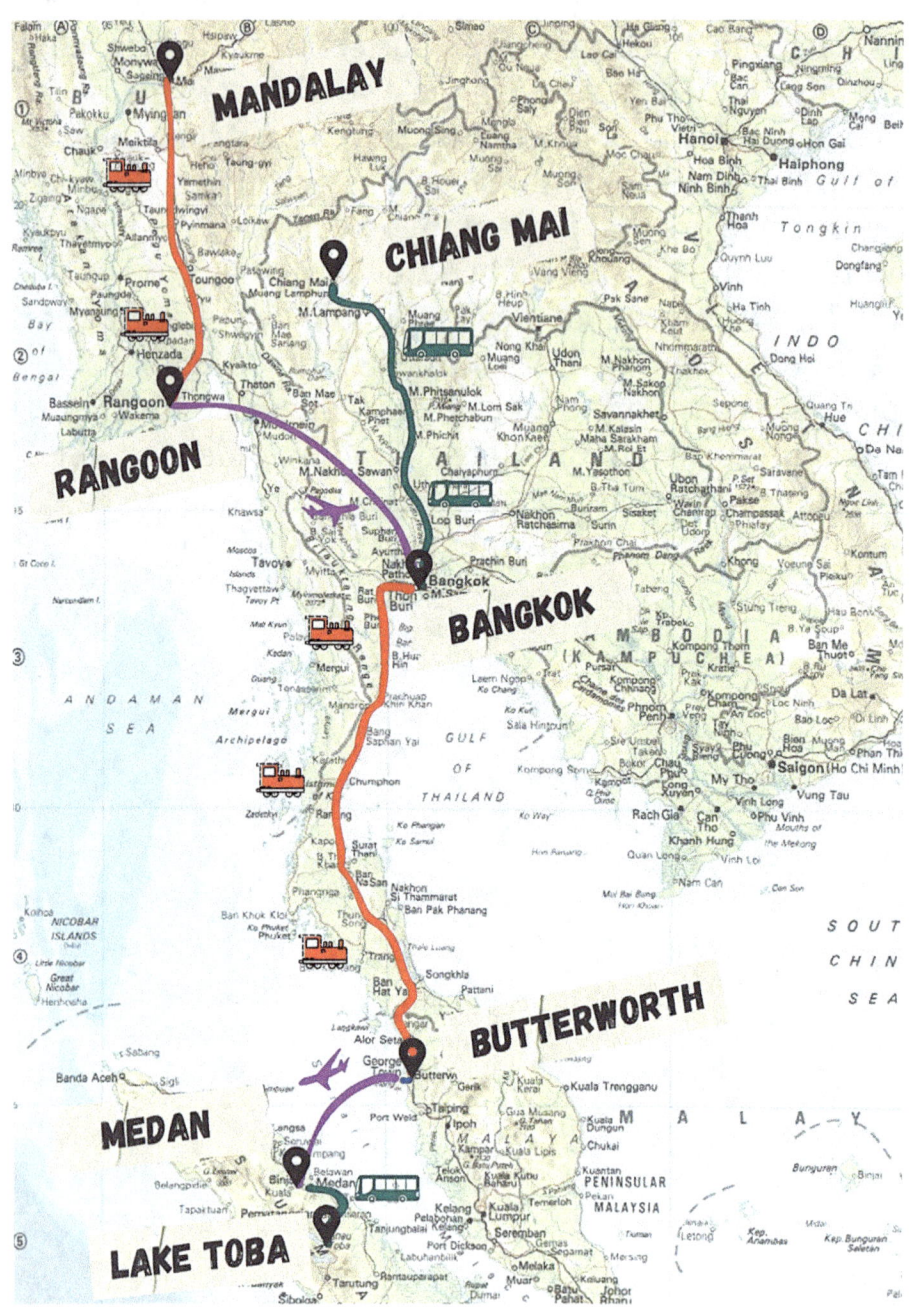

Mandalay, Burma to Rangoon, Burma (by train)
to Bangkok, Thailand (by plane) to Chiang Mai, Thailand and
back to Bangkok (by bus) to Butterworth, Malaysia (by train)
to Georgetown (by ferry) to Medan, Indonesia (by plane)
to Lake Toba, Indonesia (by bus)

Eighth Full Moon

The August full moon was due to rise on my last evening in Mandalay. That morning, Saturday the 3rd of August, I went to the Zegyo Market, the oldest market in Mandalay. The market has one main brick building full of food stalls as well as stalls outside that cover several blocks. This huge market sells fruits, vegetables, nuts, spices, beans, rice, cotton, beautiful cloth, clothing, handicrafts, jewelry, and more. I walked through the market and saw vivid colors and smelled a variety of scents while looking for the dry goods vendors. I wasn't looking to buy but to sell two items I had in my pack that weren't needed. I needed the space, but I also needed a few more Burmese kyat to get me through the rest of my week in Burma. The 85 kyat I received for the 555s wasn't going as far as I had hoped.

One item was a t-shirt with "Chicago Will" printed on it and the other was a small thermos I had bought in Srinagar thinking it would be good to have water or tea with me as I traveled through the heat of India. I was now out of India and had no problem finding drinkable liquids, plus I needed the room the t-shirt and thermos were taking up in my pack. I passed some clothing stalls, including one stall selling cloth embroidered with gold and silver thread, before coming to a stall that looked like a little flea market. The vendor had a little bit of everything, so I took out the thermos and t-shirt and asked, gesturing with my hands, if he wanted to buy them. I dickered with the man and received 25 kyat for the thermos and 15 kyat for the t-shirt, which was fine with me. I really didn't know what the value of those things were but figured that, if we were both happy with the final exchange, I was doing alright.

Directly behind the Zegyo Market stood the Eindawya Pagoda. The main pagoda sat on a large piece of property crowded with smaller pagodas and stupas. The difference between a pagoda and a stupa is that a pagoda may be entered and used as a temple while a stupa is a solid monument that cannot be entered. The main Pagoda was over 100 feet tall (35 meters) and was totally gilded, making it a huge gold structure.

Alongside many of the stupas were life-size mannequins sitting in a circle on the floor. The figures were dressed in white and appeared to be praying. I wandered quietly from stupa to stupa observing the many ornate holy figures and feeling the tranquility of the religious compound. For the past few days, I felt like I had been caught up trying to get somewhere without taking the time to just be in Mandalay. I was glad to get out of Rangoon and see another part of Burma. Before I left on my trip, I feared being lonely traveling by myself, but I had become much more comfortable making my own decisions. While walking around this peaceful setting, I started to slow down and enjoy the beauty of Mandalay.

Eindawya Pagoda

The Burmese people I had met seemed to be content with their lives whereas in India, daily life can be a challenge for many of the people and I could sense that. The local people I met here in Burma were friendly and smiling, and I felt welcome in their country. Because I felt at ease, I could better appreciate the local sights, smells (good and bad), and sounds that defined the country. My decision to stay in Mandalay and take the time to slowly roam the city and the grounds of the Eindawya Pagoda had been a good idea. I needed to slow my pace and appreciate where I was in the world.

When I got back to the hotel, I went to the common room where I met a couple from Switzerland. Bernard and Katia introduced themselves, and we started the usual conversation, trading stories of travel experiences and travel plans. After a few minutes, we agreed to go across the street where there was a stand that made delicious fruit shakes. We finished the shakes and walked down the road to a dark, quiet place where Bernard lit up a joint. No sooner had we started smoking when we saw four college-age Burmese guys coming our way. They must have smelled the pot and approached us with smiles on their faces. They were also smoking a joint. We stood in a loose circle passing the two joints between the seven of us, chatting while the August moon was rising in the east, full and bright. We had a great time laughing, smoking, talking, and just hanging with these young guys.

The young men told us about a good restaurant that wasn't too far, so Bernard, Katia, and I said goodbye to our smoking buddies and went off to have a delicious chicken and rice dinner with cold beer while sitting outside under the full moon. After the meal, we took our time and strolled back to the Man San Dar Win Hotel, where we said goodnight and goodbye. I was leaving for Rangoon early the next morning.

Before I went to the dorm room, I went to the common room and met John, an American from Boston, and Charlie from England. They were traveling together and also leaving for Rangoon in the morning. The three of us decided to get up early and catch the morning express. Traveling without an alarm clock was no problem. When I had been in a small village, the roosters started crowing early. The sun rose around 6 a.m. every morning in the tropics and would light up the room I was sleeping in, if it had a window. In dorm rooms, my dormmates were up and moving around early, which made it hard to sleep in.

Kids at a train stop

So at daybreak, I was already up and walked over to the train station with John and Charlie. We bought tickets and settled into our seats, knowing we would be on that train for most of the day. It started raining shortly after we pulled out of the station with the window still lowered enough to allow a little fresh air in while still keeping out the rain. A couple of times, we went between the train cars to smoke a joint, which helped pass the time. When we pulled into small stations along the way, vendors would come up to our window offering a variety of food and drink. We would pull down the window and buy fresh seasonal fruit; bags of roasted peanuts; rice dishes with vegetables; and, on occasion, some meat. I was happy to see roasted peanuts everywhere I went and was surprised to learn that peanuts are a crop indigenous to South America. Peanuts didn't start their worldwide cultivation until after Columbus discovered the Americas.

It was still raining when we arrived in Rangoon that evening and walked over to the YMCA to check in for the night. We were told that all the beds were taken, but they had a large open room with a stage at one end where they would let us unroll our sleeping bags for 3 kyat. Most of the people who had gone to Pagan from Mandalay were back in Rangoon, and we all met up in the Y's dining room for dinner. We traded stories and laughed at some of the tales. It was always good to bump into people whom you had met at earlier stops. Running into familiar people gave me a sense that I was part of the overland community.

The next morning, at 6:00 a.m. sharp, the local badminton team started practicing in the large room next to the stage, so that ended our night's sleep. I had breakfast and then went with David and a few of the others to the post office. I checked Poste Restante, but there was no mail waiting for me. I walked over to the Union of Burma Airways office to confirm my flight to Bangkok for the next day. The seven days in Burma had passed quickly.

When I came out of the UBA office, I saw a group gathered around someone sitting just to the side of a small square. When I got closer, I saw a snake charmer sitting on the ground with his legs crossed, using his hands to charm the snake, making it rise and move its head back and forth. The man's hand was waving in front of the snake's head when suddenly the snake struck out and sank its fangs into the hand of the charmer. The bite didn't seem to bother him and must have been what is called a "dry bite" where the snake does not release any venom. The man continued charming the snake and eventually put the head of the snake into his mouth.

Seeing a man take a cobra out of a covered basket and start to control it with hand movements made me realize once more that I wasn't in Kansas or Colorado. I left the snake charmer and bumped into John, who was checking out Rangoon on his own.

We decided to find a bus going to the Shwedagon Pagoda, also called the Golden Dagon Pagoda. While walking to the bus stop, we passed another crowd of

Snake Charmer

people gathered around a different snake charmer. We stopped to see if this charmer could charm his snake, and he did. We found the bus to the Shwedagon Pagoda, the biggest and most sacred in Burma, and got on for the 20-minute ride. The pagoda is also the oldest Buddhist stupa in the world, first built more than 2,500 years ago and believed to hold eight strands of Guatama Buddha's hair.

When we pulled up to the Singuttara Hill, we could see that the 365-foot tall (112 meter) Shwedagon Pagoda sat on top, gilded in gold and glistening, surrounded by hundreds of stupas and smaller pagodas. We enjoyed several peaceful hours walking around this special place. What a great way to get a feel for Rangoon.

Shwedagon Pagoda on far right

I spent the morning of August 6th packing and getting ready for the flight to Bangkok. The Y served a flavorful vegetable soup with noodles for lunch. Shortly after lunch, David, John, Charlie, two German guys, and I caught a bus to the airport. Arriving at the airport we had no problem getting through customs since they weren't really checking money or our packs. I had my passport stamped, got right on board, and sat down for a smooth one-hour flight to Bangkok on a Boeing 727 full of Japanese and French passengers, plus the six of us. We landed and presented our passports to the customs agents and were let into Thailand with no hassle. I went to the money exchange window and cashed some U.S. dollars for Thai baht. The exchange rate was 20 baht to the U.S. dollar. The six of us piled into a taxi and were driven through the streets of Bangkok to the Malaysia Hotel in a steady monsoon rain. Driving through Bangkok was a bit of a culture shock after coming from the quiet streets of Rangoon where there had been very few cars. Bangkok was a modern city with bright lights and was teeming with too many cars, buses, and noisy motorbikes.

The word among the travelers was that the Malaysia Hotel was the place to stay in Bangkok because the rooms were air-conditioned. After sleeping on cots, in dorms, and on the stage at the YMCA in the humid heat of the monsoon season, an air-conditioned room sounded good. And, you could score some Thai sticks right there at the hotel. Thai sticks were five-inch slices of thin bamboo covered with fresh marijuana buds and wrapped with thread.

The taxi dropped us off in front of the Malaysia Hotel, but, when we went to check in, we found that the hotel was completely full. We were told there were a few hotels within walking distance, so we went over to the Privacy Hotel across the street. The two German guys from the flight ended up staying at the Privacy, while David, John, Charlie, and I found a couple of rooms at Bungalow 27 just down the street.

We checked in, and when David and I let ourselves into the room, I looked around and saw mirrors on the walls and ceiling, paintings of nudes, stirrup chairs for the ladies, and music piped in till 1:30 a.m. in the morning. We were staying at a drive-in quickie hotel. It was clean, and we had our own bathroom, so we figured we could stay at the "No Tell Motel" for one night. We put our packs down and went to find a restaurant near the hotel. I was ready for a change from rice dishes and ordered a noodle dish called Pad Thai and a cold Singha beer. After dinner, I went over to the Malaysia Hotel and asked a traveler in the lobby where I could find some Thai sticks. He told me that Thai sticks were called Buddha grass in Thailand and that there was a guy on the third floor who had some for sale. I went up to the third floor and found the guy standing at the end of the hall selling Buddha grass for 8 baht. I bought one stick and went back to Bungalow 27, rolled up a joint, and got stoned with David, John, and Charlie. The Buddha grass was fresh and strong, and when we looked around at all the mirrors, we started laughing.

The morning of Aug. 7th David and I checked out of our mirrored room at Bungalow 27 and checked into the Malaysia Hotel for 36 baht a night, or $1.75 each. The man behind the desk gave us a key to air-conditioned room #508, where the sheets were changed daily. The hotel offered a swimming pool, piped-in-music, maid service, and grass for sale just down the hall. Very nice!

It was still early in the day, so, once we were settled in our room, I went out and found the stop for the #4 bus. Bangkok is a big city, and the bus system was the best way to get around. The bus would take me to the main train station near the center of Bangkok where I would find the main post office and the American Express office. I wanted to pick up mail at Poste Restante and exchange some traveler's checks for Thai baht at the American Express office. A #4 bus came by shortly.

The quick ride gave me my first look at the streets of Bangkok.

Not far from the train station, I noticed a group of food stalls infusing the air with the wonderful scents of cooking. I passed one street cart where the aromas were so tempting that I had to stop for a quick bite. I bought a pungent vegetable curry. As I was finishing my bowl, I saw John and Charlie headed for the General Post Office and tagged along, as I was headed there myself. I knew months before that, after traveling through India, I would eventually pass through Bangkok sometime in early August, so I had written to friends and family asking them to send letters to Poste Restante in plenty of time before I arrived. If a letter arrived at a post office after I had passed through, I would never know.

It was always a lift to my spirits to find mail from home, and I wasn't disappointed. After showing my passport to the postal clerk, I was handed a small batch of letters, which felt good, indeed. I would be able to catch up on news from home later in the hotel room. After I stashed the letters in my shoulder bag, the three of us walked over to the American Express office to exchange traveler's checks into Thai baht.

While we were in the American Express office, it started to rain, so we caught a bus back to the hotel. Before we went in, we stopped at a restaurant that served freshly pulped watermelon shakes. I always looked for fresh fruit in each country I visited. We sat out the rain by smoking Buddha grass in our room.

The visa stamps I was collecting on the pages in my passport would fill up the remaining blank spaces before I reached Australia, which meant I would have to go to a U.S. embassy to have additional pages added. Thursday morning, the 8th, I left the hotel, found my way to the U.S. Embassy, and presented my passport to the person behind the desk. I asked whether they were able to add blank pages to my passport, and he took it to a back room. It didn't take long for the embassy staff to glue in the additional pages and return the slightly thicker passport. Next, I went looking for breakfast and found a restaurant that had pancakes on the menu, so I ordered a stack with maple flavored syrup. I hadn't had pancakes for a while, and they tasted familiar and comforting. As I walked away from the restaurant, a car slid by with two prostitutes in it. They slowed down as they passed, and one young lady leaned out the car window to offer her services. I politely refused the offer and kept walking, happy that I was getting to interact with the friendly people of Bangkok.

Bangkok is a modern Asian city with all the amenities available in any Western city. Travelers found cheap lodging but took advantage of some of the things you can only find in a big city, like movie theaters showing recently released films. In Bangkok, the films were shown in their original language with Thai subtitles.

It seemed that there were food carts on every other block, so finding something to eat or drink was easy, and I didn't hesitate to stop for local street food. The Thai and Chinese street food stalls were open day and night, offering noodles, rice, vegetables, soups, fresh fruit, fruit juice, and more, for very few baht.

After running some errands and eating lunch on the go, I returned to the hotel. Later that afternoon, David and I went to see *The Long Goodbye* with Elliot Gould playing detective Philip Marlowe in a Hollywood version of Raymond Chandler's crime novel by the same name. I was seeing a recent film in English, on a big screen, in an air-conditioned theater, but missing the popcorn.

Watermelons on their way to market

Friday the 9th, I was up early and had two fried eggs, sausage, toast and butter, cold papaya, and coffee for 12 baht before heading to the Quantas Airlines office to buy a ticket for a flight from Melbourne, Australia, to

Auckland, New Zealand. To be eligible for a six-month visitor's visa for entry into Australia, I needed to prove that I would be leaving Australia when the visa expired.

I planned on flying to New Zealand in early April of 1975 after my six-month Australian visitor's visa expired. A plane ticket to New Zealand would make the Australian Embassy happy and fill the requirement for the six-month visa.

The agent at the Quantas office needed $155 for the ticket, which cut into my reserve of traveler's checks. I hadn't realized that I would need a ticket out of Australia before I even got there.

When I got back to the air-conditioned room, I wrote an aerogramme to my brother, Ron, who had just arrived in Melbourne. He had taken a job teaching history at a high school there. Australia had a shortage of teachers and was hiring recent college grads from the U.S. with teaching degrees. After living on just a few dollars a day for many months, I found that the $155 additional expense would leave me short of money to complete my journey. I wrote to my brother and asked him to transfer 200 Australian dollars to a bank in Djakarta, Indonesia.[16] When I passed through Djakarta, I would collect the money. I also asked him to send the documentation needed to retrieve the money to Poste Restante in Penang, Malaysia.

---

[16] *Djakarta became officially spelled Jakarta in 1972 and was in transition while I was there.*

I would pass through Penang on my way to Djakarta. David and I took advantage of the air-conditioned big screen modern movie theaters in Bangkok and caught another 5 p.m. flick, which turned out to be a good one. We saw *The Sting* with Robert Redford and Paul Newman, a fun movie set in 1936 about con artists pulling a big job in Chicago. Seeing a movie on the big screen took me out of the reality of Bangkok for a couple of hours before I walked out of the theater into the heat, humidity, and hubbub, where I would be snapped back from 1936 Chicago to 1974 Bangkok. After the movie, David and I found a small restaurant serving a spicy shrimp soup called Tom Yum Goong, and that was all I needed for dinner.

We had heard that up until the year before, many of the U.S. and foreign troops stationed in Viet Nam would take their R&R (Rest and Relaxation) leaves in Bangkok. Bangkok was like a small L.A., buzzing with the same hustle, bustle, buses, smoke, smog, people, cars, heat, bright lights, good food, and lots of young people. Once in Bangkok, the place to go for the GIs was Patpong, actually, Phat Phong, the entertainment district, to score sex, drugs, and rock n' roll.

I could see why Patpong was so popular once we arrived there. Prostitutes were strolling up and down the streets, and the bars were packed with young lovelies whose job it was to get friendly with the customers and keep them buying drinks. The first bar we walked into had just a few girls dancing on a platform in scanty panties. There were other girls floating around the bar who came up to us and rubbed themselves against our thighs. After we each had a beer, for an expensive 20 baht, we left that bar to try one of the other bars that lined Patpong.

We stopped at a bar that had a girl doing the Thai version of a striptease on a raised platform in the middle of the room. Shortly after we entered the bar, David bought drinks for us and for one of the roaming party girls who was being friendly. She sat with us until she finished her overpriced 7-UP and left to take her turn on the platform in the middle of the room. As soon as she climbed on the platform, she began to dance and slowly take off her clothes to the Rolling Stones' "Jumpin' Jack Flash". She was not wearing much in the Bangkok heat, so it didn't take long before she was completely naked. Our friendly server kept moving to the music when another girl handed her a cigarette that was already lit.

After a few drags, she took the cigarette from her mouth and put the filtered end to the lips of her vagina and took a drag. She continued to smoke the cigarette that way until she finished half of the cigarette. She then removed the cigarette from her crotch, stepped down from the platform and walked across the room to the spot where I was standing with David. She handed the cigarette to me and looked me in the eye. Of course, I took it from her, placed it to my lips, took a drag, and said, "It sure tastes good." The whole bar burst into applause, but my only thought was hoping that she was clean and that my lips wouldn't fall off. I could see why the GIs would take their R & R in Bangkok, but the girls were young, and the scene in

Patpong was troubling. That is not why I was in Thailand.

August 9th, 1974. OH YES! While David and I were watching one of the girls stripping to Jim Morrison singing "Break On Through (To the Other Side)", NIXON RESIGNED.

In addition to the rock music and girls stripping, there was a TV hanging off one of the walls. The volume was turned off, but I saw a new President being sworn in. It must have been Gerald Ford. This was a very historic day. Nobody else in the bar knew what was happening on the TV, nor did they care, but I was happy to see Nixon go.

When we had seen enough of the strippers and grew tired of rejecting the roving girls, we paid for our drinks and caught a bus back to the hotel. Our favorite restaurant was nearby, so we stopped in and had a nightcap of noodles, bean sprouts and meatballs, plus another watermelon shake. A small joint put us right to sleep.

Bangkok was a modern city and a good place to spend four days, but I was ready to get back on the road to see a different side of Thailand. I slept until 8:30 a.m. Saturday morning, the 10th, and then took a long hot shower. Hot water showers were one of the nice things about being in a modern city like Bangkok. Later that morning, I would be taking an overnight bus north to Chiang Mai, so I put everything back into my pack and made sure I hadn't overlooked anything before I went to the lobby to check out of the hotel. After checking out, I met David in the lobby, and we walked around a little before we wished each other "good travels" and said goodbye. David had been a good travel partner. We had first met at the Union of Burma Airways office in Kathmandu and spent time together in Calcutta, Burma, and Bangkok. We shared some meals and laughs, but now he was flying on to Hong Kong.

I went to the main post office to check Poste Restante, but the post office was closed for a holiday. Before going to the bus station, I found a quiet park to sit in and write an aerogramme to my brother, Rich, in Chicago. I was in the middle of writing when a young Thai guy approached and asked if I wanted to buy some nice Buddha grass. I bought a stick for my trip and then went to the North Bus Terminal and waited for the overnight bus to Chiang Mai, in the mountains 435 miles (700 kms) north of Bangkok.

After a sleepless night on the overnight bus, I found a hotel near the bus station in Chiang Mai and checked in for 30 baht. It was Sunday morning, and I walked around trying to get a feel for the city before I went back to the hotel and slept for the rest of the day.

Monday morning, I went to the main post office and found a note at Poste Restante from John and Charlie. They had bused up to Chiang Mai a few days earlier and were staying at the YMCA for 15 baht a night. I went back to my hotel, checked out, and went over to the YMCA to check in. I was shown a cot in a dorm room with mosquito netting over the bed for 15 baht a night. The man behind the desk handed me the *"Pocket Food Guide to Chiang Mai,"* which turned out to be a very useful little booklet showing how to say common Thai words and phrases and listing local food spots.

Pocket Food Guide from Thailand (front)

TYPICAL NORTHERN THAI FOOD DISHES WORTH TRYING:

khaaw norng	non-sweet sticky rice, eaten by hand	ข้าวนึ่ง
kheep moo	dried pork rind (ee as in at, as)	แคบหมู,
nam prick ong	chile and tomato sauce, cabbage and cucumber	น้ำพริกอ่อง
gang hungle	Burmese curry (ung as ih sung, le as in led)	แกงฮังเล
khaaw soy	noodles, meat in soup and coconut oil	ข้าวซอย

DRINKS:

nam kheeng blaaw   plain boiled water and ice (ee as in bat, aa as in baa) น้ำแข็งเปล่า

Pocket Food Guide from Thailand (page from interior)

Chiang Mai was a beautiful little city that had a slower pace than busy Bangkok. For the next few days, I was having my own R & R. I did a lot of walking, sitting, resting, and reading. I was just finishing up *Fahrenheit 451* by Ray Bradbury. It was an engaging science fiction novel where books are illegal, and firemen oversee the burning of pesky paperbacks. Would Guy ever see the error of his ways and save the classics from the flames? I didn't mind lying on my cot reading about how censorship can go to extremes and often does. I would have preferred to visit some of the hill tribes that live in the forests outside of Chiang Mai, but the monsoon weather had once again kept my exploring limited to the city.

On the evening of August 15th, I caught the overnight bus back to Bangkok. The Chiang Mai Tours bus company was only four days old, and the bus I boarded was empty, which allowed me to stretch out in the back seat and sleep the whole way.

I arrived in Bangkok Friday morning, the 16th, and caught a #4 bus over to the Malaysia Hotel, where John and Charlie had a room. They'd headed back to Bangkok a few days earlier than me. Charlie was a tall, skinny, blond guy from England who had been traveling with John, an American from Boston. They had met somewhere on the overland trail and had been traveling together for the past few months. John was an army vet who had fought in Vietnam in the early 70s. He was passing through Southeast Asia on his way overland to Australia, just like me. He never spoke about his experiences in Viet Nam, and I never asked. I had run into Charlie and John a few times over the last few weeks and found it easy to travel with them. They were into meditation, and the easy-going way they traveled fit in with the way I liked to travel. I was happy to be on my own, but I felt comfortable in the company of these guys.

Charlie and John with the locals

I left my pack in their room, and the three of us went out to find something to eat at a food stall not far from the hotel. We decided to catch a train for Penang, Malaysia the next day so we walked to the main train station and bought 2nd class seats for the 24-hour train ride, which cost us about $12 each.

Saturday the 17th, Charlie, John, and I got up late and checked out of the Malaysia Hotel. At least John and Charlie did, because I had slept on the floor without the management knowing. We arrived at the train station in the early afternoon so that we could pick up some street food for the long train ride. When the train was ready to board, we found our seats and put our packs away before we pulled out at the scheduled 4:10 p.m. departure time. There were a lot of Western travelers on the train, and we talked to some of them, but most of the trip I spent reading *Time* magazine about Nixon, or another paperback I had swapped for called *Travels with My Aunt* by Graham Green. It's a story about the easygoing retired bank manager, Henry Pulling, who starts traveling with his slightly eccentric Aunt Augusta. It would be fun to see how they traveled through Europe and beyond. I could relate to travel stories from a different perspective now that I had more experience.

Charlie pulled out a portable chess board, and we took turns playing each other to pass the time. The 24-hour train ride to Penang went through the green jungles and verdant crops of southern Thailand the entire way. If we didn't pass row after row of palm trees, we passed mile after mile of rubber trees. Every so often the constant green was broken up with a splash of beautiful tropical flowers.

I managed to get some sleep and awoke when the sun rose on Sunday morning. I knew the train would stop at the border with Malaysia. We would get off the train and go through Thai customs to get our passports stamped with exit visas and then walk over to Malaysian customs to get entry visas for Malaysia. I wondered if we would board a different train after entering Malaysia or reboard the same train that we had spent the night on. I had a little bit of Buddha grass on me, so as the train started to slow down, I went into the bathroom and locked the door. I was able to reach the light fixture in the ceiling and unscrewed the glass covering the bulb. I dropped the

Buddha stick in the glass cover and screwed it back into place over the bulb. I figured that, if we changed trains, I would lose the grass, but at least I would be clean going through customs. If they put us back on the same train, I could retrieve the grass and have a smoke on the way to Penang.

When the train rolled to a stop, we grabbed our belongings and got off to check out of Thailand and check in to Malaysia. We showed all the necessary visas and health cards, and when the Malaysian customs guard asked how much money I would be taking into Malaysia, I showed him my U.S. traveler's checks and the cash I had in U.S. dollars. The few hundred dollars seemed to be enough for the official to approve my two-week visitor's visa. Once we were through Malaysian customs, the officials led us back to the same train we had arrived on, only now it was sitting on the Malaysian side of the border. After the train pulled out of the border station, I waited until it gained full speed before I went back to the same bathroom to retrieve my stick of Buddha grass. I had probably seen someone do something like that in a James Bond movie.

At 5 p.m. Malaysian time, the train arrived in Butterworth. Malaysia was one hour ahead of Thailand, which didn't matter much to me as I had been slowly crossing several time zones as I traveled east. Butterworth is a large city on the northwest coast of Malaysia. The city is named after William John Butterworth, who was the Governor of the Straits Settlements in the mid-19th century. The Straits

Settlements was a colony of British territories that included most of the Malay Peninsula and a portion of Borneo controlled by the British from the early 19th century until 1946. We got off the train and hiked to the ferry terminal to catch a boat taking us on a short 1.9 miles (3 kms) ride across the Penang Strait to Penang Island.

Once on the other side, John, Charlie, and I stepped off the ferry in the wonderful old city of George Town, the capital of Penang, established in 1786 and named after the English king George III, the same George III who was kicked out of the American colonies by George Washington and the other colonists in 1776. After the long train ride and the ferry crossing, we were tired and hungry. We found a restaurant and sat down at a table under an awning. We were served a tasty chicken curry and rice dinner.

After dinner, we walked around searching for a place to stay and found a Chinese hotel in the middle of town with a clean room. We had to walk up a flight of stairs to reach the lobby of the Lum Fong Hotel because the hotel had its own Chinese restaurant on the ground floor with outdoor tables situated under a colorful canopy. It turned out that the Lum Fong Restaurant had the best Chinese food in George Town. The Chinese were known to have clean hotels and excellent food, which I found to be true.

George Town was situated on the Strait of Malacca, which had been a centuries-old maritime silk road for ships carrying goods from Arabia, Africa, Persia,

Southern India, and China. Ships leaving from the Chinese coast would go around Thailand and the Malay Peninsula, through the Strait of Malacca, and continue sailing to ports in India, Africa, and ancient Babylon, which is Iraq today. For hundreds of years, Indians, Indonesians, Chinese, English, and other citizens from around the world got off their boats in George Town giving the city its international flavor.

John, Charlie, and I shared a room with three beds. Once we were in the room, we each picked a bed and sat down. I noticed a large sign on the wall displaying a drawing of a durian fruit with a bold **X** drawn through it. The durian has a shape like a cantaloupe but with a skin that is covered with short spikes. Apparently eating durian in the room was strongly prohibited. When a durian is split open, the smell is similar to something rotting and repugnant. After crossing paths with a few ripe durians, I could see why they could be offensive to many. Eating them is an acquired taste and was banned in many hotels and public spaces. There were so many tropical fruits to eat that I didn't feel the need to sample a durian.

George Town was an epicurean's delight. There were food carts dotting the downtown area, and many of them had a colorful selection of cold tropical fruit, such as slices of pineapple, papaya, mango, mangosteen, star fruit, lychee, and half a dozen other fruits that I had never seen or tasted before. The mangosteen has a hard purple shell on the outside but soft white petals of deliciously delicate fruit on the inside. It is known as the "queen of fruit," and would soon become my favorite. The diversity of street food was amazing.

There were a lot of Chinese food carts, but Malaysian, Indonesian, and Indian carts were also sprinkled on corners around the city. Walking around and checking out the delicious offerings being served at the various carts, I saw noodle dishes, rice dishes, prawn dishes, and other tempting meals to choose from. After telling the vender which dish was desired, he would cook it up fresh right there in a wok or skillet. The smells that came from the small carts were smoky, cooking goodness. A few of the carts were set up around a couple of tables and chairs, so when the food was hot and ready, the cook put it on a plate and handed it to the customer, who took it over to one of the tables for a meal.

Before going out to explore the town on Monday the 19th, Charlie and I had a good breakfast of fresh papaya and eggs downstairs at the Lum Fong Restaurant. John wasn't feeling well and wanted to stay in, so Charlie and I walked around George Town until we found the office for Merpati Airlines. We told the agent behind the desk we were looking for flights from Penang Island to Medan, Indonesia, as well as flights from Bali, Indonesia to Darwin, Australia. We reserved a flight to Medan and another flight from Bali to Darwin. The flight to Australia was reserved for early October, but they wouldn't give us a specific date. The cost for the two flights was $152 worth of Malaysian dollars, which I didn't have on me at the time. I would have to come back to pay once I had the money.

Tuesday the 20th, I was up early and went to the main Post Office and found two letters from my brother, Ron, waiting at Poste Restante. He came through like a champ. In one of the letters was a bank note for $297 that I could cash right away in George Town. I left the post office and went to a bank to exchange the bank note into Malaysian dollars to pay for the Merpati flights and put the remaining $100 into U.S. traveler's checks. The extra $100 would leave me just enough money to travel through Indonesia and Australia until I reached Melbourne, where my brother was teaching. After I booked the flight to Darwin, I had to take a few moments to absorb the fact that the ticket I was holding was the prize I had been planning for since high school. I'd been traveling toward my goal for the last nine months... AUSTRALIA! To reach my brother in October, I would have to hitchhike 2,300 miles (3,740 kms) from Darwin to Melbourne, but that wouldn't take much money.

That afternoon, John, Charlie, and I boarded a bus that took us about five miles outside of George Town to Penang Hill. When we reached the bottom of the hill, we climbed into a cable car that took us up 2,300 feet (700 meters) to one of the many peaks of the tallest hill in the state of Penang. We stepped off the cable car at the higher elevation and immediately felt the cooler air. We hiked to the main peak, which was at an elevation of 2,700 feet (820 meters), and when we reached the top, we were looking out over a dense, tropical forest covering the tops of all the hills. During the colonial period, the British built houses and bungalows in the cooler hills to escape the heat and humidity of George Town. These bungalow retreats were still popular for visitors to Penang Island. There were many trails throughout the hilltops, so John, Charlie, and I followed one trail through a lush, green, tropical forest. The trail meandered for a couple of miles, and on occasion, the dense growth gave way to wide-open views. I could see most of Penang Island with the mainland of Malaysia on one side, and the blue Strait of Malacca on the other. Cameras couldn't possibly capture the panoramic views we had that day.

Friday the 23rd, John and I bought a round-the-island ticket on the Yellow Busline. The ticket allowed us to get on and off any of the Yellow buses as they traveled along the coast of the island. After a large bowl of fruit for breakfast, we boarded a bus in George Town and started our trip around the Island, heading south. We rode along the beautiful eastern coast and got off the bus when it came to Titi Krawan. The village consisted of just a few fruit stands by the side of the road. During our travels, we had heard of a beautiful waterfall dropping into a tropical pool. We asked a man at one of the fruit stands where to find the path, and he pointed us to a trail leading inland.

We hiked uphill a few hundred yards where we found a small clearing containing a beautiful freshwater pool with a waterfall splashing into it from high above. The pool was surrounded by dense tropical forest and large dark rocks that were perfect for jumping into the water. I felt that we had just walked into a picture postcard. Young Malaysians were hanging out in and around the pool, swimming or enjoying a picnic with friends. The idyllic setting seemed to be straight out of a Dorothy Lamour film. Lamour was a sidekick to Bing Crosby and Bob Hope in the "Road to" movies of the 40s and 50s. One of the most famous was the *Road to Bali*. Lamour was known for swimming in exotic locations in many of her films and this pool would have been just right.

We went back to the road and bought some mangos and mangosteens, my new favorite fruit, at one of the stands while we waited for the next Yellow bus. When the bus arrived, we boarded and agreed that our next stop would be Batu Ferringhi. Whenever I had mentioned to travelers that I would be going to Penang, they would tell me not to miss the fabulous beach called Batu Ferringhi. As the bus was approaching the small village by the water, we saw Charlie walking on the pristine shore. John and I asked to be let off the bus and joined him for a walk on the beach to the village. There were a few restaurants along the beach, and we passed one restaurant with tables right on the edge of the sand that served a baked bean dinner.

We couldn't pass up the chance to enjoy something different from the usual rice or noodle dishes we had been eating, so we sat down and ordered baked beans and beer. John was from Boston and thought our bean dinner was pretty good for a seaside restaurant in Malaysia. After dinner, we completed our tour of the island and caught a Yellow bus back into George Town.

I had traveled through many countries and cultures during the last eight months. It had been a good trip but also challenging in many ways. Meeting new people nearly every day and always being on the lookout for food and a place to sleep at night was a constant, no matter what the weather threw at me. On that Friday, the weather threw 80° F (27° C), sunny, hot, and humid at me, so I spent the day like a tourist taking a pleasant bus ride with friends around a beautiful island and stopping to see some memorable sights.

Wat Chayamangkalaram is a Buddhist temple not far from the center of George Town. Inside the temple rests one of the longest reclining Buddhas in the world, and the next morning, a Saturday, I walked to the temple by myself. The temple grounds were covered with carvings of Buddhist gods and threatening serpents painted in vibrant colors. Walking among the brightly painted mythical and religious figures to reach the temple made for a festive lead-up to the hall that held the massive, gilded Buddha.

I removed my sandals and entered the temple. The walls were adorned with wood carvings, and the magnificent figure reclined under an arched ceiling, filling one end of the cavernous room. Buddha was lying down with one arm propping up his head and looking totally at peace.

Wat Chayamangkalaram
(Credit: Emmanuel Chansarel-Bourigon / Getty Images)

According to indianexpress.com,

> "The reclining Buddha represents The Buddha
> during his last illness, about to enter Parinirvana,
> the stage of great salvation after death that can
> only be attained by enlightened souls...it also
> shows that all beings have the potential to be
> awakened and be released from the cycle of
> death and rebirth."

Sunday morning the 25th, Charlie, John, and I slowly
rose from our cots and went out to the street looking
for a food stand for a quick breakfast. We found one
stand that only sold fruit, so we ordered plates of fresh
papaya and pineapple and used our fingers to consume
the sweet treat. We returned to the hotel, washed up,

put on our backpacks, and checked out. The bus stop was close by, and we didn't wait long before the bus going to Penang Airport arrived and we climbed aboard. Already sitting in the back of the bus was a backpacker who introduced himself as Taul Paul from California.

On the way to the airport, Taul Paul told us that he had been living in the Swiss ski village of Zermatt for the last few years but was traveling to see different parts of the world. In addition to his pack, Taul Paul carried a guitar case which held his treasured Martin guitar. As we climbed off the bus, we saw how Taul Paul got his name. He was at least six-feet-two-inches (almost two meters) tall.

The four of us went through customs at the Penang Airport, got our passports stamped, and then boarded the prop plane. There weren't many passengers on the 50-seat propeller-driven plane. It took less than an hour to fly across the Strait of Malacca to Medan, Indonesia, on the east coast of Sumatra.

I already had a visa to enter Indonesia, which made clearing customs easy. Charlie, John, Taul Paul, and I got together outside the customs building and found a bus to take our little group to the center of Medan. Not far from the bus depot, we passed the Irama Hotel, which looked as good as any other hotel in Medan, so we checked in. I shared a room with Taul Paul, while John and Charlie took another room next door. We all shared a bathroom just down the hall.

Medan sits on the northeast coast of the sixth largest island in the world, Sumatra. It is the largest of the thousands of islands that make up Indonesia. I would be traveling through this island and another large island, Java, before I arrived on the island of Bali, my last stop before Australia. Indonesia has over 700 regional languages and more than 1,300 ethnic groups. As the largest country in Southeast Asia, it consists of over 17,000 islands running 3,200 miles (5,100 kms) east to west. Roughly 6,000 of the islands are inhabited by citizens who are mostly followers of Islam. Medan was just going to be a stopover on our way to Lake Toba in the middle of northern Sumatra.

We left our packs in the rooms at the hotel and ventured out to find a place to eat. It would take us a little while to adjust to a new country and a new currency called the rupiah. We found a money changer who would exchange one U.S. dollar for 400 rupiah. I knew I would be in Indonesia for a few weeks, so I exchanged a $50 traveler's check for 20,000 rupiah. Luckily, the currency came in 2,000 and 5,000-rupiah notes as well as in smaller amounts, so the money wasn't too bulky to carry. We went looking for food stands but did not see any, so we ended up at a restaurant for our first Indonesian meal of chicken and rice flavored with local spices. At first, it was hard to figure out if we were getting good value for our money, but until we were more familiar with the customs and where to find good inexpensive food, we sometimes ate at more expensive restaurants. Street food was usually the best and cheapest way to feed ourselves, and we hoped to find food stalls when we walked around Medan the next day.

Monday the 26th, we got up and asked the man behind the hotel desk for directions to the office for Pelni Lines. Pelni Lines was a company with a fleet of ships that had routes connecting many of the Indonesian islands. We asked the agent about a ship that sailed from Padang, on the west coast of Sumatra, to Djakarta, on the western tip of Java. Although it was the capital of Indonesia and the country's largest city, we would only be staying in Djakarta for one night. Most of the travelers I had talked to didn't have much to say about Djakarta. It was just another big Asian city, but once there, I could pick up letters at Poste Restante and catch a train going east to the smaller and more interesting city called Jogjakarta. The agent said they had a ship that sailed from Padang to Djakarta every Thursday costing 9,000 rupiah ($22.50), including meals. I wasn't sure what kind of food to expect on the two-day cruise down the coast of Sumatra, but I assumed it probably included fish and rice.

Sumatra is over 1,100 miles (1,770 kms) from top to bottom covered by a mountainous tropical rain forest. I had met other travelers who, along with the BIT guide, suggested that I go by water rather than trying to navigate the dense jungles of southern Sumatra. The ship seemed like a good way to travel to Djakarta. All I had to do was take an overnight bus through the rainforests and jungles of northern Sumatra, cross the equator to Padang where I would catch my ship, and then sail down the Mentawai Strait to Djakarta. The ticket agent said I could purchase a ticket once I reached Padang, allowing me to leave my travel plans open until I chose which Thursday to board the ship. That afternoon, John, Charlie, Taul Paul, and I caught the bus from Medan to Parapat for 550 rupiah, or a little over one U.S. dollar. The bus was like a minibus with cushioned seats and open windows. We enjoyed the warm humid air on the slow six-hour ride through tropical rainforest, climbing from sea level to nearly 3,000 feet (900 meters) to reach the small village of Parapat on the coast of Lake Toba.

Lake Toba is the largest volcanic lake in the world. It's 62 miles (100 kms) long and 19 miles (30 kms) wide, sitting in a massive crater created by four super volcanic eruptions some 75,000 years ago. In the middle of the huge lake sits a large land mass called Samosir Island, the fifth largest lake island in the world. There are several villages on the island inhabited by the Batak people, one of the main ethnic groups in northern Sumatra. The Batak people have their own language, customs, arts, and culture. Cannibalism was part of the Batak culture until the early 20th century, when the strictures of Islam and Dutch imperialism put an end to the eating of flesh.

I stepped off the bus in Parapat, shouldered my pack, and followed the other guys back a couple of blocks to the ferry office. We bought tickets for the next ferry to the village of Tomok, leaving in about a half hour. The village was small enough for us to see the ferry when it arrived from the island, so we walked around to check out some of the shops and restaurants. It appeared that the village had been built up to support the ferry traffic coming from and going to Samosir Island. The fresh fruit at one stand caught my eye, so I bought a few of my favorite mangosteens and a bag of freshly roasted peanuts.

We boarded the ferry and found a place to stow our packs, sit, and relax for 40 minutes while crossing to Tomok. I had been in Indonesia for only a day, but I liked the pace of life and the easy-going attitude of the people I had met so far. The four of us walked off the ferry and were met by a young man who said he would take us to a house where we could stay while on the island. He led us a short way up a dirt road until we came to two rows of Batak houses, five on either side of the road. The Batak people construct long houses that have boat-shaped roofs with intricately carved gables and upsweeping ridges. He took us to one of the houses that the village reserved for visitors and told the four of us we could stay there for 100 rupiah per person per night. He led us up a few wooden steps through the front door to a long open room with a rough wooden floor polished by years of use.

The open space had no beds, tables, or chairs, so we each picked an area on the floor, put down our packs, unrolled our sleeping bags, and made ourselves at home for a few nights. There was no electricity in the house and the outhouse was in the forest out back. The floor of the house was about five feet above the ground, which left an area to keep animals below a family's living space. This was a terrific place to stay for only 25¢ a night.

We left our packs in the house and walked back to the few shops that made up the small village of Tomok. One of the shops had a kitchen setup serving a dinner of freshly cooked chayote, spinach, and cabbage seasoned with a peppery sauce, sitting on a bed of rice. The food here was not like the curries I had been eating, and these new spicy flavors tasted good. We were having dinner at a table outside the shop when a young man from the village approached us with an offer of local grass. We pooled our money and bought a small bag of Sumatran pot for 1,000 rupiah, which we'd share while on Samosir. My travels had landed me in a beautifully serene part of the world.

Tuesday the 27th was the first full day on the remote island. The village of Tomok consisted of just the double row of traditional Batak houses on the hill where we were staying and the shops below at the water's edge. Like Parapat, Tomok grew up to serve the ferry traffic. The traditional houses had no actual doors to close or windows to shut. The inside living space was open to the elements. It was like camping on a big, open, wooden floor with a beautiful, thatched roof overhead. The roof was built to extend over the open door and windows, protecting the interior when it rained.

Lake Toba was just north of the equator, so the weather stayed mild and consistent most of the year. When we went on hikes around the island, we didn't worry about leaving our packs in the open house. We were welcomed into the village for the few nights we stayed in their guest house.

Batak House

As there was no electricity on the island, once the sun went down, we had a choice of lighting an oil lamp or crawling into our sleeping bags at an early hour, which we ended up doing. The roosters woke us up early, and to start the day, we got into our swim trunks and jumped into the cool lake. There were a few makeshift restaurants by the ferry dock where there was a choice of either eggs over-easy or rubbery pancakes for breakfast. I usually chose the eggs.

In the early afternoon, we sat down for sandwiches, and, as the sun went down, we were treated to full course dinners of fish, rice, vegetables, fruit, and tea for 200 rupiah. The lake provided fresh fish, so most meals had pan-fried lake fish, which I didn't recognize but tasted great, along with rice and a vegetable seasoned with the same peppery sauce that the Batak people liked. Half a papaya cost 25 rupiah. I had come to love the sweet orange fruit and ate it whenever I could.

On Samosir Island, I was paying, in U.S. dollars, 25¢ for a place to sleep on the floor with an outhouse out back, and less than 50¢ for each meal. It was possible to live on a tropical island for $1.50 a day. The island people grew pineapple, papaya, coconuts, vegetables, and rice.

Young resident of Samosir Island

Their cotton crop provided cloth used for many things besides clothing. On one of my hikes around the island, I came upon a woman weaving the natural cotton thread into a piece of cloth, 2 feet (0.61 meters) by 6½ feet (2 meters), which she called an *ulos ragi hotang*. Using hand gestures, she explained that the cloth is long enough to wrap around the necks of two people getting married, or it could be used by someone to keep warm on a cool evening. She had a finished piece with a red and black pattern, so I negotiated with her for the cloth and bought it as a reminder of my sweet visit to Samosir among the Batak people. Some of the best parts of my trip had been staying in small villages, interacting directly with the locals.

Our days were spent swimming in the beautiful clear freshwater lake and taking hikes to villages around the island. When we weren't swimming or hiking, we played chess with each other or with the islanders, who knew and liked the game and played it very well. In the afternoons, Taul Paul would take his Martin guitar out of its case and play instrumentals he had composed. His long fingers slid up and down the neck of the guitar and plucked the strings with precision. He was an accomplished composer and musician, and his songs were easygoing melodic riffs. We spent the last days of August enjoying life on that tropical island.

Lake Toba, Indonesia to Padang,
Indonesia (by truck) to Jakarta, Indonesia (by ship) to Surabaya,
Indonesia (by train) to Bali (by bus, ferry, and van)

Ninth Full Moon

The weather had been cloudy and drizzly since I had arrived on Lake Toba, but Sunday morning, the first day of September, dawned clear and sunny. Charlie, John, and I took advantage of the cloudless sky and went swimming and hiking around Samosir Island. I even got a little color on my shoulders.

That evening, the full moon was just rising through the low clouds over the water as we feasted on a smorgasbord of dishes at Oloan's restaurant in Tomok. The menu celebrating the full moon consisted of different kinds of fried fish, a variety of vegetables, banana, star fruit, and other seasonal fruit that I had never tasted. Of course, the feast included rice and tea, which were a constant in practically every meal. Here I was, enjoying an amazing meal, in the middle of the Sumatran rain forest with no big cities nearby to pollute the night sky with electric lights. The moon rose high into the clear black night. The evening was warm, the moon bright enough to throw purple shadows, and the orb's silvery reflection off the calm lake made for a most memorable evening.

Monday morning, we awoke to more rain. The wet conditions meant I had been spending a lot of time reading in the Batak house. I was currently enjoying *The Andromeda Strain* by Michael Crichton, a book about a deadly strain of killer microorganisms from outer space that land in Arizona. The alien organisms were killing people and had to be stopped!

Meanwhile, I had time to study a few basic Indonesian phrases. The Malaysian and Indonesian languages were very similar, and I had picked up a few phrases when I was on Penang Island and learned a few more since arriving on Sumatra. I would be in Indonesia for over a month, and I wanted to be able to say at least a few words and count to 10 in Indonesian. I learned "selamat pagi" for good morning, "selamat siang" for good afternoon, and "selamat malam" for good evening. Knowing how to say, "Terima kasih" for thank you, "sama-sama" for you're welcome, plus memorizing some numbers would help me purchase fruit and nuts at the local markets.

Taul Paul had grown tired of the rain and was eager to keep moving, so he caught a ferry off the island a couple days earlier. I was hoping to see him somewhere on Java or Bali. Marcel, a Swiss backpacker, had arrived shortly after Taul Paul left and took his space on the floor. While sitting on the floor of the village house in our sleeping bags waiting out the rain, Marcel and I got to know each other. We exchanged information about where we'd been and where we were headed. He seemed like a sincere and kind person. We could talk very easily and got along well. His home was in the German-speaking region of Switzerland, and he was traveling by himself through Indonesia on his way to Bali. We went to lunch when the weather cleared and agreed that the rainy conditions weren't going to get better, so maybe it was time to move on. To continue overland, most travelers took a 20-hour, 250-mile (400 kms) bus ride from Parapat to Bukittinggi, which was situated in the hills above the west coast port of Padang. At the port, we could board the ship bound for Djakarta. Before we had finished lunch, we decided to leave the next day for Bukittinggi.

I had been traveling with John and Charlie since Burma, and we'd had some good times, but being the third person was sometimes one person too many. John and Charlie traveled well together, but I was interacting less and less with Charlie. Our personalities didn't mesh, and I wasn't sure why. I had been to England and knew that the British always said "cheers" to everything, but somehow, the way Charlie said "cheers" didn't sound right, and it was starting to wear on me.[17] Even before I left the States, I knew that I wouldn't get along with everyone I met, and Charlie just happened to be one of those people. I thought it would be good to put some miles between us. Still, I had a good relationship with John and liked traveling with him. I would miss his subtle sense of humor, but we were headed in the same direction and would probably run into each other again. I was ready to travel by myself or with someone new. Marcel was looking for someone to travel with, so we naturally fell in together.

---

[17] *These days I find it funny that it bugged me because I have lots of English and Scottish friends who say "cheers" all the time, and it doesn't bother me. I have used the word myself when saying a toast before a drink and think of Charlie occasionally when I do.*

Tuesday the 3rd, Marcel and I woke up early to the sound of rain on the thatched roof. We started to get ready for the overnight bus ride scheduled to leave from Parapat at noon. We figured that, if we caught the 10 a.m. ferry from Tomok to Parapat, we would have plenty of time to walk over to the bus depot and buy some food before our bus left. After breakfast, I gathered my belongings and stuffed them into my pack. With the ulos cloth that I had bought from the weaver, the pack was getting full. When it was time to go, Marcel and I said goodbye to John and Charlie. They were staying on the island for another day and then taking the bus to Bukkitinggi. I would probably see them somewhere on the way to Bali.

Marcel and I put on our packs, climbed down the Batak House steps, and began walking to the ferry in a light rain. I had just taken a few steps when I slipped going down the slick grassy hill. My balance was pretty good, but, with the weight of my backpack, I went down on one knee for just a moment, righted myself quickly, and got back on two feet. I was lucky to get away with only a muddy knee as I could have had a bad tumble. I didn't mind one wet knee, but I was glad I wouldn't be riding an overnight bus through a tropical rain forest in wet, muddy pants. Marcel and I walked down to the dock and boarded the ferry a few minutes before it was scheduled to leave, which didn't matter because the ferry sat at the dock for an hour before the engine turned over and we started for the other shore.

Because of the delay I was afraid that, even if we made the crossing in 40 minutes, the bus depot was still at least a 15-minute walk from the ferry dock, cutting our departure close. When the boat landed, we were hoping to find a motorbike taxi on the other side. Otherwise, we might not catch the noon bus. Once the boat got started, the ride took the full 40 minutes. When we landed at Parapat, Marcel and I were relieved to see a couple of taxi bikes and climbed into the closest one for a quick ride to the bus station. We had just enough time to buy the tickets, a few bananas, a bag of nuts, and find a place to pee.

At noon, the bus pulled in from Medan, and, after it unloaded some passengers, we climbed on what was called a bus but was more like an army transport vehicle with rows of benches with backs like pews in a church. The windows were just the open spaces between the wooden struts that supported the canvas roof. Like other trucks I had ridden in, this truck was equipped with roll down squares of canvas over the windows in case the weather got too bad. I was glad the truck had a roof to keep us dry should it start raining, and it probably would.

Because the ferry had been late, most of the seats had already filled with local riders. I was hoping to get a place by an open window, but by the time Marcel and I were ready to climb aboard, the window seats were taken. There were a couple of seats in the third row where Marcel and I stuffed our packs under the bench and sat down.

We were just getting settled when the bus started rolling out of the depot. I was excited to be starting an all-night ride through the Sumatran rain forest. We hadn't been going more than a few minutes, when a young local guy in the row behind us started tapping on our shoulders. We turned around to see what he wanted, and he started talking to us in Indonesian or one of the Sumatran dialects. It wasn't that he was asking us questions, he was just calmly speaking to us like we were supposed to understand. It didn't take long to realize that he was not right in his head and that the best thing would be to just ignore him and hope he would turn his attention to some other unfortunate passenger. We turned around and faced forward, but he kept on talking to us. When we didn't respond to him, he stood up and his voice became louder and more agitated. After a few minutes, he turned his attention from us and started shouting out the windows to people walking on the side of the road and to the other passengers on the truck. Nobody would engage with him. He kept up his endless ranting for long periods until he was tired of shouting and then sat down for a rest. Before the truck entered the deep rain forest, it made a few stops and filled up with more passengers.

While waiting for the driver to fix a flat tire, Marcel and I took the opportunity to crawl out one of the windows to smoke some weak weed that I had bought from an English guy I had met hiking on Samosir Island. When the tire was fixed, we climbed back into the bus and were able to tune out the fact that we were on a cramped, breezy bus, traveling too fast down a narrow track, which was sometimes made of dirt and sometimes, if we were lucky, potholed asphalt, through the Sumatran jungle with a crazed man sitting behind us.

The disturbed young man was quiet for a couple of hours, but when the sun went down and the moon came up in the clear night sky, he turned into a lunatic and began to shout, rant, and rave, all through the night. Marcel played what Americans would call soccer but what he and the rest of the world called football. He was in good shape, and, although I never felt threatened, I was glad to be sitting next to the athletic Swiss. The rants from the unbalanced passenger would go on nonstop, for hours. It was probably a good thing that I didn't understand what he was saying.

We made stops for fuel, food, another flat tire, and a battery change. Luckily, the driver carried a second battery in case the first one quit, which it did. The unhinged passenger would jump out of the bus and harangue whoever would listen, or he would walk up the road and continue his tirade, shouting into the black jungle. The only way to sleep was to find the least uncomfortable position and try to ignore the incessant yelling. That was impossible because he was sitting, or sometimes standing, directly behind us shouting into our ears. This truck ride had turned into an ordeal.

I calculated that the truck would be crossing the Equator early on the morning of September 4th. I asked the bus driver, or thought I had asked the bus driver, if he would stop at the marker indicating the Equator. I wanted to get out of the bus and have a picture taken of me at that momentous point in my journey. Around 6:30 a.m., we passed an opening in the rainforest, and I thought I saw the marker indicating that we had left the Northern Hemisphere. I ran up to the bus driver pointing back toward the marker, but all he did was nod and continue to drive.

Marker for Equator where the driver didn't stop
(Credit: Alan Ingram)

I leaned out a window and gave a shout to announce and celebrate my arrival in the Southern Hemisphere. After the verbal abuse of the previous 18 hours, I didn't think my shout of joy would bother anyone.

A few hours before we reached Bukittinggi, the truck made a stop, and someone in authority got on board and sat next to the disturbed young man. In a calm voice, the man talked to him for the last few hours of the trip. For those few hours, the ride seemed unusually quiet. Nobody said a word.

After two flat tires, a battery failure, and a wild 21½-hour ride through the Sumatran rain forest, we pulled into Bukittinggi at 9:30 a.m., only an hour and a half late. The poor young man was now quiet and looked confused as he was led away by the police with his hands tied behind his back. A mad, sad, bizarre truck ride to be sure.

We didn't know how long we would be in Bukittinggi, but it would be at least one night, so Marcel and I checked into the Roda Baw Hotel and were shown a simple room with two beds. We left our packs in the room, went downstairs to the hotel restaurant for an early lunch, and ordered ikan bakar, a roasted fish on a bed of rice. After lunch, we took turns taking showers in the bathroom down the hall and found a tub behind the hotel to wash a few items of clothing. There was also a clothesline to hang the clothes in the sun, when it came out.

Bukittinggi, a city in the hills above the coast, was still a couple of hours away from the port of Padang, where the ship sailed for Djakarta on Thursdays. Since we arrived on a Wednesday, if we decided to spend more time in Bukittinggi and miss the following day's ship, we'd have to wait a week before the next one sailed. We had the afternoon free to see what Bukittinggi had of interest for the passing traveler.

We were walking along the central area of the city when a student came up to us, offering to show us a deep canyon not far from town. He introduced himself as Endi, and we agreed to follow him on a short walk up a hill that led to a panoramic view of the canyon and the hills surrounding the city. Endi told us the canyon was known as "The Grand Canyon of Sumatra." He asked me if I had ever been to the real Grand Canyon, and I told him that I had visited the Grand Canyon once when I was younger. He asked how the Bukittinggi canyon compared, and I told him his canyon was an impressive canyon but not as big as the Grand Canyon. The canyon he showed us wasn't much deeper than the ravines in Highland Park, where I had played as a kid, but it was a beautiful area, and we were happy to have a local guide.

Next, Endi took us to a zoo with a lot of scrawny animals and birds, and then we followed him to the local market. Like many of the markets I had seen, this one was bright and colorful and had food stalls with good things to eat. For dinner Marcel and I tried a dish that originated from the Minang people who populate this part of West Sumatra. It is called *Rendang*, which is beef slow cooked in curry paste, coconut oil, coconut milk, lemongrass stalks, and kaffir lime leaves until the meat is tender. The Rendang was served with white rice and a cabbage side dish. It was comforting, warm, and just what we needed after the last couple of days.

If we didn't board the ship to Djakarta, we would be spending the week around beautiful Bukittinggi, hiking up to the local volcanoes. Two of the three kinds of volcanoes were within hiking distance from the town. The first type, the extinct volcano, was not expected to erupt in the future. The second kind was the dormant volcano which hadn't erupted in a long time but was emitting steam and sulfurous fumes and had a chance of erupting in the future. I would try to stay away from the third kind, the active volcano, which spews molten lava and hot rocks.

When I got up the morning of the 5th and looked outside, Bukittinggi was engulfed in a dense fog. I realized that we wouldn't be able to see much while climbing up the volcanoes, so I suggested to Marcel that, if we packed and checked out, we could catch the 8 a.m. bus to Padang and get tickets for the ship to Djakarta, which was scheduled to leave that evening. Marcel agreed, so we caught the morning bus, which took a little more than two hours. It was a nice, gentle ride down the green hills to the coastal city. Once we arrived at the Padang bus depot, Marcel and I shouldered our packs and went looking for a bank. Padang is a good-sized port city, so it was easy to find a bank nearby.

Marcel exchanged Swiss francs, and I exchanged U.S. dollars into rupiah. We knew that we would need around 10,000 rupiah for the tickets to Djakarta. Once we had the Indonesian currency, we found our way to the docks and located the office for the Pelni Lines, where we bought tickets for the two-night sailing to Djakarta. It cost me 9,557 rupiah ($23.50) for a place to sleep somewhere on the large ship, plus meals. I wasn't sure if the ticket came with two or three meals a day or what the menu would be. I wasn't too worried, though, because I was enjoying the usual Indonesian diet of fish, vegetables, and rice. Except for a couple of meals over the past few months that made me nauseous or went right through me, I was thriving on local diets.

Before boarding, Marcel and I found a restaurant within sight of the ship and ordered a rice and vegetable dish and some tea. We were just finishing lunch when John, Charlie, and another couple walked by our table. We paid for our meal and found out that John and Charlie had left Lake Toba the day before on the overnight bus and were just arriving in Padang without stopping in Bukittinggi. They had met Terry from England and Marilyn from Australia on the truck, and all four had tickets for the ship to Djakarta. I thought I would run into John and Charlie along the way, but this was sooner than expected. It looked as if Charlie and I would continue to travel together for a while, and I was fine with that.

We still had some time before the ship started boarding passengers, so the six of us found a market where we spread out and bought bananas, peanuts in the shell, dried fruit, cucumbers, and bread to take onboard the ship. The peanuts I bought at the market were freshly roasted, dark, and smelled great. Several stalls had a variety of bananas for sale in different sizes and colors. I particularly liked the small yellow bananas that had a creamy, sweet flavor.

We walked up the ramp and boarded the upper deck of a ship called the *Le Havre Abeto*. It was a large ship with several lower decks that could be reached by flights of metal stairs. We were directed down a couple flights to our assigned deck and sleeping space.

When we reached the deck, we saw it was a huge open space the size of a large warehouse filled with row after row of triple bunk beds. There had to be hundreds of the three-tiered beds with ladders attached to the side. Stairwells and large bathrooms were located at each end of the deck.

Le Havre Abeto
(Credit: Gerolf Drebes)

After seeing all those bunk beds, I realized that the *Le Harve Abeto* was designed for the pilgrimage to Mecca for the Muslims coming from Indonesia making their Hadj.[18] The large bathrooms had long rows of sinks and toilets. Each bunk bed had a sleeping surface made

---

[18] *The Hadj is an annual pilgrimage to Mecca, Saudi Arabia, the holiest city for Muslims. All Muslims are required to travel to Mecca at least once in their lifetime, providing they are physically and financially capable. The voyage from Djakarta to Jedda, Saudi Arabia could take nine days.*

from a piece of plywood measuring 3 feet x 6 feet x 3/8 inch (1 meter x 2 meters x .95 cm). Passengers had to provide their own bedding, which was no problem for us.

In addition to our group, there were only a few Indonesian passengers on board, so we had our choice of bunks. We spread out, and I picked one of the triple bunks where I had my choice of top, middle, or bottom. I threw my pack on the middle plywood plank and my sleeping bag on the bottom bunk. There was plenty of room on our deck, and since the bathrooms had enough toilets and sinks to accommodate hundreds of people, we were comfortable, though it did get a little stuffy traveling in the belly of the ship. I could only imagine what it would have been like sailing with the entire deck of bunk beds filled with pilgrims as they journeyed to Mecca.

No dinner was offered that first night, so we went up to the open upper deck and smoked some Sumatran grass. We casually walked around the railing, getting a feel for the ship and looking out at the horizon as the sun set over the calm Indian Ocean. When it started to get dark, we went back to our lower deck, pulled cucumbers, bread, peanuts, and bananas out of our shoulder bags and shared a picnic. Just before I turned in, I went to the upper deck for some fresh air and there was a gentle rain falling.

The ship sailed smoothly as I crawled into my bag on the bunk bed and waited for sleep. The ship was so big that I didn't feel much motion, but the vibrations made by the engines reverberated through the hull creating a low soothing hum that lulled me to sleep.

I slept soundly, and when I awoke on the 6th, I wasn't immediately aware of where I was. It took a second to realize that I was in the belly of a big ship, sailing along the coast of Sumatra on my way to Djakarta. I took some time to think about where I had been and what it took to get me to this point in my journey. There had been many challenges and adventures, and I was happy with my trip so far. I felt positive, peaceful, and ready for my day.

I eventually rolled out of my bunk, cleaned up, and climbed the metal stairs to the upper deck. It was a beautifully clear morning, perfect for a stroll around the railing in the salty sea air. Because I would be spending another full day on the ship, I spent as much time on the upper deck as I could, enjoying the experience of sailing on the open ocean.

We weren't offered anything to eat in the morning, so when noon came around, we were ready for our first meal. Our group had gone to the mess window where we were told food would be served. But when the window slid open, the man on the other side told us that although the kitchen had plenty of rice and vegetable curry, the kitchen staff wasn't providing plates to put it on. We should have guessed that if the pilgrims provided their own bedding, they would have also brought their own plates, utensils, and cups. We weren't prepared for that information in the middle of the ocean. If the passengers used and cleaned their own plates, utensils, and cups, the kitchen didn't have to. It made a lot of sense, but we weren't happy with the thought of no food and started grumbling. The kitchen staff eventually found tin plates, which they piled with a fair amount of rice, vegetable curry, and one-third of a whole fried fish. A whole fish was cut into three parts and at random the man at the mess window would place either the head, body, or tail of a fish on top of the rice and curry. I didn't know it at the time, but the head of the fish is the prized section. The head contains the eyes, soft cheeks, and forehead of the fish, which are considered delicacies. We ate with our fingers and picked clean whatever part of the fish was put on our plate. The ship's kitchen served a pretty good, filling meal.

We kept our plates and utensils and cleaned them after we ate, ready to use for the next meal. I had picked up a deck of cards at one of the street markets along the way, and Marcel mentioned that he liked to play card games, so I broke out the deck and shuffled. We both knew how to play gin rummy 500, but he taught me a game called Casino. It's a good game for two people, and playing cards helped pass the time while the boat sailed southeast along the coast. I liked traveling with Marcel and was getting to know him better as we played cards and paced the open deck of the ship. He told me that he worked in a Swiss bank and was taking some time off from work to travel and see new parts of the world. Marcel was a good traveling partner and an easygoing guy who laughed at my jokes.

I had plenty of time for reading *Caravans* by James

Michener, which took me back to the time I had spent in Afghanistan. Two days on the ship gave me time to relax and take the occasional nap. The ship didn't offer any food or drink other than at mealtime, but luckily we had our peanuts, fruit, and a few other provisions to snack on while we sailed.

Charlie, Marcel, Marilyn, Terry, and John

Friday night the ship was showing a movie for 250 rupiah (60¢) and raffling off a two-burner gas stove worth about $50. We were looking forward to the diversion of movie night, so after dinner Marcel, John, Charlie, Marilyn, Terry, and I gathered with other passengers and a few members of the crew in the makeshift theater room, which had rows of folding chairs lined up in front of a screen. Before the movie began, one of the crew walked around selling raffle tickets for 20 rupiah. We all bought raffle tickets and sat down, expecting to see a full-length Abbott and Costello movie – what we had heard was being shown. We had only watched five not very interesting short films when the projector was suddenly turned off and the lights were turned on. Movie night was over after 30 minutes, and they never did show the Abbott and Costello film. It felt like a rip-off for 250 rupiah (60¢). Then, to add insult to injury, when the winning number was called for the raffle, one of the ship's crew was holding the winning number and won the two-burner stove. I'm sure that the raffle was fixed and that the two-burner stove had been raffled off many times before and would be raffled off a few more times on future voyages.

Saturday the 7th was a beautiful sunny day. I woke up late and had just enough time to write a letter to my folks and strap the sleeping bag to the bottom of my backpack before the ship docked in Djakarta at 9 a.m. The six of us got off the ship and walked to the bus station by the dock. We bought tickets and boarded the bus going into the center of Djakarta where we could find banks, the main post office, and train station. When we got off in the city center, we said goodbye to Terry and Marilyn, who were going to stay in Djakarta for a few days. John, Charlie, Marcel, and I found a table outside a small café and put our packs down. Marcel agreed to stay with the packs while the three of us ran some errands before we went to the train station to buy tickets to Jogjakarta. I had met several travelers who had passed through Indonesia but didn't take the time to stop in Djakarta. They said that it was just an overcrowded city with not much to see or do. They advised it would be better to pass through Djakarta and take the train to Jogjakarta, which was a smaller city and had many cultural and historic sights to explore.

Jogjakarta is the center of the Indonesian, or at least the Javanese, culture. Travelers just called the city Jogja and said that the city and region would be the place to see Indonesian art and centuries-old crafts. Ancient ruins from lost Hindu and Buddhist cultures were also easily accessible from Jogja.

I left Marcel with the packs and went to the main Djakarta post office to collect the mail being held at Poste Restante. I knew I would be passing through Djakarta and had written my parents and siblings weeks before, giving them plenty of time to send letters. After picking up a couple of letters, I stopped at a bank to exchange some traveler's checks for more rupiah. Marcel was having a Coke when I got back to the café, so I sat down and ordered one for myself. If I wasn't sure about the purity of the drinking water, I drank Coke, which was safer than the unknown water. John and Charlie arrived at the café after stopping by Merpati Airlines. John was confirming our flight together from Bali to Darwin, and he said we had been confirmed for the October 3rd flight. That was four days earlier than I had expected but would still give me plenty of beach time on Bali. I finally had the exact date I would be arriving at the destination I had set for myself a decade earlier: AUSTRALIA!

I had left my straw hat on a chair next to me, but when the four of us picked up our packs to walk to the train station, my hat was gone. I liked that hat but would have to find another to cover my head in the hot September sun.

The four of us were on the train when it left at 6:16 p.m. We found our seats and stowed our packs in the overhead rack. John and Charlie elected to stay with the packs while Marcel and I went to explore the train. One of the train cars was set up as a small casino with a roulette wheel, craps table, and some card games that I had never seen before. At one table, a dealer was dealing Blackjack, a game I was familiar with. The seats in our train car didn't look conducive to sleep, so we knew we wouldn't be getting much rest that night. Marcel and I sat down at the Blackjack table for a while before moving around the gambling car trying some of the other games hoping to win some quick rupiahs. Around two in the morning, we had finally gambled enough.

With a few less rupiah in our pockets, we returned to our seats to try and get some sleep. We couldn't stretch out, and after four long hours of trying to sleep in an uncomfortable position, we gave up at 7 a.m., just as the train pulled into the station.

On Sunday the 8th, John, Charlie, Marcel, and I walked off the train, out of the station, and into central Jogjakarta. We found rooms at the Indonesia Hotel nearby. Marcel and I took a simple room with two cots, a fan hanging from the ceiling, and the bathroom down the hall. John and Charlie got their room and went to bed. Marcel and I left our packs in our room and went to find a restaurant called Gado Gado 71, or Mama's, which we had heard served good omelets. We ordered the veggie omelets, which were served as hot, fresh, and delicious as we had heard. After breakfast, we passed a street vendor selling fresh fruit drinks. I bought a glass of mango juice which was the perfect way to finish breakfast.

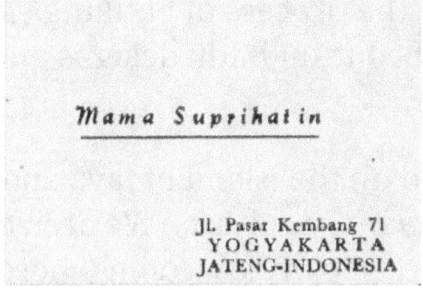

Mama Suprihatin

Jl. Pasar Kembang 71
YOGYAKARTA
JATENG-INDONESIA

Restaurant with good omelets

Between gambling and the uncomfortable seats, we hadn't slept much on the train, so Marcel and I went back to the hotel and crashed till early afternoon. We got up, showered, shared a joint, and played a few games of Casino before going out for dinner. Not far from the hotel, we found a street stall that served tender frog legs. We then strolled around Jogja to get our bearings before returning to the room for an early evening.

Marcel and I got up with the sun the next morning and knew that the day was going to be warm. We figured it was a good day to do the laundry that had been accumulating in our packs. We found a faucet, tub, and a clothesline strung up behind the hotel. I had a small amount of powdered soap which I threw into the tub, washed a few things, and hung them up to dry on the clothesline. Most of the clothing I had been wearing had been made of light-weight cotton and could be washed at night, hung over a chair, and would dry by the morning.

Marcel and I went back to Mama's for a couple more veggie omelets before walking over to the Batik factories to see the process of batiking. Jogja is well known for the beautiful Batik designs and patterns produced there.

Batik originated on the island of Java and is very important to Javanese culture. We arrived at one Batik factory and were shown to a room where the artists drew ornate patterns on cotton cloth using a hand tool called a *canting*. The canting held warm liquid wax which was applied to the cloth. The wax sealed the cloth and blocked the dye from penetrating the waxed areas, leaving those areas in the original color. The freshly waxed cloth was taken to a room with hot vats filled with different colored dyes. Red, blue, green, yellow, orange, and other colors waited in covered vats scattered throughout the room. The cloth was dipped into a vat of dye and hung to dry. After the fabric dried, an artisan would scrape off the wax leaving whimsical designs on the cloth where the dye had not penetrated. The material could then have new patterns added using the warm liquid wax and the process repeated many times using different colors. Several of the finished batiks were exquisite.

After spending the past few weeks traveling through Malaysia and Indonesia, I felt comfortable thanks to the combination of experience and the gentle people I had been meeting. I had less than 30 days left to travel overland, and I wanted to explore this new country without rushing. The people were friendly, the food fresh and delicious, and the weather hot without the intensity of India in July. I had a few traveler's checks left and figured that the money would be enough to get me to Bali and the beach life I had been looking forward to since passing up the Greek Islands in April. Once in Darwin, I wouldn't need much money to hitchhike the 2,500 miles (4,000 kms) south to Melbourne, and I hoped to have at least 10 Australian dollars in my pocket when I arrived at my brother's door. Traveling with Marcel seemed to make the trip more enjoyable. The first day we traveled together was on the overnight bus ride through the Sumatran rain forest with the disturbed passenger. After that experience, we knew things couldn't get much stranger.

Making decisions with Marcel had been easy, and our similar temperaments and senses of humor meant that we got along very well. We spent many hours sitting next to each other on various modes of transportation, sharing meals, drinks, and the good and the bumpy times. When we weren't exploring, we put the deck of cards to good use and swapped stories about our lives back home. Marcel loved to talk about the great hiking and skiing in Switzerland. He loved the outdoors, and it was clear that he loved his home country.

Tuesday the 10th, John, Marcel, and I decided to check out the ruins of Borobudur some 25 miles (40 kms) outside of Jogja. We took one bus from the center of the town and changed to a second bus halfway to Borobudur. It was a pleasantly warm day, and we enjoyed the bus ride with the windows open observing the lush countryside of the southern part of Central Java.

After a while, we came around a corner, and just ahead, the large ancient site of Borobudur loomed above the green treetops.

Will at Borobudur in new batik shirt

Borobudur is a huge ninth century Buddhist temple, the largest in the world. In 1974, 260,000 tourists visited the site, and I was one of 36,000 foreigners among them.[19] We slowly climbed up the nine levels of the temple using large steppingstones to reach the next level. Every level had hundreds of reliefs carved into the stone telling stories about Buddha's life. We walked around each part and saw dozens of stone stupas containing a sitting Buddha.

The temple site was shaped like a pyramid, so as we climbed, the upper levels became smaller until we reached the large stone stupa at the top. The government of Indonesia was just beginning a massive restoration of the entire temple.

While we were trying to interpret the stories being told by the reliefs, crews were working to create parking areas. Once the parking areas were completed, work would begin on the restoration of the temple itself.[20]

---

[19] *Twenty years later, 2.5 million tourists visited Borobudur annually, of which 20% were foreigners. Currently, every year on a spring full moon, Vesak, a day commemorating the birth, death, and the time when Siddhartha Gautama attained the highest wisdom to become the Lord Buddha is observed at Borobudur and two other temples.*

[20] *Between 1975 and 1982, the Indonesian government and UNESCO funded the Borobudur Restoration Project, after which the monument was listed as a UNESCO World Heritage Site in 1991.*

Relief at Borobudur

Relief at Borobudur

I hadn't been taking the time to explore historical sites over the past few months, but the Jogjakarta area presented both a Buddhist temple and Hindu temple in close proximity. The Jogjakarta region had been the center of religious practice and artistic expression for centuries. After non-stop travel from northern Sumatra, it felt good to take a few days to do some serious sightseeing and learn something about Indonesian culture.

Marcel, John, and I retraced our route back to the hotel on a couple of slow buses, and the leisurely pace was just fine for us. When we walked into the hotel, we heard music coming from the common room. We went over to see who was playing. It was none other than Taul Paul and a couple of other guitarists jamming to a melody and taking turns improvising. I was happy to see him and to listen to good musicians. When they took a break, we said hello to Taul Paul and were introduced to Tony and Chris, Australians who traveled with their guitars and happened to be staying at the same hotel. We saw Charlie sitting off to one side with two young women. He introduced us to Beth and Lorraine from Sydney. Lorraine let us know they were selling Buddha grass at 600 rupiah ($1.50) a stick. To show us how good the grass was, Beth rolled up a joint, and we went out back to pass it around and get nicely stoned.

When we went back to the common room, we ordered a plate of fresh fruit from the hotel restaurant and were served sliced mango; mangosteen; banana; and rambutan, which is related to the lychee.

It was a perfect way to spend the rest of the afternoon: talking with friends, old and new, and listening to good music.

There had been very few women traveling overland, so I was a little taken aback with these two vibrant Aussie backpackers and their big city energy. They had taken a flight from Sydney to Djakarta and were going to travel through Java on their way to Bali before returning to Australia. They wanted to check out the silver factories just outside of Jogja, so John, Charlie, Taul Paul, Marcel, Beth, Lorraine, and I chipped in to cover the 200 rupiah (50¢) needed to hire two horse-drawn carriages for the day. We split up, climbed into the carriages, and sat on wooden benches. The horses took us slowly from the city center to the more rural outskirts where the silver shops were grouped together. Lorraine lit a joint, passed it around, and started singing "Me and Bobby McGee" with Beth, so naturally, we all joined in. Janis Joplin had only been dead a few years, and the Kris Kristofferson song brought us together. The carriage drivers let us off near a group of shops, and I went with Marcel to check out a few along the road. I saw beautiful earrings, bracelets, and other fine silverwork, but I wasn't really interested in buying silver jewelry, and it seemed that the bracelets and other silver pieces were pretty much duplicated at every factory. Although Beth and Lorraine were hoping for more variety, they each found earrings that they liked and bargained with the shop owner until they mutually agreed to a price.

Not far from the silver shops, we found a few leather

factories that produced nice bags, belts, and purses, but, again, I wasn't interested in making a purchase. My pack was already completely full. It didn't take much time to cover the silver and leather shops, and we climbed back into the carriages and let the horses walk us back to the hotel. I sat with Beth, Lorraine, and Marcel on the way back, and, in getting to know the Aussies, we discovered that Beth and I shared the same birthday, January 8th. Lorraine celebrates her birthday on January 13th. They were in their early 20s and full of energy. The three of us were all Capricorns, and I had usually gotten along with most of the Capricorns I'd met. Even though it was hard keeping up with their Aussie accent, constant smoking, and high energy, there never was a dull moment hanging out with them.

Marcel, Taul Paul, and I thought it would be a good idea to rent bicycles on the 12th and ride the 11 miles (17 kms) to Prambanan, the ninth century Hindu temple compound and the largest Hindu temple in Indonesia. Before pedaling over to the temple site, we stopped at the Indonesian immigration office so that I could extend my Indonesian visitor's visa. The visa in my passport would expire before October 3rd, the date I was scheduled to leave for Darwin. There were no short-term extensions, so I paid the 9,000 rupiah ($22.50) for a three-month extension, although I would only be in Indonesia for a couple of weeks past the original exit date. The extension visa was a big expense that cut into my remaining resources.

While waiting at the immigration office, we met another Swiss traveler, Hans, who had lived in

Australia for three years and said that the carpentry work there was plentiful, easy, and paid well. Hearing that put my mind at ease about finding work in Australia.

Once I had my expensive visa extension, we got back on our bikes and continued to pedal toward Prambanan. The road was flat, but after a few miles I could feel my legs start to fatigue. I hadn't been on a bike since grammar school, and I could feel it. I was in good shape for hiking and carrying a pack, but not for riding a bike.

Still, arriving on bikes was a great way to silently approach the temple compound. As we rode closer, the ancient ruins looked jagged, coming to a point at the top. The structures were of different heights, but the main Shiva temple was at least 150 feet (45 meters) tall.

The construction of the first temple began in 850 CE, and work on other temples continued for another 80 years until there were 240 temple structures, making the Prambanan temple compound the center of Hindu art and architecture by the early 900s CE. It wasn't long after the final temple was completed that the compound was abandoned because the political dynasty in control at that time shifted their capitol from central to eastern Java.

Prambanan

Over time, most of the temple structures fell apart from earthquakes and were covered by volcanic ash. Later, the art and building stones were harvested from the temples by local people and early Dutch colonials to be used for their own structures. The ruins were rediscovered in the early 19th century, and the Dutch colonial government started reconstruction in the early part of the 20th century. The reconstruction stopped during World War II, but after the war, the Indonesian government continued and completed the reconstruction of the main Shiva temple in 1953. In addition to Shiva, other deities venerated in Prambanan included Vishnu, Krishna, and Ganesh, among others.

Marcel, Taul Paul, and I wandered around exploring what was left of the intricate structures and looking at the bas-relief panels. The carved reliefs narrated stories from epic Sanskrit legends. One relief, called the Ramayana, followed the life of Prince Rama. The other relief, also in Hindu Sanskrit, was called the Bhagavata Purana and narrated several topics that included astronomy, cosmology, genealogy, geography, legend, music, and dance. This site must have been magnificent hundreds of years ago, and, judging from the few temples that had been rebuilt by 1974, I was sure the compound would be spectacular once the restoration was completed.[21] The compound was originally laid out in a mandala circle, and, although it was far from being restored, I could feel the spirituality

---

[21] *The restoration of Prambanan was completed in 1991 and designated a World Heritage Site the same year.*

of the temple. *Mandala* is Sanskrit for circle, and the geometric shape is supposed to focus the worshiper and pilgrim's attention on spiritual, emotional, or psychological work.

Since arriving in Jogja, I had visited a Buddhist temple site and a Hindu temple compound, both supported by a Muslim government and its people, out of respect for their heritage.[22]

I knew the bike ride back would be a challenge, and about halfway back to the hotel, I ran out of steam. We found some shade and took a break. The heat, humidity, and miles of pedaling sapped my energy. After a rest, we hopped back on our bikes. I sure was happy to finally get back to Jogja and return the bikes to the rental shop.

I staggered back to the hotel for a cold shower and took it easy for the rest of the day. I was bushed from bicycling over 20 miles and would think twice before getting on a bike again to go for more than a ride around the block.

On Friday the 13th, Marcel and I got up bright and early and had breakfast with Taul Paul, who was leaving for Bali that morning. We wished him luck and said that we hoped to see him on Kuta Beach when we reached Bali. Marcel and I went for a walk around the old city and were surprised when we turned a corner and came

---

[22] *Today, in 2023, there are still small Hindu and Buddhist communities in Indonesia. The people of Bali have remained true to the Hindu faith, even as the rest of Indonesia converted to Islam.*

upon a big, colorful, open-air market. The market covered a huge area with several rows of stalls selling tropical fruit, vegetables, clothing made with Indonesia print patterns, and other dry goods. Someone at the market came up to us and said that a cock fight was going to take place at a nearby corner. I had never seen a cock fight and wasn't so sure that I wanted to see two roosters trying to tear each other apart. We went to the corner where the fight was supposed to happen and milled around with some of the locals. It was an experience that would have to wait because the gamecocks never showed.[23]

Just after leaving the market, we passed a man who was standing behind a small table with three cards sitting face up on the tabletop. We walked up to the table and saw the 2, the 3, and the Jack of Hearts. The dealer turned the 2 and 3 face down and held up the Jack to the crowd. He then proceeded to toss the three cards one over another, slowly and deliberately, until all three cards lay on the table face down. He bet anyone in the crowd to guess where the Jack of Hearts had landed. Anyone who could pick the Jack from the other two cards would be a winner.

A local guy stepped up to the table and put down a 100-rupiah note (25¢), which the dealer matched with his own 100-rupiah note. If the guy picked the Jack from the three cards, he would pick up both notes. If the gambler didn't pick the Jack, then the dealer would pocket the notes. The guy who had walked up to the

_____

[23] *I am happy to say I have never seen a cock fight.*

table guessed correctly and picked the Jack out of the three cards. He took the two 100-rupiah notes and stayed to play the game a couple more times and won each time. It looked easy to tell where the Jack landed because the card shark was moving the three cards slowly, and even I could see where the Jack ended up. It was just too easy. The dealer was no fool, and, as soon as some big money was put down, the card shark would show his talent.

Marcel smiled at me and said he was sure that he could follow the Jack and win some money. He stepped up to the table and put down a 5,000-rupiah ($12.50) note. The dealer matched his 5,000-rupiah note, picked up the Jack, and showed it to Marcel. He then started moving the three cards, one over the other, until his hands moved so fast it was difficult to follow the Jack and see where it landed. I had no idea where the Jack was, but Marcel looked down at the three cards and pointed to the card in the middle. The dealer turned over the card showing the 3 of hearts, not the Jack. Marcel lost 5,000 rupiah, and he wasn't happy about it. I had seen that trick before, probably on TV, and was leery of it. A hard lesson for Marcel. I was sure that the first guy who had stepped up to the table and picked the Jack three times was working with the dealer. He made it look easy and tricked Marcel into betting. The scam worked, and Marcel was poorer for it, but richer for the experience. I know I was richer for the experience, although, sadly, it was at Marcel's expense.

The next experience we would have that day would sting me and not Marcel. I carried a medical vaccination card with me because some countries, including Australia, required proof of up-to-date vaccinations before allowing travelers to cross their borders. The vaccinations guarded against certain diseases, and I was due to get booster shots for cholera, typhoid, and paratyphoid. We found out where the vaccination center was located and walked over so I could receive one shot containing all three boosters. The cost was 300 rupiah (75¢). With the information updated on my vaccination card, I had all the documents I needed to enter Australia, and now it was time for dinner.

Nasi Goreng is a very popular dish in Indonesia, and that's what we ordered that evening. Nasi Goreng, which means "fried rice," is very similar to any fried rice dish in that it is mainly rice with a little meat or onion and vegetables. The difference is the sauce, which is made with a sweet soy sauce that darkens and caramelizes the rice in the cooking.

Marcel, Beth, Lorraine, and I found a restaurant that served Nasi Goreng with chicken. The waiter brought out a side dish called *Gudeg*, which he explained was young jackfruit boiled in coconut water with local spices. The food was delicious, and a bottle of cold Bintang beer was the perfect way to wash down the flavorful, spicy meal.

After dinner, the four of us decided to take in some Indonesian culture and went by trishaw to a hall that was presenting classical Javanese dance. The trishaw is a bicycle-powered rickshaw that has the driver riding behind the passengers and pushing them through the streets, instead of pulling the passengers in the way that I had experienced in India.

That night the dancers were performing the *Ramayana*, the same epic story of Prince Rama that was told in the reliefs on the walls of the Prambanan temple. We arrived at the hall, bought our tickets, found our seats, and sat down with just a few others in the audience. The performance started late, and once the dance began, it was hard to see the dancers because the dim lighting left some of them in the shadows. I expected live musicians to accompany the dancers, but there was only a recording played over a pair of tinny speakers.

The *Ramayana* is a classic story that has great meaning for Indonesians, but that production was not even close to being interesting. The four of us were so disappointed that we walked out after 10 minutes. We went up to the man at the box office and demanded our money back, but after a little back and forth, we finally accepted that he wouldn't return our money and went looking for another trishaw. Beth said that the traditional dances on Bali were 100% better, so I would have to wait until I was on Bali to see the *Ramayana* with live musicians and better lighting.

Saturday the 14th, Marcel and I got up and had a quick breakfast before leaving for the train station. We bought tickets and boarded the 9:30 a.m. train taking us 200 miles (325 kms) to Surabaya in eastern Java. I hadn't realized when I bought the ticket that the train was not an express. It was the slow local, stopping at every small station. In addition, the train left an hour late and pulled onto sidetracks quite often to let other, faster trains pass. At many of the small stations, vendors would walk up to the open car windows offering food and drink for sale. At one of the stops, a young woman came up to our window offering small skewers holding grilled chicken. The popular dish called "*satay*" consists of small bits of marinated chicken, goat, beef, or fish stuck on a skewer and grilled to a crispy goodness. I would be looking for more satay before I left Indonesia.

When we finally pulled into the Surabaya station at 8 p.m. that evening, we were three hours late. I had been on many trains over the past few months, but that all-day experience was one of the most boring rides I had taken so far. Marcel and I played a lot of Casino that day. I had heard from other travelers that the Bamboo-Denn Hostel was a good place to stay in Surabaya, so we checked in for 300 rupiah (75¢) a night and were shown cots in the men's dorm room. We left our things at the hostel and went out to find a nearby restaurant for a quick meal. We found one serving *Gado-Gado*, a delicious salad made with veggies, hard-boiled eggs, tofu, potato, and tempeh, a patty of fermented soybeans. After dinner, we walked around Surabaya to get the feel of the city, which was a little disappointing after the vibrancy of Jogjakarta. When we got back to the hostel, I went to the shower room and found a plastic cup to pour water from a big cistern over my head and body to wash off the grime of the day before going to bed. Sleep came easily that night.

I woke up thinking about the train ride the day before. Had I taken so many buses and trains that I was jaded, thinking that a daylong train ride through the beautiful volcanic countryside of Java was boring? I had been on longer train and bus rides over the past few months but never felt bored. I was always excited to be traveling through a new country, village, and landscape, confronted with things unfamiliar and stimulating. I had been in Indonesia a few weeks and moving through the country had been easy without extreme weather or unusual incidents to challenge me. Perhaps I was taking things for granted. The scenery was always lush and green, and, being so close to the equator meant that the weather stayed pretty much the same every day: pleasantly warm with high humidity saturating the air, making it feel thick and heavy. The tropical climate probably slowed me down a little, but it wasn't the weather that caused me to be impatient with the slow train. Maybe, instead of exploring more of Java, I was ready to move on to the beaches of Bali before my overland adventure was over. However, every traveler I met who had passed through Surabaya suggested that the zoo was worth visiting because it held a broad selection of animals from around the world.

On Monday the 16th, after a breakfast of questionably fresh eggs at the Glory Restaurant, Marcel and I started walking from the city center to the zoo. We walked for 30 minutes before we realized that the zoo was much farther away than we thought, and, as the day was warming, we flagged down a rickshaw and jumped in. The rickshaw driver was in no hurry, and neither were we as he pedaled slowly through the streets of Surabaya.

Surabaya is on the Madura Strait and had been an important port city for eastern Java since the tenth century. It was the largest city in the Dutch East Indies, and many of the buildings are from the Dutch colonial period. The Dutch East Indies, what we know today as Indonesia, was a Dutch colony from 1816 until 1949, when Indonesia gained independence. The mix of colonial Dutch architecture and local traditional buildings made for a visually stimulating ride.

The Surabaya Zoo took up a surprisingly large area in the middle of the city, which had grown up around it. The zoo sat on 37 acres (15 hectares), providing more room for the animals than I had seen in other zoos. We took our time and wandered around from enclosure to cage and got to see a Sumatran elephant, a Javan leopard, proboscis monkeys, apes, orangutans, baboons, chimps, lions, tigers, and bears. "Oh my!" The zoo had a wonderful aquarium building containing several large glass tanks where dozens of colorful tropical fish glided through the water.

Marcel and I wandered through a building that displayed a variety of reptiles. Just outside the reptile building, we came to a large open pit with a fence encircling it to keep people from falling in. We walked up to a railing overlooking the pit containing one huge lizard the size of a grown man - the Komodo dragon. The oversized lizard was the main reason I wanted to visit the zoo. These man-size predators will eat just about anything that moves. The Komodo dragon can grow up to 10 feet (3 meters) long and weigh over 300 pounds (136 kgs). They can run as fast as 12 mph (20 km/h). A human running very fast might be able to outrun a Komodo dragon. Good luck!

When young and light, the dragons can climb trees looking for a meal. We watched the large beast walk casually up and down the enclosure, sticking its arm-sized tongue in and out, the way smaller lizards flick their tongues, only slower. It was a little unnerving, to say the least, and I was glad the giant reptile was down in the pit.

The impressive lizards live on Komodo Island and a few other remote islands east of Bali. The name Komodo dragon was coined by an American. William Douglas Burden led an expedition to Komodo Island in 1926 collecting the hulking lizards, dead or alive, for the American Museum of Natural History. The Burden expedition was the inspiration for the original *King Kong* movie of 1933 starring Fay Wray. Catherine Burden, William's wife, was part of that expedition. On the way to Komodo island, the expedition's ship picked up a film crew in Singapore to record the historic meeting of large lizard and American reptile collector. Sometime during the five-week stay on the remote tropical island, Catherine got between a mother Komodo dragon and her baby dragon, creating some drama. Thanks to quick thinking, disaster was averted, and a storyline was created. I guess Hollywood thought a giant ape made for better theater than a giant lizard. I had been to a few zoos, and, in its display of animals, I would say that the Surabaya Zoo came as close to providing a natural habitat as is possible in a city.

After spending a hot day at the zoo, we took rickshaws back to the hotel and doused ourselves with cold water from the cistern. Marcel and I played Casino until 8 p.m., when we went down to the restaurant and had a delicious bowl of *Bakso*, a dish of noodles and meatballs swimming in a broth flavored with ginger, garlic, cinnamon, cardamom pods, cloves, peppercorns, and fried shallots or green onions or whatever the chef has on hand. Yum!

While Marcel and I were at the zoo, John and Charlie had caught an early bus and would be in Bali by the end of the day. I was also ready to move on, but Marcel said he wanted to stay a little longer in Surabaya. My plan was to get up early and catch the 5 a.m. express bus from Surabaya to the eastern tip of Java. I could then board the ferry at Ketapang and ride it across the Bali Strait to Gilimanuk on Bali. However, I overslept but got up in time to board the 7 a.m. local bus. It would take longer than the express, but it was early in the day, and I knew I would get to Kuta Beach by sunset. The bus ride would be one of the last I would take on this trip, and I wanted to enjoy it. I got on the bus with a few of the locals ready for the slow ride down to the water with the windows open. I was glad to be taking this last bit of travel by myself.

Besides the few local passengers on the nearly empty bus, there were four other Western travelers. Once I stashed my pack, we said our hellos and I met two Swiss students and a Swedish electrical engineer and his wife. It was an uneventful but pleasant morning ride to the very end of Java Island and the ferry terminal.

While looking out the window, I thought about the many bus, truck, and train rides I had taken over the past few months. Very few had been as peaceful and calm as this ride. Most of those rides had been packed with people, chickens and goats, bundles, and belongings, and I missed being part of the jumble. I think that's why the train ride to Surabaya was so boring. There was no jumble.

When we arrived at the terminal, I grabbed my pack, got off the bus, and got in line with the other travelers to buy a ferry ticket. When the ferry arrived, we boarded for the short ride across the strait. I had reached my last destination on the Asian continent before flying to Darwin.

I walked off the ferry and was immediately greeted by a Hindu shrine to the elephant god, Ganesh, the same statue I'd purchased from my friend Anish's brother in Kathmandu. I'd bought the small statue of Ganesh to remember the sense of hospitality I'd experienced in Nepal during my time hanging out with Anish and all he shared with me. Now, all the people arriving from Java by boat, including me, were being greeted by Ganesh, the god of new beginnings and the remover of obstacles. Travel creates new beginnings every day, so I felt being greeted by Ganesh was very appropriate. It is said that he provides fortune, prosperity and success.

Hinduism was first brought to the islands that would become Indonesia in the first century CE. Buddhism reached the area a short time later, and the people adopted a blend of Hindu and Buddhist ideas, mixing them with their own folklore and Animist beliefs. Islam reached the archipelago in the 13th century and is still the main religion throughout most of Indonesia. After all the time I had spent in southeast Asia, seeing the elephant god on Bali felt welcoming and familiar.

The Swiss students and the Swedish couple joined me near the Ganesh shrine, and we agreed the best way to get to Kuta Beach was by minibus. I had heard about beautiful Kuta Beach soon after I started traveling. The warm sands, sunny skies and surfable waves were where I wanted to spend my last few days in Asia. On a beach!

We found a minibus and eventually came to an agreement with the driver on the cost for a ride to the beach. No sooner had we climbed on board with our packs when a local police officer started talking to the driver. Before I knew what was happening, I was standing with my pack by the side of the road, and the minibus was pulling away with the Swiss, the Swedes, and a cop. The needs of the cop took precedent over one bearded traveler. This was not a happy moment on the road to Bali.

I was now looking at taking a couple of local buses to reach Kuta. First, I would have to take a local bus to Denpasar, the main city on the island, and then make a connection to a bus bound for Kuta. I went to the bus depot and was told there were no more buses that day and that none of hotels in the area had any vacancies. It looked like I was left high and dry at the ferry dock. I started looking around for a place to roll out my sleeping bag when the driver of a mini truck drove by and stopped. He saw that I was stranded and offered to drive me about 15 minutes up the road to the small village of Negara. I thanked the driver when he dropped me off in the middle of the small village. I wasn't sure where there was lodging, but it didn't take long before a couple of college-age guys walked by and started chatting. I felt lucky that so many people in the world speak English. One of them left and returned in a few minutes with a bunch of small bananas and a couple of rice cakes. I found out later this offering is a Balinese custom. The two young men walked me to a small lodge where I took a room with clean sheets, a bath, toilet, and solitude for 750 rupiah ($1.80). If I hadn't been kicked off the bus in Gilimanuk, I wouldn't have met these guys and had such a tranquil evening.

I woke up early on Tuesday the 17th, to make sure I could catch the 7 a.m. open air minibus, called a *Bemo*, that stopped in Negara on the way to Denpasar. A Bemo arrived not long after I got to the bus stop, but it didn't have enough room for me and my backpack. Every 15 or 20 minutes, a Bemo would stop, but they were always full. Finally, one stopped around 8 a.m.

and had enough room, so I paid the driver 300 rupiah (75¢), climbed in, and rode across beautiful green Bali for two hours before arriving in Denpasar.

I had a few errands to run while in Denpasar before taking a bus to Kuta Beach, the most talked about beach on the whole overland journey, and where I planned to kick back. I went to the main Post Office and checked Poste Restante for mail and then walked to the Merpati Airlines office to confirm my flight to Darwin on October 3rd. The airline office wasn't far, and I was able to get back to the bus depot around noon. Just outside of the bus depot, the smell of sizzling street food drew me to a stand that had a hot grill covered with browning sticks of satay. I ordered chicken satay and dipped the pieces of chicken in a peanut sauce. Street food had been a constant source of mostly excellent hot meals. It was easy to find a Bemo to Kuta, and I was finally on my way to the beach.

The Bemo dropped me off at the Kuta stop. Before I could put on my pack, a young man approached me and asked humbly if I needed a place to stay. I agreed to follow him to his family's guest house called Warta Losman. A losman was usually a family-run accommodation located on their property.

The Warta Losman had a few small individual guest bungalows behind the main house. I picked one and put down my pack by one of the beds. The room was very basic with just two beds, but it had a small porch in the front with two chairs and a table. There was no electricity, but I did have my small flashlight after the sun went down. I think that the lack of electricity added to the tranquility of Kuta. I had access to an open-air bathing space that was just a brick cubicle with walls built chest high. When I walked into the cubicle, there was just enough wall height to give some privacy while I took a standing bath using a cup to toss cold water from a large stone basin all over my head and body. Once wet, I would soap up and then rinse off with more cups of water. The temperature each day was at least 80° F (27° C), so the water in the stone basin was a refreshing way to wash off the ocean salt water after a day of swimming. Each morning and evening, someone from the main house brought a tray with tea, bananas, and some sweets, just like the ones I received from the young men who led me to the lodge in Negara. The Balinese people had a tradition of being kind, generous, and welcoming to strangers.

Once I got settled in the room, I changed into my swimsuit, grabbed my travel towel, and followed a dirt path a short way before turning left onto another dirt path. I only had to go about 30 yards (27 meters), and the path emptied onto a beautiful white sand beach and the dazzling Indian Ocean. I had been hearing about Kuta Beach for months, and I had finally arrived. There weren't many people, so it was easy to spot John and Charlie. They had arrived the day before and wasted no time getting into the surf and sand. I went over, said hello, and spread my towel on the warm sand. There were only a few people scattered up and down the beach, tanning or body surfing. This is what

I had been waiting for. I had passed by the sunny beaches of the Greek Islands and those of Goa on the west coast of India so that I could keep traveling overland and end up at one of the most incredible beaches anywhere in the world. Because Bali was so close to Australia, there were more women on the beach than I had seen in a few months. Many of the women sunning and swimming were topless. I had seen a few of the Balinese women walking around with nothing covering their tops, and it seemed that many of the vacationing Western women had adopted the topless custom. Wow! I took off my glasses and dove into the surf. I swam and lay in the sun all afternoon.

There were only a few of us left on the beach when the sun went down, and we were treated to a beautiful sunset. Kuta Beach faces west, so the sun was overhead all afternoon until the last flicker of light disappeared below the horizon. I had heard that, if I was lucky, the last instant of sunlight would produce a green flash on the horizon. I looked for the elusive flash but didn't see it that evening. If the weather stayed clear, I had a couple more weeks of sunsets to try and catch the green flash.

The following afternoon, while we were sunning, Marcel walked onto the beach with his backpack. I was glad to see him. After saying hello, I told him about the Warta Losman and walked him back to the room. We found our host and asked if Marcel could take the other bed in the bungalow. The host agreed, and Marcel quickly changed into a swimsuit, pulled his towel out of his pack, and we retraced our steps to the beach for a swim. I had been happy to travel by myself, but I was glad to be spending these last few days with Marcel, John, and even Charlie.

Bali was the vacation I had promised myself at the end of my overland journey. Compared to the constant traveling of the past few months, life on Kuta was very tranquil. There wasn't much to do but relax and enjoy beach life. I had no decisions to make or buses to catch. I was ready to put down my pack for a couple of weeks before hitchhiking from Darwin through the outback and down the east coast of Australia to Melbourne.

Charlie, on the other hand, was ready to leave for Australia. He was blond and had very fair skin and said he never tanned but only got redder. Beach life wasn't for Charlie. On Thursday the 19th, John went with Charlie to the airport outside Denpasar and waited to see if Charlie would get a seat on the plane to Darwin as a standby.

Flying standby meant that the list of passengers who would pay full price would go first, and, once they were seated, a standby could buy a ticket at a reduced price if there was a seat available. When John got back to Kuta, he told us that Charlie managed to get on the plane as the 19th standby. I had been traveling with Charlie on and off the past few months, and, even if we didn't always get along, it was strange that he wasn't around.

There was one main dirt path that ran parallel to the beach. All along the main path were side paths that either led to the beach or to the main road where Bemos were easy to find. After a while, I knew how to find little outdoor restaurants and shops up and down Kuta. Flipflops, swimsuit, and a towel were all that was needed for life at the beach. Sometimes I would go to the beach with a book, passing the leisurely day reading and napping. I had read Ernest Hemingway's *The Old Man and the Sea* in high school and had recently traded for a well-worn copy. I remembered that the old man went on a long fishing trip, but I wasn't sure if he succeeded in catching a fish, or if it even mattered.

Young Balinese guys walked up and down the beach selling drinks, small bits of food, suntan lotion, or occasionally, a piece of art to the backpackers who were sunning themselves between occasional swims. Bali was known for its arts and crafts, and sometimes a vendor would stroll down the beach showing the sunbathers a painting or a small sculpture. The Balinese were known as excellent craftsmen, and woodcarving was one of those crafts. One day I was stretched out on a towel when a teenage boy came up to me carrying a cloth sack over his shoulder. He said hello and told me that his father was a woodcarver in the hills in the middle of the island. The teenager had come down to Kuta to sell his father's sculptures. He pulled out an object wrapped in cloth from his sack and unwrapped it to reveal a 15-inch (38-cm) rosewood sculpture of a woman carrying a basket on her head. It was a beautiful little hand-carved figure and unlike anything else I had seen. It was just the right size to squeeze into my pack, so I asked the boy how many rupiah he wanted for the carved beauty. We traded numbers back and forth until we agreed on 1,000 rupiah ($2.50) for the little statuette. I had waited to find just the right object to purchase as a reminder of my trip, and she was the one.

Rosewood Sculpture

We had heard from other travelers that, if we went to the beach early, we could find a guy selling freshly picked magic mushrooms. Friday, the 20th, Marcel and I were on the beach by 7 a.m. and found the magic mushroom vendor. We bought about 10 mushrooms in a paper bag for 125 rupiah (35¢). We also were told that The Garden Pub restaurant would take the mushrooms and cook them into a savory magic mushroom omelet. When we sat down, the waiter gladly took the mushrooms, and soon we were served a magic mushroom omelet, fresh fruit, and tea. After breakfast, we had time to change into our suits, go to the beach, and jump into the surf before we began to feel the buzz of a silly psilocybin high.

As the mushrooms started coming on, I felt a warm glow inside and a sense of peace and calm. Everything around me was clearer and sharper. The ocean surface was alive, sparkling from the sunlight, and the sand seemed to rise and fall as if it were taking a breath. The surfers slid down the watery slopes with great skill and balance. Growing up in Illinois and going to school in Colorado didn't give me much of a chance to try surfing with a board. I had body surfed and knew what it was like to catch a wave and let it propel you toward the shore. Surfing on a board would just intensify that feeling. I knew from when I worked as a framing carpenter that I had good balance and could carry a sheet of plywood across a row of narrow wooden joists 20 feet (6 meters) off the ground. I was inspired to test my balance on a surfboard, if I got the chance.

Monday morning the 23rd, I dug out the packet of

stones I had been collecting over the past few months. I brought out the red ruby I had bought in India, the turquoise stone I had purchased in Iran, and four of the 20 jade stones I had traded gold for in Burma. I had admired another traveler's ring and he told me he had the ring made by a silversmith named Nyoman Wanon. Nyoman's small shop wasn't far up the main dirt path from where our losman was located. I put the stone packet into my shoulder bag and walked over to Nyoman's open air stand. After saying good morning, I brought out my stones and laid them on the wooden board where Nyoman did business. I told him I would like to have six silver rings made. The four jade stones would go into rings for my three siblings and myself. The rings would be very similar and identify us as siblings. I would have the ruby and turquoise set into rings for myself. Nyoman suggested some designs for the rings which I liked. I picked simple designs that would show off the stones. The cost for the six rings would be about $22 and was well worth it. The silver work in Bali was known to be very good, and the rings would make great gifts and good reminders of my trip.

Card from Balinese jewelry maker

The more I heard about Bali, the more I wanted to explore the interior of the island. Bali was more than just a beach, and I needed a break from the repetition of sleeping in, going to the beach, and getting stoned. I was enjoying myself, but it was already the end of September, and I would be leaving for Australia soon. I wanted one more adventure before leaving this part of the world.

So, on Wednesday the 25th, Marcel and I rented a 125cc Honda motorcycle and headed north for a little tour of the island. Marcel had ridden motorcycles in Switzerland, so he did the driving, and I hung on behind him. We packed light for a three-day trip to visit villages known for their skilled craftsmen, a smoking volcano, and a few of the many Hindu temples sprinkled around the island.

Once we were through the flat, noisy city of Denpasar, the road started climbing into the green hills, and we saw very few cars or motorbikes. We drove up to an area that had several villages, each known for a specific craft. Silver and goldsmiths, stone carvers, weavers, and basket makers each had their own village. I wanted to see Mas, the village where the woodcarvers had their shops. We parked the bike and went into a few of the shops where we saw some beautiful carved pieces. I didn't see anything that looked as beautiful as the little rosewood statuette I had bought on Kuta Beach. After seeing the expensive woodcarvings in Mas, I was very happy with my little carving. She would make a good present for my parents.

Marcel and I got back on the bike planning to make two more stops before ending the day at the edge of a smoking, recently active volcano. The first stop was the well-known painter's village of Ubud. Both Balinese and European artists had studios around Ubud, where they displayed canvases capturing the color and diversity of Bali. Some painters used vivid blues and frothy whites to capture the crashing waves, while others used a variety of greens to depict a glen in a tropical forest on a sunny day. Tourists could take home a painting to remember their visit to beautiful Bali, but we would take home memories.

Our next stop was about 20 minutes away at the Elephant Cave near Bedulu. Goa Gajah, or the Elephant cave, was a temple created sometime in the 11th century for spiritual meditation. The temple contained stone carvings telling both Hindu and Buddhist stories. Above the entrance to the cave was a wide-eyed creature carved out of stone that made me feel as if I were going down its throat. Descending into the cave by way of a long staircase, I found the air full of fragrant smoke from the burning incense in the temple below. The freestanding stone carving in the main temple had lost much of the fine detail that must have once defined the figure.

Originally, the stone was thought to be an elephant which gave the temple its name. The Hindus believe that the figure was of Ganesh, the elephant god, and used the temple regularly for prayer. Foreboding faces, fierce enough to scare away bad demons, look down from the sculptures on the walls. The natural cave in the hillside made for a unique and spiritual temple visit.

Across the road from the cave entrance was a basket market where dozens of beautiful handmade baskets were on display. We walked over to see the handiwork but didn't buy anything. We had heard from another visitor at the temple that there were more stone carvings at Yeh Pulu on the other side of Bedulu. It didn't take long to find the path and park the bike. We walked down a narrow dirt path on the edge of rice patties until we came to a stone wall. When we got closer, we could see the wall was covered in carvings. The wall and carvings were said to be all that was left from a 14th century Hindu temple. I could see that the craftspeople of Bali come from a long line of talented artists.

We thought it would be a good idea to stay at the edge of an active volcano in the mountain village of Kintamani on the rim of a caldera overlooking Mount Batur (Gunung Batur), which had just erupted earlier in the year. Calderas are basin-like depressions created when the old volcano collapses. Mount Batur is a volcanic mountain rising out of the depressed remains of a larger extinct volcano. The road took us up to the edge of the large caldera, and we continued around until we reached a look-out point sitting on the rim of the huge extinct volcano. The sun was just setting, the high clouds were colorful, and the waxing moon was directly overhead.

We looked down into the caldera and saw the remains

of a smaller volcano in the middle of the older one, plus a big lake called Lake Batur, also within the caldera of the extinct volcano that had erupted 20,000 to 30,000 years earlier. The volcanoes that created this part of Bali must have been massive. The dramatic setting made for a beautiful sunset of reds and oranges. We got back on the bike and kept going before it got too dark. We rode up to the small village of Kintamani and found a quiet losman that had a small room with a couple of beds. We were tired from the long ride on a small motorcycle, so after a simple dinner, we went back to our room for an early night.

Mount Agung (Gunung Agung) is an active volcano and the highest point in Bali. It was only a few hours walk from our losman, and on the 26th, Marcel and I woke up early so that we could hike to the smoking mountain. Mount Agung had erupted in 1963 and continued to percolate into 1964.[24]

The owner of our lodging introduced us to a boy named Wayan, who would be our guide around the volcanic area. Ken, a dentist from Toronto, was also staying at the losman and joined us for the hike. Wayan led us over the uneven black lava fields that had been left from a series of eruptions spewing molten lava for thousands of years. We slowly climbed the barren side of the mountain to reach the rim. It was like walking through a cluster of earth's heat vents. The smell of sulfur and the warm vapor rising from the

---

[24] *More recently, the volcano erupted in 2017 after hundreds of earthquakes rocked the region. The seismic and volcanic activity continued into 2019 causing disruption to air traffic around Bali and the surrounding region.*

ground gave me a real sense of how alive planet Earth is. This was the smell of the earth growing. After we hiked to the edge of Mount Agung, Wayan took us back over the lava field and down into the caldera surrounding Mount Batur. We hiked down until we came to Lake Batur, stripped down to our swimsuits, and jumped into the cool, clear water. It was a wonderful experience to swim in a large lake at the bottom of a massive bowl-shaped crater created by an enormous blast thousands of years ago.

Wayan, our guide to the volcano

When we were done frolicking in the water, we followed Wayan back to the losman. We paid him what we had agreed to and thanked him for showing us the volcanoes. We packed up our things and got back on the bike to continue our tour. Marcel and I took the coastal road at the top of the island going west until we reached the 15th century Pura Beji temple in the village of Sangsit. The large compound contained several separate buildings covered with intricate stone carvings. Again, the carvers and craftsmen had created a Hindu temple that has been maintained in a beautiful, lush green jungle setting for hundreds of years.

The coastal road took us to the old port town of Singaraja, where we took a left turn and headed south back up into the volcanic mountains. We hadn't climbed far when the sky clouded up. There was a slight sprinkling over us, but the sun shone bright as it approached the horizon. We pulled into the mountain village of Bedugul for the night and found a small losman on the edge of an old caldera lake called Lake Bratan. We were shown a small separate room behind the house, which had two beds with thin mattresses where we threw down our sleeping bags. Once the sun had set, the evening turned gloomy and overcast. After dinner, we played some Casino and went to bed. With no electricity, evenings ended early, and the day started with the sunrise.

Friday morning started out gray. The rain was pattering lightly on the roof, but we got on the bike anyway and headed south to Batuan because we had heard about two mountain temples near the village that we wanted to see. After fixing a flat tire and following bad directions down rough and bumpy roads, we eventually found one of the temples. Pura Puseh was on the edge of a jungle, and the carved dark lava rock was striking against the wet green. We drove among a scattering of abandoned structures, passed a lake, a river, fountains, and came to the prayer temple. Once we turned off the engine and got off the bike, we saw the temple's true beauty. The scene was tranquil and serene. The ancient setting had just the right atmosphere to change our moods after the morning's hectic ride on the buzzing bike. It rained on and off while we explored the temple grounds, but we were able to find places to keep dry and were content with the day.

The 125cc bike had worked hard to take Marcel and me up the cobblestone road to the Pura Puseh Temple at the top of the hill. Marcel got on the bike, started it, and I got on behind. We left the dirt parking area and immediately started going downhill. As soon as the bike reached the wet cobblestones, I could sense the narrow tires didn't feel steady under us. Marcel was having a hard time keeping the bike from slipping on the uneven cobblestones when suddenly the front wheel veered sharply to the left toward a ditch. Marcel, the bike, and I went into slow motion as we toppled into a jumble of bodies and machine, landing at the bottom of the ditch. The motor had died leaving us in silence. We had both landed hard and I slowly took account of my limbs to see if anything was broken. I asked Marcel how he was, and he said he was okay. We untangled ourselves from under the lightweight bike, stood up, and made sure we had no other injuries. We pushed the bike back onto the cobblestone road and looked it over. We couldn't find a scratch or a dent. It could have been bad if either of us had been hurt, but luckily both the bike and our bodies came through the tumble unscathed. The close call and rainy weather convinced me that our tour of Bali was about over. We thought about visiting one more temple called Tanah Lot on the southern coast but agreed to head the bike back to Kuta for the sunset, dinner, and an early evening.

Pura Puseh Temple, Bali

Marcel wasn't finished touring Bali and the next morning he extended the rental and got back on the bike to explore the island by himself. He said he would be gone for a few days. I thought that more days on the beach would be better than riding on the back of a bike. John came over to my bungalow later in the morning, and we walked to the beach looking for a spot to put down our towels. The warm sun and sand were welcome after my ride through the cool, wet volcanic mountains. John and I were body surfing in the warm water, when we saw Beth and Lorraine, the Aussies whom we had met in Jogja, walking down the beach. We all saw each other at the same time, so John and I got out of the water to say hello. They had just arrived on Kuta and had found a losman nearby. They put down their towels and proceeded to tell us their adventures of the past few days. Beth reminded us of the Balinese dances she had told us about and was excited to see one of the performances. The four of us agreed to buy tickets for the next day's performance of the Barong Dance starting at 8 p.m.

The next evening, Beth, Lorraine, John, and I met for dinner before the show. While we were ordering, Lorraine brought out a small paper bag holding a few magic mushrooms. She handed the bag to the waiter and ordered a magic mushroom omelet for dinner, which she split with Beth. They were preparing for the wild colorful costumes depicting mythical animal spirits and the exotic gamelan music that accompanies the dancers. John and I ordered something a little less psychedelic.

The Barong Dance is a traditional dance of Bali and Java pitting Barong, king of spirits and leader for good, against Ranga, the demon queen. A gamelan orchestra has a unique sound starting with a metallophone that looks like a xylophone but uses metal instead of wooden bars that are struck with a mallet to produce a metallic sound. Added to that were drums, wooden flutes, stringed instruments, and some instruments that I had never seen before. I didn't need magic mushrooms to be mesmerized by the bright colors, intricate costumes, and the banging of the metallophone. We were told that the dance performed that evening was in celebration of the coming full moon.

Full moons are a time for celebration on Bali, and we wanted to be part of the festivities. The moon had been an important part of my trip; it is also an important part of Balinese culture. One of the two Balinese calendars is based on the phases of the moon. The new moon, *tilem*, is just as important as the full moon, *purnama*, and ceremonies are observed on both days of the month. When the moon is full, people pray to *Chandra,* the moon god, for blessings received from the moon's light. The new moon is a time when the Balinese celebrate the darkness of a moonless night and pray to *Surya*, the sun god, for the light that guides them in the darkest hour. Here I saw a culture that celebrates the balance of light and dark and all aspects of nature which we must live with each day.

We were treated to an evening of beautiful costumes and dance punctuated by highly choreographed finger movements, intricately refined foot movements, over-the-top gestures, and wild facial expressions. The theater had a full gamelan orchestra, which accentuated the drama with increased volume and banging when two of the ornate figures were in conflict. The story was a little hard to follow, but King Barong clearly outdid the demon queen in the end. Attending a live performance of Balinese dance and music with friends, I thought, was a great way to end a month of travel through Indonesia.

Marcel wasn't back from his tour of the island, so on the evening of September 30th, Beth, Lorraine, John, and I went to the Sunset Restaurant on Kuta Beach. The restaurant sat on the edge of the white sand with tables spread across a patio facing west, so the diners had an excellent view of the sunset each night.

We all agreed to order one large grilled fish for the main course with lots of side dishes, rice, tea, and fresh fruit. We watched as the sun shown its last glimmer of light and fixed our attention on the horizon to see if one of us could catch a glimpse of the green flash. No one did. When we got up to leave, the mostly full moon was rising behind us in the east.

Bali, Indonesia to Darwin, Australia (by plane)
with a customs stop on Timor

Tenth Full Moon

A trip that started out solo was ending solo but surrounded by strangers who had become friends, if only for a short time.

I remembered the dream I had in Florida about meeting an unfriendly man who wouldn't give me directions and then, a friendly man who took me where I wanted to go. I had met all kinds of people on the overland trail, and most of them were helpful and friendly. Except for a few stone-throwing kids in Turkey, I had never felt any bad vibes.

The past few months showed me that the world was a safe place to explore. The October moon marked the end of one part of my journey and the beginning of another.

John and I stopped by Beth and Lorraine's losman on the way to the beach, and Beth was excited to show us the LSD she had scored from an Aussie she met. She had two kinds of acid and wanted to share them with John and me. She pulled out two small squares of Windowpane and a couple tabs of Sunshine. I had dropped both Windowpane and Sunshine a few years before, and had good trips on both acids, so I wasn't apprehensive about tripping on the beach in Bali. The best trips for me were the ones taken outdoors. John and I bought one tab of Windowpane which we would split and take later. We had heard that there was to be a Full Moon gathering that night on Legian Beach, about a 30-minute walk north from Kuta, and acid would be the perfect way to enjoy the celebration. I expected I would be smoking grass and hash as I traveled east but didn't expect to come across LSD on Bali. Young Australians were finding their way to Bali for a vacation in the surf and sun and brought along something different to get high on.

On the way to the beach, we stopped by Nyoman's silversmith shop to see how he was progressing on the rings he was making for me to hold the Burmese jade, an Indian ruby, and a piece of Iranian turquoise. He had assured me that the rings would be finished before I left for Australia, and he seemed to be making good progress.

John and I split the tab of Windowpane at about 3:30 p.m. on the afternoon of October 1st. We went back to Beth and Lorraine's losman to pick them up on our way to the gathering on Legian Beach. The half-hour walk would give us time to watch the sunset as the acid started to kick in. Beth and Lorraine each dropped a tab of Sunshine before the four of us walked onto the beach as the sun approached the horizon. We were all starting to feel the buzz of the acid coming on by the time we got to an area of the beach where a few dozen people were milling around. Many of the travelers who happened to be on Bali that day were gathering to see what was going to happen.

I couldn't see who, but someone had a conch shell and

started blowing, which seemed to signal that something was going to begin. As additional conch shells joined in, the acid came on strong. There were dozens of us on the beach, and more were drifting in from all directions.

People started moving and chanting, and I was caught up in the group energy, the warm night, the full moon directly overhead, and the acid. I became part of the moving human mass and lost contact with the others from Kuta. We started weaving through and around each other. I remember bright skirts, sashes, colorful clothing, arms moving, people twirling, smiles, and dancing under the moon. I remember that at one point in the celebration we all started chanting, "Spirit-Spirit-Spirit running 'round my head - makes me feel glad that I ain't dead" over, and over again.[25] The beach gathering was exactly where I was supposed to be. I couldn't have arrived at a better place in the whole world for celebrating the full moon and life. I eventually passed by John, and we looked but couldn't find Beth and Lorraine. We headed back to Kuta walking along the beach with the moon reflecting off the gentle waves rolling ashore.

I don't know when I got to bed, but I only slept for a few hours and woke up just before sunrise feeling more spaced than when I went to bed. I got dressed and followed the path to the beach. No one was around, and the beach was quiet as I crossed the sand

---

[25] *That night's chant was similar to an ancient peyote chant called "Witchi Tai To" adapted by songwriter and saxophonist Jim Pepper, who fused his Native American culture with his love of jazz.*

to the waves coming ashore. As I walked up the beach, the waves crashed against my legs. I had come a long way and thought about some of the sights I had seen and the people I had met. The gentleness of the people and tranquil beauty made Bali the tropical paradise that I had heard it would be.

After clearing my head in the ocean breeze, I went back to my losman and repacked so that I would know every article in my pack. If the customs agents in Darwin wanted to check my pack, they were welcome to search. After lunch I went back to Nyoman's shop and picked up the six beautiful rings he had crafted out of silver and stone. The rings would be great keepsakes reminding me of the last few months.

John and I were catching a plane out the next day, so we agreed to have a party to celebrate the time we had spent together. We would be going our separate ways shortly, and this would be a going-away party for all of us. Marcel was back from his road trip, so he, Beth, Lorraine, John, and I got together for a special evening. We first met at Beth and Lorraine's losman to start the festivities passing around a fat joint of Buddha mix. The Aussies always had good smoke.

The five of us slowly walked to one of the nicer restaurants on Kuta beach. We all ordered beer and then a variety of local Balinese dishes to share. We started with Lawar, a chopped coconut and chicken dish spiced up with garlic and chili pepper. We couldn't resist the duck, Bebek betutu, stuffed with spices, wrapped in banana leaves, and cooked in a pit of embers. I can almost taste it as I'm writing. I purposely ordered the Balinese satay spiced with local flavors. An order of a Balinese rice dish called *Nasi Bali*, which blended a variety of veggies served on steamed rice, rounded out the feast. We added fresh fruit and tea for dessert. The food was delicious, and the beer tasted great. The evening passed quickly with our tasting of each new dish, telling stories, laughing, and saying how we hoped to see each other again someday.

Our party was the perfect send-off feast for all of us, but particularly for John and me, since it was our last night on the overland trail. I looked around the table at the people who were sharing this moment with me and knew that I didn't want to be anywhere else.

My goal would be reached tomorrow, but today I had completed a journey that had changed the way I saw the world.

***

October 3rd arrived! I woke up at 5 a.m. to get Marcel up because he was going fishing.

He had met an Austrian guy on the beach who owned a sailboat and was looking for a crew to help sail his boat from Bali to Singapore. The Austrian skipper admitted he didn't have enough experience to navigate the route by himself and was taking the sailboat out for a fishing trip with a few curious travelers to see whether they would join him on the longer sail. Marcel would know by the end of the day whether or not he would sign on as a member of the crew.

The day started out rainy and looked like it would be the worst weather we had seen on Bali since arriving a couple of weeks earlier. It seemed like the perfect day to be leaving. The rains were getting more consistent, and everyone I knew was moving on. Marcel and I took a few minutes to reminisce about the past few weeks which started with the wild bus ride through the Sumatran jungle with a disturbed young man shouting at the night. We laughed at some of our adventures, but we were sad to be parting company. We had become very close in just a few weeks The rain let up long enough to let Marcel get on his motorbike and take off for the boat dock. A good travel partner can enhance the experience, and Marcel was the right person at the right time. We were headed in different directions, and our time together would become just memories, but good memories.

John came by at 7 a.m. to pick me up. He had his pack on and was ready to go. I lifted my pack, grabbed my shoulder bag, and we went out to the road to flag down a Bemo for a ride to the airport.

It took only 30 minutes to get there, so we had plenty of time before the scheduled 8:30 a.m. flight. John and I found a tea stand in front of the airport terminal and were having a cup when Beth and Lorraine got out of a Bemo and joined us at a table for tea. They were kind enough to come to the airport for one last goodbye. After we finished our tea, they took us outside for one more joint before it was time to board the prop plane.

Beth gave me the address and phone number of their flat in Sydney and invited me to stop by if I wanted to visit. We all hugged and said our goodbyes. They had been good to travel with, and whenever I had bumped into them over the last few weeks, they were always ready for a party, an adventure, or both. I hoped to see them in Sydney.

They caught a Bemo back to Kuta while John and I boarded the Merpati flight and took off over the water. The plane made one stop at Kupang, Timor, where we were asked to get off the plane and go through Indonesian customs. Timor is an island that sits at the eastern end of the Indonesian archipelago. Indonesia shares the island with the sovereign nation of East Timor. With exit visas stamped into our passports, we were ready to reboard the plane. I took a moment to look around and knew that I had completed my journey. I felt confident that I could go wherever I wanted.

I looked forward to traveling through Australia, New Zealand, Fiji, Samoa, and Hawaii before returning to Colorado and completing my circumnavigation of the globe.

I climbed up the metal stairway onto the plane, sat down, and buckled up for the two-and-a-half-hour flight. I was about 300 miles (500 kms) away from Darwin, Australia, the beginning of a new adventure.

Epilogue

The world has changed since I started that journey 50 years ago. 1974 was a relatively safe time to travel to some of the more remote parts of the world. The U.S. Department of State usually issues Travel Advisories for individual countries, but in January 2024 they issued a "worldwide" Level 2 Travel Advisory which suggests travelers "Exercise Increased Precautions". The countries where I traveled freely such as Iran, Afghanistan, and Burma (Myanmar) are now listed at a Level 4 Advisory, which warns, "Do Not Travel".

I was fortunate to explore the world at a rare time when the route between Istanbul to Bali was open to those who dared to travel several thousand miles/kilometers across Asia on the cheap. I met kind, generous, and friendly people wherever I went and I'm sure the same is true today of the people living in inaccessible Iran, Afghanistan, and Myanmar (Burma).

John's travel partner, Charlie, hitchhiked to Darwin airport to pick up John and me. The driver was nice enough to drive us all to the crash pad where Charlie had been staying. The house was full of travelers on their way to Bali, or just arriving in Darwin, like me. After a 30¢ spaghetti dinner on the first evening, a few of the people staying at the crash pad picked up guitars and a flute and started singing. A great first day in

Australia. After dinner, Charlie packed his things, said goodbye, and walked to the edge of Darwin to start hitchhiking to Perth. He wanted to travel at night to avoid the heat.

John and I took Friday the 4th of October to wander around Darwin, and on Saturday morning, we walked to the edge of town to the dusty dirt road leading into the outback. John was going west to Perth, and I was heading south to Melbourne, so we split up and promised to see each other again. I took off my pack and waited for vehicles heading south.

There were very few cars passing because the next town was hundreds of miles away. I had been waiting a couple of hours when a van drove up and stopped. It was equipped with a kangaroo catcher on the front because there was a good chance a kangaroo would jump in front of the van. The driver asked me where I was going, and I said I was trying to get to Melbourne. He told me to get in and I joined the four men already sharing the van. There were no seats in the back, so I sat on my pack, thankful to be on my way to Melbourne. The van was equipped with an eight-track tape deck which kept us entertained with the familiar Stones, Who, Deep Purple, and Led Zeppelin. My van mates liked to listen to Neil Diamond's *Hot August Night*.[26]

Along the way we picked up another guy and two

---

[26] *Hot August Night was one of the most popular albums in Australia in 1974, and, as I made my way south, I heard "Sweet Caroline" in just about every car, truck, or van that picked me up. "Holly Holy" and "Song Sung Blue", too!*

women from New Zealand. We took turns driving or riding shotgun, keeping whoever was behind the wheel awake. We drove all night through the outback of the Northern Territory and entered the state of Queensland in the morning. I was dropped off in Townsville on the Pacific coast. Thanks to using my high school study hall for memorizing Australian geography, I knew I would still have to hitchhike through the states of New South Wales and Victoria to reach Melbourne.

After several rides and a few more days, I eventually arrived at my brother's house with not much more than 10 Australian dollars.

I stayed with my brother for six months. John came to visit, and we went to Tasmania hitchhiking around the island for several days. A few weeks after that I hitchhiked up to Sydney to visit Beth and Loraine. They had a flat in Bondi Beach, which was a vibrant part of Sydney full of young people, like us. The three of us enjoyed the great beach, good restaurants, and lively bars. After a few days I hitched back to Melbourne.

Marcel and I didn't meet again in our travels, but he wrote me a letter when I was living and working in New Zealand. He told me about his sailing adventure to Singapore with the Austrian captain. The crew consisted of Marcel, an American, and a young Indonesian man. The captain didn't know how to read the charts, and on the second day out, he put the boat up on a reef. In trying to get off the reef the captain got the anchor stuck and had to cut it free, which left the boat without a way to hold a position. The American and Marcel quickly learned how to read the charts. There was smooth sailing until they laid down for a rest and the skipper took over navigation. Once again, he put the boat up on a reef.

Trying to get off the reef the captain burnt out the motor and the ship was stuck. Luckily, a fishing boat approached to investigate the situation.

Marcel, the American, and the Indonesian man grabbed their gear and quickly jumped onto the fishing boat, leaving the Austrian captain cursing the abandoning crew. When the fishing boat landed, Marcel and the American were arrested for entering Indonesia without a visa. Marcel contacted the Swiss Embassy, and after a few days, he was released. He immediately went to Singapore and found a nice beach to shake off the misadventure before flying back to Zurich. I felt bad because I had encouraged Marcel to have an adventure, but it turned into more of a nightmare.

While visiting Boston a few years after returning, I met with Ellen, whom I traveled with in Greece. Ellen told me that shortly after I left for Turkey, Mike had returned from the Greek islands hoping to find me. He wanted to talk me into joining him on one of the other Greek islands. That would have been fun and there was a small part of me that was sorry I had missed him.

As to the swami and his fortune telling, I can say that none of his predictions came true. He had told me I couldn't keep a secret and I guess he was right.

The internet has made the aerogramme, which was so important for communicating with my family, all but disappear. Many countries still provide aerogrammes, but the United States Postal Service discontinued the aerogramme in 2006, as did the Royal Mail of the United Kingdom in 2012. Poste Restante is still available at many post offices around the world, as is General Delivery which is available at certain post offices in the United States and Canada.

I spent six months in Australia, and another six months traveling and working in New Zealand before crossing the South Pacific. I stayed on one of Fiji's beautiful tropical islands for three weeks before making stops in Western Samoa, American Samoa, and Hawaii. I landed in Los Angeles in November of 1975 and from there I flew to Chicago, completing my trip around the world.

In total, I had been traveling for one year and 11 months. I had traveled with people from dozens of countries through a variety of cultures using local transportation. I sipped salty tea with a water buffalo farmer and his family in the cold Himalayan mountains of Kashmir and shared a kava bowl with villagers on a lush Fijian island in the sunny South Pacific.

When I returned to America in late 1975, the Viet Nam war had ended, and a new President was in the White House. America had changed, and so had I. I was more confident in who I was and in the decisions I made. I had been apprehensive about traveling by myself, but wherever I went people were helpful, and I never felt alone.

After nearly two years I had crossed four continents and met countless numbers of people. My goal had been to reach Australia, but by taking the slow route, living out of a backpack, eating street food, and sleeping anywhere, I found that the real prize was learning who I was and how to live in the world.

Acknowledgements

I would like to thank:

My wife, Jenny Jones, the first reader and best editor who thought my scratchings had promise. With her urging I started to put more of myself into the story. I would also like to thank Jenny for her delicious and imaginative cooking, artistic input, and playful sense of humor.

Bill Carlsen, author and journalist, read an early draft of the first five chapters and encouraged me to complete the journey.

My first editor, Richard Gottlieb, asked insightful questions challenging me to clarify and fill out the story.

Jessica Prichard, who used her technical expertise to wrangle a ragged 90,000 words into the memoir I'm proud to share.

Paul Chutkow for his sharp eye and much appreciated suggestions.

Brent French for his collaboration on the cover that communicates the sense of adventure and travel that I felt in 1974.

Thanks to my nieces and nephews who inspired me to write this memoir and waited patiently for the results. I would like to thank my siblings, Richard, Ron, and Nan.

I would like to thank Wikipedia for being a wonderful resource. I support Wikipedia and I hope all who use the site will also support it.

About the Author

Will Furth is a Baby Boomer, born in Chicago, IL just after the end of World War II. His spotty college career in Colorado, Florida, and Illinois eventually earned him a BA degree in film from Columbia College Chicago. After college he moved to Evergreen, CO where he and his brothers owned a small tea and spice shop. After that, he worked as a framing carpenter until January 1974 when he decided to take the overland route to Australia.

During his 30s and 40s, Will was a co-founder of a dance company in Tucson, AZ, the manager for a dance production company in Seattle, WA, and the director of an art center on Vashon Island, WA. After retirement, he began sculpting and moved to Paris where he enjoyed two successful gallery shows.

Will is the proud uncle to two nieces and six nephews for whom he wrote this memoir: Carly, Jody, Scott, Rob, Alan, Ryan, Ray, and Rusty.

He is married, currently living in Sebastopol, CA, and continues to travel when possible.

Email: furthereditions@gmail.com